Heavenly Tribe Hoondok

Heavenly Tribal Messiah Special Textbook |

| HOONDOK STUDY TEXTS |

Heavenly Tribe Hoondok

Heavenly Tribal Messiah Academy

PREFACE

When it comes to the care of their children, parents have a spontaneous sense of responsibility that flows out from their original mind. They want to embrace their children and grow them to perfection with the love that pours out naturally from the depths of their hearts.

In the same way, Heavenly tribal messiahship begins from the spontaneous sense of responsibility to embrace their tribe members as their own children. Heavenly tribal messiahs hope to see tribe members be reborn as mature children who deeply feel the parent–child relationship in our True Parents' and Heavenly Parent's embrace of them.

Heavenly tribal messiahs also wish for their tribe members to understand Heavenly Parent's and True Parents' circumstances, hopes and hearts. They hope that their tribe members will learn to see the world from their (Heavenly Parent's and True Parents') standard and point of view and accomplish human salvation and build ideal families and an ideal world. If you live like this, you will one day realize you have come to possess a parent's heart that resembles the hearts of Heavenly Parent and True Parents.

If the heavenly tribal messiahs take the lead and pioneer this path, and if awakened people from the tribe families come to help, then absolute good spirits and Heavenly Parent will begin to reside there. When these tribe members—as Abel tribe members—work together with and become one in heart with the heavenly tribal messiahs, they become the pioneers of the community. Through loving and embracing the heavenly tribal messiahs and the tribe members, they come to understand the hearts of the heavenly tribal messiahs, and they come to develop the characteristics that an original human being should have. Then they can become the elders of the tribe, and they can move onto the next stage where they themselves come to walk the path of heavenly tribal messiahs. They are reborn as children who understand the heart and situation of Heavenly Parent.

This hoondok compilation contains speeches which document True Parents' victories of restoring God's children on earth and subjugating Satan by going (back and forth) between the spirit world and physical world during the early days of the church. Those who read these words can gain the standard of living needed to be victorious against Satan every day and Heavenly Parent's original attributes will settle within them.

In their daily lives, heavenly tribal messiahs and new tribe members will face questions like the following:
- How can we realize the original ideal of creation in our lives?

- How can we separate from selfish fallen nature and sinful nature?
- How can we experience the existential Heavenly Parent and attend Him in our lives?
- What kind of people are the True Parents who restored us as Heavenly Parent's children and blessed us?
- What is the core of True Parents' salvation of humankind, and what kind of course have they walked?
- What is the value of the Marriage Blessing that we have received, and how can we apply the ideal of the original family to our family?
- What is the mission of the messiah who attends Heavenly Parent, and how can I participate in that?
- What is the relationship between the spirit world and the ultimate mission that we must complete while on the earth?
- Through what stages and methods must we live our life of faith so that we can stand before Heavenly Parent?

This compilation consists of a selection of 84 topics broken down into 11 comprehensive chapters answering these questions. We hope to offer content that heavenly tribal messiahs and new tribe members can read on their own every day to gain answers they seek and to put the lessons learned into practice.

Some of the topics included in the readings are: The Fallen World and I, The Relationship between Heavenly Parent and Human Beings, The Ideal World Heavenly Parent Hopes For, The Value of the True Parents and Their Ministry for Salvation, True Parents' Life Courses and Achievements, The Significance of the Marriage Blessing, The Basic Building Block of the Ideal World of Creation, Blessed Central Families, Heavenly Tribal Messiah and I, The Spirit World, and Life of Faith.

If you go through this hoondok process, you will mature in your life of faith and will receive the energy of Heavenly Parent's blessings.

Each chapter comprises first with "True Parents' Words," followed by "Sharing Thoughts," and "Points for Contemplation" that facilitate self-reflection. Each hoondok topic will provide you with ways to resolve issues within your family and society and how to build a world of happiness according to the way of the Divine Principle.

We hope that through this book, heavenly tribal messiahs and new tribe members will understand the will of True Parents and the teachings of the Divine Principle correctly, and learn about the value and legacy of Heavenly Parent and True Parents. We also hope that everyone will naturally master the ideals of Family Federation for World Peace and Unification and the lifestyle for being reborn as their original selves. We hope this book will be an asset and strength to the heavenly tribal messiahs and new tribe members who play leading roles in realizing a peaceful, ideal world overflowing with love through attending True Parents and embodying the Holy Spirit and the Truth.

February 1, 2018
Family Federation for World Peace and Unification
International Headquarters

CONTENTS

PREFACE 4

As You Begin
1. Introducing the Family Federation for World Peace and Unification   15
2. The Value of Doing Hoondokhae 21

Chapter 1   The Ideal Family
1. Experiencing Heavenly Parent's Love in a True Family 29
2. Experiencing the Most Beautiful Love in a True Family 34
3. Showing Filial Love to Parents in a True Family 39
4. Siblings' Love at the Center of a True Family 45

Chapter 2   Heavenly Parent's Ideal Created the World
1. Finding a Substantial Being to Realize Love 53
2. Heavenly Parent Who Wants to Appear Substantially 58
3. The Substantial Embodiment of
   Heavenly Parent's Dual Characteristics, Adam and Eve 64
4. True Parents Who Have Completed the Purpose of Creation 69
5. The Root of True Love, True Life, True Lineage 74
6. Heavenly Parent's Ideal World and Cheon Il Guk 80
7. Cheon Il Guk Is a World Where People Live for
   the Sake of Each Other 85
8. Let Us Become True Parents, True Teachers, and True Owners! ... 90
9. Toward the World of Unity, Peace, Happiness, and Freedom 95
10. One Family under Heavenly Parent 101

Chapter 3 Heavenly Parent

1. One Must Experience the Existing Heavenly Parent 109
2. The Relationship between Heavenly Parent and Humankind Is That of a Parent and Child 114
3. Heavenly Parent Who Is the Eternal Owner of the Heart 119
4. Heavenly Parent Is the Starting Point of True Love 125
5. Heavenly Parent Invested Everything 129
6. The Realization of the Kingdom of Heaven That Attends Heavenly Parent 134
7. We Have to Experience the Sorrow of Heavenly Parent 139
8. Heavenly Parent Has Worked to Save Humanity for Thousands of Years as If It Were Only a Day 144
9. The Providence of Restoration Is the History of Re-Creation 149

Chapter 4 Seeking the True Self

1. The 6,000-Year Battle Within 157
2. A World Trapped in a Materialistic Civilization 163
3. The Culture of Pleasure That Has Lost Life's Compass 167
4. Fallen Nature That Cannot Be Eliminated, No Matter the Effort 172
5. The Fundamental Principle That We Must Live for the Sake of Others 178
6. Before You Seek to Master the Universe, First Attain Mastery over Yourself   183
7. Desires Should Be Denied, Centering on the Conscience 188
8. Seeking the Vertical Parent and Connecting to Love 193

Chapter 5 Humankind Needs True Parents

1. History of the Struggle between Cain and Abel 201
2. Foundation of Faith and Foundation of Substance to Receive the Messiah 208

3 The Ultimate Purpose of Human History Is the Manifestation of
   True Parents 214
4 World Religions Have Continued to Enlighten the
   Human Spirit and Intellect 219
5 The Only Begotten Son and Only Begotten
   Daughter Were Finally Manifested 225
6 A New Horizon in History, the Marriage Supper of the Lamb ... 231
7 From Wild Olive Tree to True Olive Tree 237
8 Life of Blessed Families Living in Attendance to True Parents ... 244

Chapter 6 The Meaning of the Marriage Blessing
1 The International Marriage Blessing and
   the Salvation of Humankind 253
2 Absolute Sex and True Love 258
3 Blessed Families and Three Spiritual Children 264
4 Holy Wine Ceremony and Change of Lineage 269
5 Indemnity Stick Ceremony and Change of Lineage 274
6 Three-Day Ceremony and First Love 280
7 Conjugal Love in Blessed Couples 285
8 Blessed Couple and Blessed Children 291

Chapter 7 The Basic Building Block of the Ideal World of Creation: Blessed Central Families
1 What Is Family? 299
2 Introduction to the Family Pledge 303
3 Restoration of the Original Homeland Centered on True Love 308
4 The Path of the Central Representative Families of the Cosmos 313
5 The Path of the Original Family 318
6 Perfecting the World of Freedom, Peace, Unity and Happiness 324
7 Progressive Development 329

8	Life of Conveying the Blessings of Heaven	333
9	Living for the Sake of Others	338
10	The Ultimate Task of Blessed Families	343

Chapter 8 Life of Faith

1	True Meaning of Life of Faith	351
2	Stages in a Life of Faith	356
3	Life of Faith and Spiritual Experience	362
4	Living for the Unity of Mind and Body	367
5	Inheriting the Traditions of Cheon Il Guk	373

Chapter 9 True Parents' Remarkable Achievements

1	True Parents and Declaring the New Truth	381
2	Interdenominational and Interreligious Work	386
3	The Victory over Communism Movement and the End of Communism	391
4	The Korean Reunification Movement	397
5	Working for World Peace	403
6	Financial Activities for the Construction of a World of Interdependence	408
7	The Ocean Providence	414

Chapter 10 Spirit World

1	Human Life That Spans Three Stages	421
2	Life and Death	426
3	The True Identity of the Spirit World	431
4	Experiencing the Spirit World through Prayer and Jeongseong	436
5	Life in the Physical World to Prepare for Eternal Life	441

Chapter 11 The Path of the Heavenly Tribal Messiah

1. Heavenly Parent's Standard of Jeongseong 449
2. True Parents' Standard of Jeongseong 454
3. Sincerity Moves the Universe 459
4. Sincerity Moves People 463
5. Sincerity Moves People 467
6. Sincerity Moves People 472
7. Sincerity Moves the Self 477
8. Sincerity Moves Heaven 482
9. Sincerity Raises Your Status 487
10. Heavenly Tribal Messiah 492

Bibliography 497

A GLOSSARY OF KEY TERMS 500

As You Begin

1
Introducing the Family Federation for World Peace and Unification

Heavenly Parent created us human beings as His children. He wished for us to meet a mature partner with a perfected character, become a couple together, give birth to children and realize a happy family in a peaceful world. However, due to the Fall of human beings, Heavenly Parent's purpose of creation could not be realized.

Heavenly Parent's ideal of creation was for all humankind to become His true children, share beautiful true love, realize families filled with laughter and happiness leading to harmony and balance, and create a peaceful world where flowers bloom. In today's society, which cares only for individual benefit and materialism, the only way to forgive and embrace the enemy is through the true love of Heavenly Parent. The vision of the Family Federation for World Peace and Unification is to inherit that true love and realize the ideal of creation. Even today, we are moving forward to realize that dream.

The history of the Family Federation officially began on May 1, 1954, when True Parents established the Holy Spirit Association for the Unification of World Christianity. True Parents knew very well that if the headquarters were established based on the will of human beings, it would not be able to stand in a position of authority with regard to the Will of Heavenly Parent or the historical mission. That is why they first established a new religion based on faith in Heavenly Parent and had it manifest as the Abel-type religion. After that, they restored the Cain-type religious organizations, and from the inter-religious position, after completing the providence in stages, they concluded the era of religions and established a plan to lead all humankind into the presence of the original Heavenly Parent.

The significance of the establishment of the Holy Spirit Association for the Unification of World Christianity was that it was to take on the mission originally meant to be fulfilled by Christianity. The Holy Spirit Association for the Unification of World Christianity is the parent religion that ultimately must take charge of the providence of restoration of Heavenly Parent. That is why the words "World Christianity" are in the name. The term "unification" signifies unifying Christianity as well as other religions and bringing together all humankind. "Holy Spirit" signifies building the foundation for the kingdom of heaven on earth and in heaven together with the truth and through the harmony of the physical world and spirit world. "Association" means that this is an organization that will realize the ideal world of the original creation by completing the unification of the physical and spiritual worlds.

Jesus came 2,000 years ago to complete restoration on a worldwide level and become the king of kings of the prepared chosen people of Israel. However, that mission could not be completed because the Israelites and Jews could not accept Jesus. The True Parents, in the position to take on the mission of Jesus, had to establish the principle of restoration through indemnity and place the chosen people of Korea as the second Israel, in place of the Israel that could not unite with Jesus. They had to find and establish the second Israel and second Judaism. Therefore, since Korea is the second Israel, the Family Federation for World Peace and Unification symbolizes the second Judaism because Christianity could not fulfill its responsibility. In conclusion, Korea and Christians should have become one with the Holy Spirit Association for the Unification of World Christianity, attended True Parents, and realized the realm of the nation. And when this realm of the nation was achieved, they should have united the divided world and fulfilled the mission of realizing Heavenly Parent's Will. Today's Christian democracy realm is the environment and foundation prepared by Heavenly Parent so that True Parents could march forth into the world.

However, this prepared foundation of democracy and Christianity could not attend and become one with True Parents. That is why True Parents had to find and restore the entire lost foundation on their own. They first established the foundation in Korea, which was the chosen nation, and, based on that foundation, they should have gone out into the world. True Parents had to walk a lonely course of suffering for 40 years, from 1945 to 1985, and lead the providence to again find and establish the lost foundation.

First, internally, the Korean people, who were the chosen people, had to recognize True Parents. After being divided into north and south after World War II and undergoing suffering during the Korean War, which started in 1950, Korea was in a state of despair. To awaken the broken, chosen people, True Parents mobilized the young people internally and initiated a movement to educate and enlighten all the rural people throughout Korea (the movement that inspired the New Village Movement).

Externally, they established the Victory over Communism movement to educate and awaken the chosen people about the attacks of North Korea, which was in the position of Satan. In this way, the foundation to welcome True Parents, who have led the providence internally and externally, could be established in the nation.

After that national foundation was established, True Parents established the foundation for worldwide missionary activities by focusing their work on the United States. During the time when they were victorious in the national foundation of the 40-year wilderness course, they finally predicted in 1985 that the era of communism would end soon. They met privately with the president of the Soviet Union, Mikhail Gorbachev, in 1990 and with the leader of North Korea, Kim Il-sung, in 1991. Through this, they were able to persuade Gorbachev, the representative of the communist realm and the symbol of the Cain realm, to move forward with removing the statues of Lenin and bringing the Soviet Union out from under the control of communism. This victory of True Parents was recognized by Satan and the Cain realm on the worldwide level, and they were able to take the victorious substantial position of the True Parents.

Based on that foundation, the era of the Family Federation for World Peace and Unification, in which there is no need for religion and we can return to the original world, was opened. The family that was lost due to the Fall of Adam and Eve in the beginning was restored centering on Heavenly Parent. And because what began with Adam and Eve's family was expanded to include people around the world, True Parents opened the era for blessed central families, who have been restored to original families, to come together and unite.

The great victorious foundation of True Parents was a foundation to be able to proclaim before humankind that they came as the True Parents, Messiah, Savior and Lord of the Second Advent. Furthermore, they could proclaim that ideal true families that can attend Heavenly Parent have settled on the earth and that true children have appeared. The significance of the proclamation of true parents, true family and true children is that the era of the ideal family that attends Heavenly Parent has arrived.

The True Parents, who led this significant change in providential eras, concluded the era of religion centering on the Holy Spirit Association for the Unification of World Christianity on May 1, 1994. In 1997, they clarified that the world manifesting the ideal of creation is not based on the foundation of religion but that it can take root through ideal families, and directed that from April 10, 1997, the name of the Unification movement should be changed to Family Federation for World Peace and Unification.

The name Family Federation for World Peace and Unification consists of five concepts: world, peace, unification, family and federation. The word "world" signifies the combination of the incorporeal world and corporeal world, which together form the cosmos. The Family Federation for World Peace and Unification means that blessed families unite on the cosmic level and carry out activities with the goal of peace and unification.

The environment in which we are living is the era after the Foundation Day of Cheon Il Guk in 2013, an age in which there is no indemnity. Our role as blessed families is to attend Heavenly Parent and build a world of happiness, joy, freedom and unification, as the original Adam and Eve were meant to. From now on, as members of the Family Federation for World Peace and Unification, we have become members of the ideal family of Heavenly Parent and members who must train to live as ideal families. It is the author's hope that we can become people who can attend Heavenly Parent and True Parents as our parents in our daily life, think of the members of our heavenly tribal messiah community as our brothers and sisters, and embrace the spiritual children of the Cain realm with true love.

2
The Value of Doing Hoondokhae

True Parents have bequeathed to us many teachings during their lives. Their words constitute textbooks on the Principle, given for all humankind. They reveal the essence of Heavenly Parent's creation and the secrets of salvation for all people. True Parents established hoondokhae (gathering for reading and learning) on October 13, 1997, asking everyone to read True Parents' words and make them part of their daily life. [CBG 12.1.2: Intro]

You need to place great importance on hoondokhae. It should be more important for you than eating. And you should feel an interest and a liking for hoondokhae. If you were to ask yourself the questions "Where am I going now? How am I living my life?" what grade would you give yourself? You need to grade everything. [CBG 12.1.2:27]

You absolutely need this hoondokhae that you are doing on this earth. You need to settle down in accord with it. The spirit world is already carrying out this work. We are now living in an era in which the family can settle through hoondokhae. That is why hoondokhae is important. It is a program for liberating your ancestors in the spirit world and also for liberating your descendants. [CBG 12.1.2:22]

The significance of hoondok is as follows.
First, hoondokhae is a tradition of the Family Federation for World Peace and Unification to inherit the word. [Sermons, 302-280]

True Parents began hoondokhae in order to pass down the tradition. The words we read when we do hoondokhae are not just passing words but the textbook that must take root in blessed families on the earth. Through hoondokhae, blessed families must become the ancestors of the Word to transform their relatives into citizens of Cheon Il Guk. [Sermons, 294-330]

The mother and father of a family should set an example that they enjoy the tradition of hoondokhae so much that they forget to eat. When children see their parents eagerly awaiting this time with joy, they should be able to say, "We want to learn what our mother and father are learning!" This is how to put your family on the right path. You must establish such a tradition for your sons and daughters. [CSG 11.2.3:4]

Second, hoondokhae sets the standard we should follow in our daily lives and is the mirror where we can check our status.
The words in hoondokhae are a record of the victory of True

Parents and the record of the victorious tradition. You can win over any fight with Satan by reading True Parents' words. We can start by being victorious in the conflict between our mind and body. We also can get rid of the fallen nature that remains within ourselves so that we can come to resemble the attributes of Heavenly Parent. You must apply that tradition to your daily life, check your lifestyle every day, reflect and make right the wrong parts in your deepest selves. [Sermons, 301-080, 358-216]

I have lived according to the Will, trying to build the kingdom of heaven on earth and in heaven by fulfilling the dutiful way of loyalty and filial piety and the dutiful way of saints and divine sons and daughters. This has brought me into a precious relationship with Heavenly Parent. In order that you do not fall short of that standard, each of you must establish and uphold it within your family. To bequeath the tradition of the True Parents, I started this tradition of hoondokhae. [CSG 11.2.3:16]

Third, hoondokhae is like bringing people the word and letting it flow like water. Therefore, we must convey the word to those around us.

The Chinese character hoon (訓) of hoondokhae consists of two characters combined: "words" (言) and "stream" (川), which mean "the words that flow." Therefore, these words do not die. If water remains still for just one week, it will begin to stagnate. Therefore, water needs to flow. They should flow like water, from higher ground to lower. Hoondokhae is the eternal business of sharing Heavenly Parent's words. The Chinese character dok (讀) consists of two characters combined: "words" (言) and "sell" (賣). It means to sell the words. Even if you give these words to 1,000 people, you will not suffer any loss. This is an eternal undertaking. The money you gather eventually will run out, but these words never will run out. [CSG 11.2.3:6]

If you do not know my words well, buy a collection of my speeches and share it with them. The more you share the words, the greater wealth you will accumulate. By conveying the words to people, you become their eternal ancestor. Your heavenly fortune, position and rank in heaven will be determined according to how often you shared the words and how much effort you made to re-create people into citizens of the heavenly kingdom. That is why I am teaching you this incredible truth. [CSG 11.2.3:8]

True Parents also explained in detail about the way to do hoondokhae. They emphasized that there should be a uniform program around the world in which words that are related to each of the 365 days in a year are selected beforehand and read. [CSG 11.2.3:10]

If you come across words that are important or that need to be questioned, you should go back to them and establish them as the standard in your life.

From now on, whenever you do hoondokhae, do it in a group and share the reading aloud among multiple readers. One person should read one section and then designate another person to read the next section by calling out his or her name. Establish the tradition of calling each person to read next by name. You can address important points or questions the group wants to raise. You can set the standard, saying, "In today's hoondokhae the content to be studied is this, and we must absolutely maintain such-and-such as our principle." [CSG 11.2.3:15]

How can you get the maximum benefit from doing hoondokhae? After passing out the hoondokhae books, begin by having one person read aloud. Then have the reader call on someone else to read, and so on. Train them to do it this way. If ten people gather to do hoondokhae, make sure that one-third of them ask questions on the parts they are interested in. If there is not enough time, allow just a few people to ask questions and then discuss each one. [CSG 11.2.3:13]

Husband and wife as a rule do it together at home. If the husband attends hoondokhae service at church, he should tell his wife which part he read that day. Then she should read that same part, so they can keep on the same page. [CSG 11.2.3:12]

Next, let us look at an example of how a hoondokhae session be structured.

Order of Hoondokhae (Example)
1. Light the candle on the altar.
2. Offer a bow before the altar.
3. Recite the family pledge.

4. The leader, the emcee or a member offers a representative prayer.
5. Read the word. The leader should select words from the three Cheon Il Guk Holy Scriptures that are appropriate for the guests or the providential environment.
6. The participating members can ask the leader about any part from the reading that they did not understand.
7. Have a lively discussion on the topic. A few people can speak about what they felt and how their perspective must change. The participants should gain strength from the word, and present a renewed determination. (If this is a big group, divide into smaller groups for this.)
8. Present what you gained from today's words and what you would like to put into practice, what should change in your family (three minutes for each participant).
9. Sing holy songs and then the leader gives a closing prayer.
10. Offer a bow before True Parents' picture.

We are now living in an era in which the family can settle through hoondokhae. That is why hoondokhae is important. It is a program for liberating your ancestors in the spirit world and for liberating your descendants. The past, the present and the future are one. [CBG 12.1.2:22]

We hope this textbook can help you uphold the tradition of hoondokhae that True Parents have shown us, thus leaving behind for your descendants a model of living by the word and becoming a family that can be proud generation after generation.

Chapter 1

The Ideal Family

1
Experiencing Heavenly Parent's Love in a True Family

— Parents' Love

True Parents' Words

Children are the substantial manifestation of their parents' love and investment. They are an extension of their parents' life and the embodiment of their parents' ideals. Those who have given birth to children and loved them know this. They say to their beloved children, "You are the embodiment of my love, the extension of my life and the realization of my ideals. You are a second me." Because children are born on the basis of the parents' love, life and ideals, the more the parents see their children, the more they find them lovable, the more vibrant their lives become, and the more they discover in their children their ideal object partners.
[CSG 3.2.2:1]

The most precious love of all is parental love. This is because true love travels by the most direct route. Parental love is the vertical expression of true love. Vertical love occupies only one point and cannot be divided. If you change that position, you are turning heaven and earth upside down. No matter how capable you are, no matter how skillful you are, if you shift the position of vertical love, you make heaven and earth grow dark; you turn it into hell. Since love travels along the shortest route, it intersects the horizontal plane at a perpendicular angle. You cannot damage this love; you can't put it aside. It is only one. It is absolute. Because the parent–child relationship is vertical and perpendicular, no power can sever it. [CSG 3.2.2:3]

A mother and father do not keep accounts of their sacrifices for their children, how much they worked at night to feed them and send them to school. They don't calculate their investment or expect a return, saying, "I have spent this amount on you; in ten years it will be worth this much, including interest." Instead they invest everything without keeping track of it and forget what they have invested. The principle of creation tells us that only in sacrifice can you find true love. This is why parents are good. Parental love is the best thing. People without parents are called orphans. Being an orphan is very sad. An orphan has no roots and so cannot set his or her direction in place. [CSG 3.2.2:5]

To satisfy a baby's hunger, its mother's breasts swell with milk. When the milk accumulates, the breasts begin to hurt and the mother's entire body feels pressure. The feeling of a mother as she embraces and breastfeeds her child is beyond expression. When the swollen breasts empty, the mother feels relieved and happy. Only mothers can understand this feeling. Moreover, as a mother watches her baby nurse at her breast and caresses it, love springs up in her heart. At that time, joy and sadness intertwine in a mother's heart in a way that only a mother can comprehend. [CSG 3.2.2:14]

Sharing Thoughts

The Japanese novelist Kenzaburō Ōe is a well-known writer. While in university, he already debuted in his literary career as a young writer with a promising future. As soon as his talent was recognized, he was not envious of anything.

However, that kind of life changed for him in a moment. After he married, in the year in which he turned 26, he had a son who had a congenital deformity of the brain. In a moment, the color of Kenzaburō Ōe's life changed to gray. His son had surgery but remained a disabled child who would not be able to live a normal life. Still, Kenzaburō Ōe was not discouraged. He determined to start his life again and live together in that world with his child. His son appears in many of his novels. One of these describes his life with his son, and the shock he felt at his child's illness. His literary works usually deal with the problems of life, love and the salvation of humankind, but the influence of the work about his son has spread beyond Japan out to the world.

Ultimately, in 1994 he received the Nobel Prize in Literature. Due to his unfortunate son, his life had turned around. Later it was discovered that this son to whom he had given so much love had musical talent; he now is active as a famous composer.

If we look at the allegory above—before marriage Kenzaburō Ōe must have had many dreams about his life! After marriage, when he found out that his child was disabled, he might have felt despair, as if the sky were collapsing. On his own, however, he chose the role that as a parent he had to take; at the same time, he was able to distinguish between his conscious role as a parent and some fateful, destined life course. Maybe because of that he was great. He did not work hard for himself or his own honor. However, by raising and taking care of his child, eventually he was able to attain a result that he had not anticipated.

Parental love is possible only after giving up and sacrificing oneself. Love for our children is not something that comes about through human power. That fact makes us experience a desperate heart and makes our character grow. Giving birth to and raising a child who resembles them gives parents an experience as if they are living a second life. While loving the child in their heart, the parents experience the child's growth process. The parent and child can find perfection if they live for and love each other. Parents cannot become parents by themselves. This is not something that a parent can decide by him- or herself. The parent must have a child, and when the child calls him or her "my parent," the parent can become a complete parent. However outstanding a character or personality one may have, without marrying or having a child, one's position as a parent cannot be set. Ultimately the value of a parent rests on how perfectly the parent has raised the child.

Therefore, parents worldwide also live sacrificially if it is for their children. Of course, they take care of their clothing, food and shelter, and they invest everything for their children's future. Why do they do that? It's because they must help their children become perfect before they can say they lived their lives well as parents. They are assessed as parents according to the successful position of their children. Moreover, we who are living and attending our Heavenly Parent hardly need to say anything more. Accordingly, our Heavenly Parent also comes to us, the children, so that we will respond as children do to their parents. and Heavenly Parent's position then will become perfected.

❋ Points for contemplation
1) Let's think about why we feel that the love of parents is great.
2) What kind of love did Kenzaburō Ōe fulfill?
3) Let's think about when the value of parents' love can be recognized.

2
Experiencing the Most Beautiful Love in a True Family

— Conjugal Love

True Parents' Words

Sacrifice goes hand in hand with love. The way of love flows downward, making sacrifices. This makes everything smooth. Without sacrifice, everything is thrown out of balance. It is the same for what we call conjugal love, which is the working of the heart that provides balance in the family. If you move alone and independently, problems arise. But as love grows bigger, it spills over to fill even the lowest places. Thus, even people living in a slum can nurture the dream of love. They can say, "Since we came here because of our search for love, happiness is right here," and they will want to settle and live there. [CSG 3.2.3:1]

Man was born for woman; woman was born for man. A woman keeps a man's most precious treasure; a man keeps a woman's most precious treasure. They exchange these treasures with each other. Because a man entrusted his treasure to the woman, he cannot separate from her. Because a woman entrusted her treasure to the man, she cannot separate from him. This is the linkage of love. Therefore, a woman is the owner of a man's love, and a man is the owner of a woman's love. Throughout history, men and women have been unfaithful to each other. Furtively they steal from the owner, and now the whole world is corrupt and in decline. The woman has the key to the man's love, and the man has the key to the woman's love. [CSG 3.2.3:14]

The place of conjugal love is the flower of the whole universe. A wife is a composite of all people in the museum of human history. She is the flower of her entire lineage. God is present on her wedding night. After waiting throughout history, finally God can settle in the joyful place of a man and woman's love. How awesome is this place! She must think, "I have the role to open the way, to reconnect the broken path and to explode in love as a perfect minus where this has never been done before." From here, the bright sun of love rises above heaven and earth. When a man enters his wife's room, he should do so as the embodiment of love and of the ideal. [CSG 3.2.3:21]

Sharing Thoughts

If we talk about the most beautiful love in the world, it would be when a man and a woman meet in their youth, marry, and share their first love.

A man and a woman who have become a couple and love each other can conceive a new life because the union of Heavenly Parent's dual characteristics (the male character and the female character which exist inherently in Heavenly Parent) become one and manifest themselves. Furthermore, when they meet each other, the moment they share love, yin and yang achieve harmony because they become one body, and they can experience the joy of becoming completely one. Like this, a man and woman achieve the love of a couple and conceive a child and develop through the love of becoming parents. Giving birth to and raising a child who resembles the parents gives them an experience as if they were living life a second time. That is because while loving the child from their heart, the parents experience together with their child the growth process and experience their own (as parents) growth process as well.

Among Shakespeare's plays, the most beloved work is *Romeo and Juliet*. The leading characters were born into families that were feuding. They fell in love at first sight and shared a burning love. To protect that love, they were even willing to die. Through Shakespeare's outstanding writing ability and poetic expression Romeo and Juliet's pure yet passionate love is portrayed well. Going beyond time and space, this work has reached the modern age and is considered a representative work about love.

When our Heavenly Parent created humankind, the human beings who were created as His children, one as a man and one as a woman, were to grow up, become a couple, become parents, and become grandparents. Our Heavenly Parent had designed their life course so that their characters could grow and become perfect. He had wanted to participate together with them on that course and share love and joy. Our Heavenly Parent's purpose for creating humankind as His children was that He wanted to see them live to realize a society, nation and world based on the foundation of a family centered on true love.

Accordingly, the love of a couple is very important. Heavenly Parent wanted Adam and Eve to grow and, as children who resembled Him, become one with Him in thought and will. Therefore, in the Bible it is recorded that after creating Adam and seeing that he was lonely being by himself, Heavenly Parent took out one of his rib bones and created Eve. Here Adam being created first and then Eve being created later should not be interpreted as the order of the relationship. Having taken one part of Adam and making Eve is to stress that they were one body.

In a couple, the perfection of the husband's love depends on the wife. The only person among the many women of our world village who calls him her husband and who recognizes his value is his own wife. Only if she recognizes him as her husband, can his position as a husband be perfected. In the same way, the wife's position also becomes perfected through the husband recognizing her. Therefore, in the love of a couple, my partner completes me. By the partner having that kind of authority, in order to perfect my position, I have to match myself to my partner. If I put myself at the center, my partner cannot perfect me.

The work that only I can do is to provide what my partner needs, and when I help my partner to grow, my position also can go up as high as my partner's perfection becomes. The level of perfection of the wife's position does not depend on the wife; she stands in the place matching how much her husband raised her. The degree of perfection of the husband's position also is shown by the husband showing how much the wife raised her partner. Therefore, both sides raise each other, and when they concentrate on filling what is needed, they become the ideal couple that Heavenly Parent dreamed of.

❋ Points for contemplation

1) Try meditating on what actions need to be done for a couple to perfect each other.
2) The love of a couple is the substantial manifestation of Heavenly Parent's dual characteristics. As substantial beings born in the form of a couple who resemble Heavenly Parent, what can couples do to live according to Heavenly Parent's purpose of creation?

3
Showing Filial Love to Parents in a True Family
— Children's Love

True Parents' Words

My mother and father's lifelines are connected to me; their "love line" is connected to me, and their "ideal line" is connected to me. No one can cut this off. Even God cannot cut this off, and the universe also cannot cut this off. To the contrary, all the power of the universe protects this. Thus, wherever I go, my parents follow me. My parents always want to be with me, even in the spirit world. Thus, it is the greatest sin if you dislike your parents accompanying you. This attitude is destructive to the entire universe. If you dislike the company of your parents, it means you are off track from the universal principle and are going the way of the Fall. Hence, thinking of and loving your parents as if they were your own body and carrying out your filial duty are of the highest value for human beings. That's why it is said, "Heaven's blessing comes to the harmonious family." [CSG 3.2.4:9]

What kind of person can we call a filial child? The son who treats his parents as they treated him is a filial son. A filial son moves Heaven. Even though parents devote themselves to raising their children, if the children don't care about their parents, that family will go to ruin. In order to ensure that the family will remain strong and intact, they need to establish an objective standard based on the principle of giving and receiving. When that happens for the first time, God will come and dwell in that place and the kingdom of heaven will be realized. What kind of children can reside in the kingdom of heaven? They are those who pay the debt of parental love on their own. When their parents become old and senile, the sons and daughters should endure the difficulties of their care without feeling it is difficult. They should possess the same heart their parents had toward them when they were little, cleaning up their urine and feces. This is what it means to be children of filial piety. [CSG 3.2.4:12]

Fulfill your filial duty to your parents; become a filial son or daughter and a patriot. It is your parents who have led the nation and the world. Before becoming a patriot, become a filial child, and before becoming a filial child, become a proud family member who truly loves your brothers and sisters. "Family member" is the name by which siblings can praise each other. You must show filial piety to a degree greater than when men and women married and had children, created a family, and fulfilled their filial duty to their parents in ages past. You cannot be a truly devoted son or daughter before you get married. You can become a truly filial son or daughter only after getting married. You can establish the realm of true filial piety only after you have married and the wife's filial piety is added to the husband's in front of his parents. Only through this foundation of devoted attendance to the parents can a true realm of filial piety be established. [CSG 3.2.4:14]

Sharing Thoughts

Han Yoo of the Chinese Han dynasty was being beaten by his elderly mother, and he burst into tears. When his mother asked the reason, it is said he answered, "When you were young, your beatings were very painful, but the beating of today does not hurt at all. Isn't that because you have become old and your energy has become exhausted?" Then for the sake of his mother who had suffered much hardship, he did not eat for a day and with a humble heart thought about his mother's hard work.

Long ago in the countryside there was a home widely rumored to have a filial son. To officially commend that filial son, the nation sent a government official to check on him. The government official, who appeared dressed as a traveler, met the elderly mother and began to investigate whether the rumor was true. However, while waiting for the son, who had gone to the mountain to gather wood, though he made the elderly mother talk, the government official could not find any real examples about how the son had been filial.

As soon as the son came down from the mountain, his mother had him sit on the edge of the wooden floor and put his feet in a basin of warm water; she made a commotion while she washed and dried his feet. Then that son, not even knowing how to refuse, was waited on in many ways just like a newborn baby. At the meal table when his elderly mother filled his spoon with rice to feed him, he just eagerly opened his mouth and ate.

The government official thought this rascal wasn't a filial son, and he considered him to be someone who just gave his mother hardship. At the same time, the strange thing was that the elderly mother looked so very happy; and the son did, too. The fact that the elderly mother believed her son was the most filial son in the world was confirmed.

This story tells us about another method of filial piety for one's parents. It is a kind of filial piety that is not the textbook method of just giving something to one's parents and making sure they are comfortable. The story leads us to understand that allowing parents to do something that they can do, and letting them be happy for it, is also filial piety. Another kind of filial piety is feeling empathy for our parents' difficulties when they become old and weak.

Parental love which goes beyond the self in caring for the child is the largest, greatest, and most devoted love. On the other hand, the love that should be given in return for this kind of parental love is filial piety. This filial piety is not just the duty of returning love because love was received. It must come from the heart, and that heart must be one of sincerely respecting one's parents and loving them.

Moreover, True Parents say that we must repay the debt of our parents' love by ourselves. Even when our parents become old and senile, we should think of our childhood and attend our parents without complaint. This is a teaching from True Parents that we can apply to our lives. They see that only if we live with that kind of heart can we fulfill the duty of filial piety before heaven. Soon, the children will be able to become parents. Children who have received sacrificial parental love should respond to that love with a heart of filial piety. Just as their parents love their children, the children should live for their children and their parents. Therefore, the perfection of the child does not come by asserting oneself; it is possible when the child is recognized by the parents as having inherited the right to be able to participate together with the parents, and the child's position and value have been established.

❋ Points for contemplation

1) More than having a feeling of duty that we must repay the love that our parents gave us, when we become parents we should live thinking about the parents' situation. This is the child's proper attitude. Please meditate together about what kind of parent you want to become.

2) A parent–child relationship is one of growing together. While raising their children, parents become parents, and while growing, the children come to understand their parents. Mutual discussions change many things. Today at this time, please tell your parents what you want to say.
3) Let's think about the kind of love that children and parents should give and receive.

4
Siblings' Love at the Center of a True Family
— Love of Brothers and Sisters

True Parents' Words

Why do we need brothers and sisters? It is so that a brother, by looking at his younger and elder sisters, can understand, "Oh, that's how our mother was as she grew up!" Through them he sees the process of his mother growing up. Also, a sister observes carefully how her elder or younger brother grows up to understand how her father grew up and lived. This is the love among siblings; you become one by growing up like this. That's the value of loving your brothers and sisters. [CSG 3.2.5:1]

The relationship of brothers and sisters is connected to both the vertical and horizontal planes. If we say the relationship between Adam and Eve is horizontal, then that between God and Adam and Eve is vertical. East and west form only a horizontal line. This is why two linear dimensions that form a plane are necessary. And then the front–back aspect gives the required third dimension. Only the love between brothers and sisters expands the love of the family to a new dimension. Only through adding that love can a sphere of love come into being. That ideal sphere represents the highest standard of hope for men and women. Sons and daughters in substance are the embodiment of the love God hoped for at the time of creation. These sons and daughters will be able to inherit heaven and earth and the love that represents God. These sons and daughters grow up as brothers and sisters, and they mature. When these children grow up, they must find their father and mother, and the father and mother must find their sons and daughters. Through this encounter, they become complete. This is the principle of counterparts. [CSG 3.2.5:2]

Man is the subject of life who contains the seed of life that woman receives. This is why we say that man represents the east and woman the west. The sun rises in the east, and the west receives the sun. An axis plus east and west together make four directions. Up and down, east and west form a cross but not a sphere. That's why we need brothers and sisters. Through brothers and sisters, a nation arises and all humankind arises. So, it is brothers and sisters who form the sphere. Brothers and sisters expand to become a people and the world. So, the love of siblings relates to the love of the world. A family in which many brothers and sisters grow up is like the model needed to create the ideal, the kingdom of heaven, the kingdom of God on earth and in heaven. [CSG 3.2.5:4]

Sharing Thoughts

This is a story about what happened in a poor seaside village of the Netherlands. A strong hurricane bared its white teeth, and the roaring waves became stronger as night came. All the people of the village came out to the seaside. They were anxiously waiting for the rescue team which had gone out to save the people who had gone out fishing and could not return. As time passed, the boat that the rescue team had taken pushed through the ferocious waves and thick darkness and approached the shore. The rescue team that came up on the land said there was still one person they had not been able to save. That was because the rescue boat was too small, and they could not help but leave that person there and come back.

"If we had saved that person and brought him back in the boat, the rescue boat would have sunk, and we all would have died. That one remaining person must be saved quickly. We are short of helping hands, so people who will go together to save that person, please come forward."

The captain of the rescue team looked around at the people who had gathered and pleaded with them, but no one came forward readily.

"My son, please don't go. Ten years ago, there was a shipwreck, and your father died. And a few days ago, your elder brother went out to catch fish, and since then we haven't had any news of him, have we? Now you are the only one I have left."

"Mother, nevertheless I will go. If we all think that this kind of dangerous work must be done by someone else, what will happen? Mother, this time I will definitely save that person and come back. When there is something that can be done for someone else, no one should ignore that."

The boy embraced his mother, went forward and followed the captain. The rescue team went out into the dark sea. After some time had passed, the boat that the rescue team had taken appeared.

"Mother, we saved the person who remained alone in the sea. It was my elder brother who went out fishing several days ago and about whom we had no news. I rescued my brother!"

The people who had been watching the dark sea with tense hearts cheered and shouted hurrah together. The sacrificial attitude of the young boy who, despite his own danger, went out on the rough sea, brought about the rescue of his elder brother.

In this story, the young boy in the face of danger followed the rescue team captain. Because of that, he was able to rescue his elder brother who had gone out to catch fish but was in danger of dying. In our world there are also many cases of people who boldly leap into situations, despite the risk to their own life, to save other people's lives. In a life-and-death situation, a friend who puts his life on the line and saves us becomes the savior of our life; even if we want to, throughout our entire life we can never forget that friend.

Brothers and sisters should live for each other. My individual position is not made just for or of myself. When my brothers and sisters give me recognition, I can receive it and become perfect. We should be able to receive the recognition of people, saying, "That brother is really a true person." Ultimately my individual perfection does not come from myself alone; it depends on my counterparts.

Accordingly, we should think of our neighbor not as someone different but rather as our own brother. When this kind of brotherly love develops to love of humanity, that neighbor becomes a brother like me and the same kind of citizen as I am. We can become people who live together on our earth. As our True Parents' words indicate, brothers develop and become national citizens and world citizens. Accordingly, he said, "Brotherly love flows through love for the world" and "A family where many brothers and sisters are growing up is like the model for making the ideal kingdom of heaven, the kingdom of heaven on earth and the kingdom of heaven in the spirit world."

❋ Points for contemplation

1) When we think of humankind as brothers and sisters sharing love, how does this compare to the way we have looked at people until now?
2) Let's think about what kind of ideas the young boy had who followed

the rescue team captain.

3) Think about situations where and when brotherly love can develop into love for humankind.

Chapter 2

Heavenly Parent's Ideal Created the World

1
Finding a Substantial Being to Realize Love
— The Object Partner of Love

True Parents' Words

God created human beings because of love. Love cannot be experienced by one being alone. Therefore, the only thing that God absolutely needs is an object partner to whom to give love. In other words, God needs an object partner of love. [CSG 1.1.2:9]

God exists as the origin of true love. But in order to experience love, even God needs a partner. Love is an experience and a joy that is possible only through the relationship between a subject partner and an object partner, that is, through a relationship. No one can ever feel love by himself or herself in isolation. God's motive for creating was to realize true love through object partners of true love. God created human beings so they would be object partners with whom to freely exchange love, as partners for total love. Hence, we human beings are sons and daughters of God, the Creator, who is our True Parent. God hoped that Adam and Eve would remain pure and grow up to become true persons based on true love. [CSG 1.3.3:9]

God treasures human beings above all else because they are the object partners of His love. That is why God's love is the most precious thing for us. No matter how much love God may have within Him, He cannot feel it without having partners to love. He can experience His own love only in relationship with a partner. It is because we are in the position of these object partners that God cherishes human beings the most. [CSG 4.1.4:3]

Sharing Thoughts

Once there was a person who visited France. While there, he bought a cheap necklace at a marketplace and returned to his country, where he was charged a high tariff by the customs officer. Perplexed, he insisted, "This is a very cheap item." But the customs officer merely replied, "No. It is a very expensive item." The man then had to pay the high tariff for the item before he could continue into his country. The man thought it strange and took the necklace to a jewelry appraiser for an appraisal. The appraiser closely observed the necklace under a magnifying glass for some time and was then astonished. "Mister, this is no ordinary necklace.

Have a look yourself." So, the man also took a look through the magnifying glass and saw some writing etched into it. The necklace had the inscription "To Josephine from Bonaparte." Having been signed by the man who once laid claim to an entire century made the necklace priceless.

Perhaps the same is true for us. We do not realize just how precious certain things are when we go about our everyday lives. There may be aspects of our lives that we push aside because we did not scrutinize them under a magnifying glass. Heavenly Parent is always by our side, but we may have lived without that realization. This is because Heavenly Parent has become a part of me and stays near me as a Parent.

A partner exists in our lives; therefore, we can form relationships, love, and be fruitful. There is nothing so valuable that it can be exchanged for that partner. Heavenly Parent felt lonesome without anybody to love, and that is why humankind was created as object partners for love. One's value and significance are reaffirmed through interacting with a partner. Therefore, humankind, who can become a partner to Heavenly Parent, is of absolute value to Heavenly Parent. Hidden in the picture of the creation of humankind is the inscription that confirms the authenticity of the children of the Heavenly Parent and the expectations of the Heavenly Parent. The external form and the amazing plans of Heavenly Parent are always disguised. The fact that each one of us exists as a person and was born as a child needed by Heavenly Parent is a reality that holds infinite value and grace.

In addition, we were created so that Heavenly Parent can visit and live within us and experience the world through our external form, through our eyes, ears and bodies. Also, being object partners in a parent–child relationship, we become Heavenly Parent's everything.

When parents have children, those children become the most precious thing in the world to the parents, even more than their own lives. The same is true for Heavenly Parent. And all parents desire their children to be better than themselves. Among normally functioning parents, there are none that wish that their children be worse than they are themselves. Heavenly Parent as well desires that we become extraordinary. This is why, after creating humankind as beloved children, Heavenly Parent has continued to invest love in us and has experienced infinite joy from observing us, His beloved children.

With such lofty dreams in mind, Heavenly Parent invested absolutely everything in creating humankind. Creation took a very long time, but it was a labor of love by Heavenly Parent. This was because the ultimate moment in the process of creation was the creation of beloved children, the son and daughter, Adam and Eve.

Knowing that this moment would come after a long, patient wait, Heavenly Parent created humankind with a heart of loving others, of bearing the fruits of love, of anticipation. Therefore, it was possible for Heavenly Parent to imbue all of creation with divine love. The goal of Heavenly Parent was creating the love that could create a substantial partner. Love was present at the start and throughout the process, and the result was also love.

We are the substantiation of Heavenly Parent's love. We must live with the filial heart to fulfill the dream of creation of our Heavenly Parent.

❋ Points for contemplation

1) What was the heart of Heavenly Parent when He was alone prior to the creation?
2) What kind of life should we live to become an object partner of the substantial love of Heavenly Parent?

2
Heavenly Parent Who Wants to Appear Substantially

— The Relationship between Heavenly Parent and Humankind

True Parents' Words

God's last step in realizing His purpose of creation was to assume a form. The incorporeal God cannot govern the physical world directly, so to be the Father and Mother of all humankind, God has to manifest in physical form. He has to embody Himself in the physical forms of human beings, so that when these human beings relate to one another as subject partners and object partners and are stimulated through their sensory organs, He also will experience that stimulation. [CSG 4.1.1:7]

When God created heaven and earth, He did so with absolute faith and absolute love, based on the absolute, unique, unchanging and eternal ideal. The reason God created was to find the partners whom He desired. The invisible God, the God without form, wanted partners of love who would be His visible manifestations, and having form they would be His representatives in the world of form. God would have become embodied in them. This was God's first purpose of creation. It is the same with regard to the spirit world. Although God is incorporeal, God can become the Father and King in the spirit world as well, once His ideal of creation is fulfilled through human beings with form, Adam and Eve. That will occur when Adam and Eve, who have bodies, and their sons and daughters, who have bodies, come to the spirit world. It would be impossible for God to do this without assuming form. Then, whose form would that be? God's face would be none other than the faces of Adam and Eve, who would have reached perfection and become one in conjugal union after receiving God's Blessing. Adam and Eve are the partners of God's love. [CSG 4.1.3:1]

People up to now generally have asserted that created beings cannot stand in a position equal to the Creator. However, if that were true, it would be impossible for the Creator to realize His ideal of love. God's ideal of love is to relate to His children, Adam and Eve, as His corporeal substantial object partners and attain oneness with them for eternity. God wants to dwell in human beings. The moment that those human beings reach perfection as His object partners is the starting point for the incorporeal God to realize His ideal of love through substantial human beings. [CBG 1.1.4:16]

Sharing Thoughts

After the fall of humankind, it is true that the incorporeal Heavenly Parent was living in the same position as humankind. We could compare it to thoughts we have heard from Helen Keller, who had three disabilities. She said that blind people could offer a clue to those who are not blind.

Tomorrow, try covering your eyes to resemble the disability experienced by a blind person and reflect upon that. Then try experiencing what it is like to be devoid of the sense of touch. The following day, reflect about the disability experienced by a deaf person. Imagine being incapable of hearing any sounds but able to only imagine the pleasant sounds you once enjoyed hearing, such as the happy chatter of children, the chirping of birds, and the howling of the wind. Then the day after that, try to imagine what it would be like to experience the disability of no sense of smell. You would not be able to enjoy the beautiful fragrance of flowers or the smells of tasty food.

It is a blessing to have a body that you can move as you please, eyes to see, a sense of touch and hearing to experience sound. Also, you live life capable of enjoying the fragrance of flowers that smell the best. But, why is it that you are not singing praises? Have you forgotten to be grateful? On the other hand, there could be someone unable to move, who has no sense of touch, and cannot see or hear. But that person has realized something that is immensely precious. [Source: True Happiness and Gratitude of Helen Keller: A person with three disabilities (Korean publication)]

The American author and activist Helen Keller (1880–1968) lived with three disabilities; she could not see, hear, or speak. She possessed a body but lived her life as if she were without one. Thanks to the devoted care of her parents and her teacher/caretaker, Anne Sullivan, despite suffering physical disabilities, she was able to enjoy an unfettered mental existence.

Heavenly Parent does not have even a physically disabled body such as Helen Keller's. Helen Keller longed to have a healthy body, so just think how desperately Heavenly Parent must have longed for human senses. The incorporeal Heavenly Parent has no physical body. What is the dream of Heavenly Parent? Heavenly Parent's purpose of creation, in fact, can be for the incorporeal Heavenly Parent to make use of the corporeal body of humankind. Heavenly Parent did not create people from a distant position from which to experience happiness by merely looking upon them. Heavenly Parent desired to live, present in the heart of humankind in His form, using their physical bodies and experiencing the invigoration of love among them and love among all creation. In this instance, Heavenly Parent becomes human, and human beings become Heavenly Parent, attaining divinity; Heavenly Parent comes to experience character, and human beings become the entities with character that will attain divinity. Likewise, living a life in which the love between humans and Heavenly Parent becomes one, and the incorporeal and the corporeal worlds become one, is the embodiment of the relationship between Heavenly Parent and humankind, the parent–child relationship.

We treasure the desperate Will and desire of the incorporeal Heavenly Parent to use the body of humankind. From this point forward, we will strive to attain a mind and body within which Heavenly Parent can reside. We must realize that Heavenly Parent's fervent desire to use the body of humankind can be realized through us and that we should become true people who can attain oneness with the love of the Heavenly Parent.

Heavenly Parent does not require money, power or might, only love. Heavenly Parent created this world in order to establish a corporeal partner with whom to share love, and in particular created humankind for this purpose. The greatest desire of Heavenly Parent is to attain a substantial relationship of love with humankind, who were created in His image.

What kind of relationship is a love relationship between the Heavenly Parent and humankind? Love itself is like a magnet that has the power to stick to something once it attaches to an object of desire. True Parents have used the metaphor of honeybees when describing love. "In spring, the honeybee awakens from its long hibernation and has a taste of fresh honey. The honeybee is so intoxicated by the taste of honey that its stinger can be removed with tweezers. Even with its stinger removed, you will see honeybees that cannot separate themselves from the honey. What about you? Once you have experienced the taste of the true love of Heavenly Parent, even if you flee from it, you will return and stick to that true love."

Once we come to know this true love of Heavenly Parent, we will strive to never lose it.

Then, how is it for Heavenly Parent? He too would wish to never part from His children. He would want only to be completely one with them. That is because Heavenly Parent resides within our hearts and minds. Heavenly Parent dwells within my heart, and when I become one in body with my incorporeal Heavenly Parent, Heavenly Parent will walk alongside me, and when I am in thought, Heavenly Parent is in thought with me, and when I am joyful and sorrowful, Heavenly Parent will be joyful and sorrowful with me; this is the parent–child relationship that was formed between Heavenly Parent and me.

✻ Points for contemplation

1) Where would Heavenly Parent, who loves us, desire to remain ultimately?
2) Let us deeply meditate on the significance of my heart and Heavenly Parent's heart becoming one, and my body and Heavenly Parent's body becoming one.

3
The Substantial Embodiment of Heavenly Parent's Dual Characteristics, Adam and Eve

— Heavenly Parent's Dual Substantiation

True Parents' Words

God exists as the subject partner with dual characteristics. He manifested His internal masculinity to become substantially visible through Adam as His counterpart, and He manifested His internal femininity substantially through Eve. In other words, human beings represent the investment and substantial embodiment of all that is within God's internal nature. [CSG 1.3.2:2]

The Unification Principle defines God as the incorporeal, absolute subject partner, the subject partner with dual characteristics in harmony. As a being with dual characteristics, God created Adam and Eve as His substantial second selves to reflect His characteristics individually. He intended to become the center in the vertical position when they fully matured and became one flesh with each other horizontally through love. What this means is that when Adam and Eve reached full maturity, God's masculinity was to reside in Adam's heart and mind, and His femininity in Eve's heart and mind. This, however, does not mean that God is divided. He is the subject partner of these dual characteristics. He can dwell in the heart and mind of both Adam and Eve. [CSG 1.3.2:3]

Why do we marry? It is to resemble God's form. In order to connect our family (a husband and wife in resemblance to God) to God we must receive love when we are born, mature in a way that aims to love, live our lives centered on love, and when we pass on to the spirit world we should pass intent on returning to (God's) love. Unless you set out focused on the goal of living for others, your path will take you in the wrong direction. [CSG 7.1.1:25]

Sharing Thoughts

The following is recorded in an ancient document (the ancient text's original author is still unknown): "Man is at conflict until he finds the rib that has been removed from his side. And woman is at conflict until she can return to the embrace of man. The reason for this is for man to seek his half that went out from him, and for woman to return to that place. This is because the two desire to live as one."

The American self-improvement author Dale Carnegie said, "There is no person in society that has made it on his own, and true happiness cannot be found unless a man finds his other half when he returns home."

Humans were created as incomplete beings unable to perform any task on their own. Humans were made to become a pair that interact and complement each other, and to live having become one.

You may know that all things in the cosmos were created in pairs. When you look up the noun "pair" in the dictionary, it is defined as "something that comes in twos" or "a unit of counting that includes two units joined into one."

Shall we first look at the animal kingdom? In the case of animals, there are males and females, and throughout their lives they interact, mate, and bear young. Once male and female demoiselle cranes become mates, they remain together for the rest of their lives. The same is true when you look at flowers and trees. Throughout their existence, all plants have a pistil and a stamen, and produce seeds and fruit through the medium of pollen. Even in the microscopic world of molecules and atoms, there exist characteristics of plus and minus such as positive and negative ions, and protons and electrons, that survive, multiply and interact in harmony. Now can you see that everything in the world really does come in pairs?

Then what is the reason that Heavenly Parent created all of creation in pairs? There is no other reason than for love. Heavenly

Parent created everything in the world in pairs for there to be a subject partner and an object partner, and for them to engage in a subject–object partner relationship, giving love and beauty and experiencing joy.

When you see animals running on the hills, you will see male and female animals; when you see butterflies, you will see male and female butterflies. Everything is made in pairs. Things that come in pairs do not change. The concept of pairs of species based on love cannot be replaced by anything. They are there to interact and multiply forever.

Heavenly Parent had this ideal of love when He created Adam and Eve in His image. Adam was created as the embodiment of the male characteristics of Heavenly Parent, and Eve was created as the embodiment of the female characteristics of Heavenly Parent. Adam's purpose of existence lies with Eve, and Eve's purpose of existence lies with Adam. Based on the love of Heavenly Parent, when "the two halves" of Adam and Eve come together as a couple and create a family, they can live as the perfect embodiment of Heavenly Parent.

You can feel how all beings exist in pairs and create various manifestations of loving harmony. Try picturing in your mind the entire earth like a large orchestra of love with balance, peace and beautiful harmony. You will come to the realization that Heavenly Parent created this world as a world of love.

❋ Points for contemplation

1) Contemplate deeply on the statement that man and woman are manifestations of just half of Heavenly Parent. What would a world be like where only men or women existed?
2) Look around the world that consists of pairs and try to experience the hope of Heavenly Parent who sought to achieve love.

4
True Parents Who Have Completed the Purpose of Creation
– The Meaning of True Parents

True Parents' Words

God conceived the term "true parents" in His mind before the creation. [PHG 7-17:1110]

God's intention and purpose went beyond perfecting the vertical subject–object relationship with human beings in love. After perfecting vertical love, He wanted Adam and Eve to bear the fruit of their horizontal love. That moment was to be the very moment when the internal Parent, God, and the external parents, Adam and Eve, would achieve the ideal of love in complete union. Then the incorporeal parent, through the form of Adam and Eve, would have become the eternal parent in this corporeal world. At that moment Adam and Eve would have become the true parents and true ancestors of humankind. [CSG 1.3.1:30]

God is the root of love, life and lineage, and the root of the kingdom of heaven on earth and in heaven. On the day of Adam and Eve's wedding, God would enter their minds and inspire them with love that would bring them together as one. Originally God was the vertical True Parent and Adam and Eve were to be our horizontal true parents. At the time of our birth, we would be given flesh and blood from both our vertical and horizontal parents. Hence our mind would be our vertical self and the body our horizontal self. At the time of our marriage, we would create a realm where we are united with God in love. When we attained mind–body unity with God as loving couples, God's sons and daughters would be born. [CSG 12.3.5:103]

Sharing Thoughts

"One day an angel came down from heaven and looked for three things that were of the utmost beauty. Traveling here and there, looking for the most beautiful things, the angel first found flowers and placed them in the basket; then he chose the happy laugh of a pretty child; and finally he chose the love of parents as the most beautiful thing.

"The angel placed these three things in the basket and after some time returned back up to heaven, but the flowers had wilted and become ugly. The laugh of the child had turned into an adult's laugh and lost its innocent sound, no longer sounding beautiful.

But that which was eternally unchanging, both on earth and in heaven, was the love of parents. This is why the love of parents, which resembles the love of Heavenly Parent, has been handed down until now as the greatest value on earth."

It is said that young children are not conscious of the love of their parents until they grow up and become parents themselves. At that time, they feel the grace of their parents and practice love. How did you feel about the above fable? The greatest love is the unchanging love that Heavenly Parent has toward humankind. And the True Parents are the ones who have come bearing the unchanging love of Heavenly Parent in His stead.

Adam and Eve lived in the garden of Eden. Adam and Eve were the most precious gift of Heavenly Parent. Also, Adam and Eve were to become the first true parents of all humankind. However, because Adam and Eve disobeyed Heavenly Parent's command and ate of the fruit of the tree of the knowledge of good and evil, they were cast out of the garden of Eden by Heavenly Parent. The true ancestors of humankind that Heavenly Parent earnestly desired were Adam and Eve, who were supposed to become the true parents of all humankind, Humankind was supposed to be born of their blood lineage, but instead humankind inherited the seed of Satan's false love and false life.

What does humankind, which has inherited the seed of false love and false life, need the most? Humankind needs true parents, who are like Adam and Eve prior to the Fall, to come again. In other words, people who could inherit the heart, the blood lineage, and the creation of Heavenly Parent are the true parents who must return. Such a son should come and connect with true love and inherit original life. Unless that happens, we cannot be a part of the true parents' blood lineage.

Then what does the phrase "true parents" mean? It is when the incorporeal Heavenly Parent resides in the love of corporeal Adam and Eve and uses their bodies to become the parent of humankind. It means the love of Heavenly Parent becomes one with the love of humankind, and the parents give birth to children of the true love, true life and true lineage of Heavenly Parent. If this happens, all the descendants connected to the position of the true parents become part of the direct line of descent of Heavenly Parent. Through the true parents, Heavenly Parent and humankind share the affection of parent and child and can live as one body. The ultimate desire of Heavenly Parent is to find the way to make a fundamental start again. That is the fulfillment of true parents.

The words "true parents" are truly amazing words. Though there were many saints and sages in history who sought the truth and strived to live righteous lives, there was no one who could grasp the concept of true parents. This is because people had fallen into ignorance through the Fall of the first ancestors and have lived as the children of false parents.

The Family Federation calls Sun Myung Moon and Hak Ja Han the True Parents. It means they are the ones who enable us to be saved and reborn through love and the word. Now, through the lives of the couple Sun Myung Moon and Hak Ja Han, who are the manifestation of the True Parents, we have become able to experience the value and significance of the True Parents.

Now what task lies ahead of us? It is to receive the Blessing from True Parents and to live our lives as true parents ourselves. We should experience the love of Heavenly Parent when sharing true love with our spouse, perfect our conjugal love and create a true family in which Heavenly Parent would like to dwell. This is not impossible. True Parents already have shown us what a model life is. We just have to practice that model life as it was lived. Even before the creation, Heavenly Parent hoped for True Parents. We should fulfill that hope for Heavenly Parent.

❇ Points for contemplation

1) Contemplate deeply why the hope of Heavenly Parent was the True Parents.
2) Think about the significance of the True Parents, and discuss what we should do to live lives resembling those of True Parents.

5
The Root of True Love, True Life, True Lineage
— True Parents as the Ancestors of Humankind

True Parents' Words

God wanted to fulfill the ideal of true love in the family of Adam and Eve and establish the kingdom of peace and unity in heaven and on earth through the multiplication of their descendants. From Adam and Eve as the starting point, the pure, true love, true life and true lineage of God were supposed to spread out horizontally in their descendants. Then Adam and Eve naturally would have become the true parents, true teachers, true owners, and true king and queen, creating the kingdom of peace and unity based upon the true lineage. [CBG 13.1.4:13]

If the Fall had not occurred, there would be no need for religion. Holy and pure sons and daughters would simply be born through the use of the reproductive organs. That is where true love comes from. That is where true life and the true sons and daughters of the true lineage—the liberated sons and daughters whom Satan cannot accuse—come from. The reproductive organs are the palace of true love, true life and true lineage. They are the most precious things. If they disappeared, heaven and earth would disappear. Without them, God's ideal, God's family and God's Will could not be achieved. They are the source of the perfection of everything. [CSG 2.4.3:15]

True Parents are the owners of true love. True Parents are the king and queen of love. We have lost that most precious true love. The question is how we can recover it. True Parents, true love, true life and true lineage form a realm that Satan cannot touch, no matter how much he tries. Humanity must become attuned to God's Will for eternity. God and all people must constantly maintain an eternal relationship as subject partner and object partners, with true love at the core. Unless we can arrive at this goal, we cannot maintain a life centered on true love, which is God's ideal of creation. This is the Principle. No one can deny it. This is why we absolutely need True Parents. [CBG 1.2.5:21]

Sharing Thoughts

"There are two inland seas within Israel. One is the Sea of Galilee, and the other is the Dead Sea. The Sea of Galilee is a reservoir for

Israel and acts as a lifeline in the desert region. The source starts in the north in a pristine location on Mount Hermon where permanent snow melts and flows down, forming spring water. The stream of water gathers together in the Sea of Galilee. The source of the water is so clean and clear that the Sea of Galilee holds a wide variety of fish that leap and play there, and the mountains near the sea are thick with trees that evoke amazing scenery.

"On the other hand, the Dead Sea receives water from the Jordan River and is a sea that has a point of inflow but no point of outflow. Therefore, it has several times more salt content than typical seawater, which makes it an unbearable environment for life. Therefore, it is called the 'Dead Sea.' There are no fish there, and no plant life is near the sea in the desert surrounding it.

"All other seas have water constantly flowing into them and out of them, because there are points of inflow and outflow. The Dead Sea is the only sea that has only a point of inflow and no point of outflow. Accordingly, the water evaporates naturally through vaporization, and salt accumulates in the water. This is why it is called the 'Dead Sea.'

"These two seas provide us with a valuable lesson. When it comes to people, those who are giving to others live a life that gives new life to their neighbors, but those who seek only to receive and place their greed above everything else are unable to breathe life into others. We are able to feel many things through the lessons nature has shown us."

Adam and Eve were born in the garden of Eden, a place full of life and beauty. Heavenly Parent made them as His children and blessed them to "be fruitful, multiply and have dominion over creation, and to become the source of blessings." Adam and Eve were born to pass on the true love, true life and true lineage granted to humankind as implied in Heavenly Parent's ideal of creation. For humankind, life in the garden of Eden was a heavenly existence where they resembled Heavenly Parent, lived for the sake of each other and shared love by giving well and receiving well.

But this was interrupted when the ancestors of humankind, Adam and Eve, succumbed to Satan's temptation. Their eyes were opened in a way that they could focus on their desires, centering on themselves. Humans were to perfect themselves through completing periods of growth in stages. After they accomplished that, Heavenly Parent naturally would have had humans inherit everything. However, there is a process for that. That is the period of growth, in which humans obtain the authority to have dominion over the creation. However, immature humans succumbed to Satan and to their self-centered desires and fell. They ended up being expelled from the garden of Eden. That exile was the result of having severed the ties of true love, true life and true lineage connected with Heavenly Parent. The aftermath of the Fall of humankind was a self-centered society that was focused on the self, like the Dead Sea. Therefore, humankind is making a dark society that continues endlessly with ongoing strife and discord.

Then where does life come from? Life comes from love. Plants, too, were created by the love of Heavenly Parent upon fertile soil supplied with the clean water of life. It is the same with human lives. Humans receive pure love from Heavenly Parent, and when a new life is conceived, the lineage of Heaven can be continued.

Such a process of love, life and lineage began in the very beginning when Heavenly Parent created humankind. In other words, the lives of Adam and Eve were conceived through the love of their parent, Heavenly Parent. Yet, Heavenly Parent alone cannot ensure that "life" is passed down the family line. Only if Heavenly Parent uses Adam and Eve's bodies and enters them to realize the oneness of Heavenly Parent, humankind and love, and a life is conceived, for the first time the lineage of Heavenly Parent and humankind can be passed on.

However, humans, who should have been children of the lineage of goodness of Heavenly Parent, ended up becoming fallen humans of the lineage of evil of Satan. New lineal roots are required to correct this. This is why there must appear the manifestation of a true man, born of the love of Heavenly Parent and free from the fallen lineage. In other words, the last Adam and last Eve, who are the only begotten son and the only begotten daughter, must appear and become the true parents of humankind.

Fallen humans can be reborn as the sons and daughters of the True Parents by merely attending them. From that point they can be redeemed by receiving the Blessing and being changed to Heavenly Parent's blood lineage. The True Parents of humankind, who have come as the roots of the true blood lineage, are Reverend Sun Myung

Moon and Dr. Hak Ja Han Moon. We who have received the Blessing from True Parents can be called the true branches that grew from the roots of true love, true life and true lineage. Blessed central families were able to live after forming a blood relationship with the True Parents, who are the founders that separated themselves from the Fall. We should be proud of our True Parents, from whom we have inherited true love, true life and true lineage, and we should preserve the value that is continuously flowing within us. We must play an active role in the movement of informing others about the True Parents, having people be redeemed by receiving the Blessing and thus purifying their blood lineage.

❈ Points for contemplation

1) Let us reflect deeply on the significance of the words that life comes from love and lineage comes from life.
2) We must find a mentor who can provide us with life coordinates to enable us to return to the state of original humankind. Those mentors are the True Parents. You must lead your neighbors, relatives and tribe to receive the Blessing from True Parents and become people with a transformed blood lineage. From that standpoint, I ask that you think carefully over what roles we must play in our surroundings.

6
Heavenly Parent's Ideal World and Cheon Il Guk
– The Theory and Reality of Cheon Il Guk

True Parents' Words

God's vision of the ideal of creation included the kingdom of heaven in the spirit world, but He created all things because He wished for a concrete kingdom of heaven in the physical world, where He personally could reside. In other words, God created the world and everything in it to experience the glory of both the spiritual and the physical kingdom of heaven, with Himself and Adam and Eve as the center. He did not plan on establishing the kingdom of heaven in heaven and on earth just for Himself; He created them for humankind as well. God's purpose for creating heaven and earth was so that human beings could live in the kingdom of heaven on earth and afterward in the eternal world of the kingdom of heaven in heaven, centering on Adam and Eve.
[CSG 7.1.4:15]

The Chinese character for heaven, *cheon* (天), is formed by combining the characters for two (二) and *people* (人). Thus, Cheon Il Guk (天一國) means the nation where two people, Adam and Eve, become one with each other horizontally and become one with God vertically. From that point sons and daughters appear. [*CSG* 12.2.1:1]

Cheon Il Guk is a place where parents and children, husbands and wives, and brothers and sisters become one. God dwells in each family where two become one. Hence, two people in a parent–child relationship, which is a vertical relationship, have to completely become one; the same is true for two people in a husband–wife relationship, which is a right–left relationship, and in a relationship between older and younger siblings, which is a front–back relationship. Those who live for the sake of others bring such unity, whereas those who ask others to live for them will fall by the wayside. [*CSG* 12.2.1:5]

Sharing Thoughts

A certain woman prayed fervently, "Heavenly Parent, please bring me to the kingdom of heaven, where You are." Soon after, an angel appeared and declared before vanishing, "Heavenly Parent has heard your prayer and said, 'I will gladly answer your prayer, but I would just like to see you neatly organize your garden where you are living.'" The woman diligently cut the grass and trimmed the bushes before praying again, "Heavenly Parent, will You call me now?" This time an angel replied, "Plant trees in your village to create shade, and have people rest in the shade." The woman then planted trees along the road of the village and began planting beautiful flowers around them. Once again, the woman desperately pleaded to Heavenly Parent. Her plea, "Now will You call me?" was met with "Yes, you have worked hard. But there is a beggar standing at your door. And look at your family members." So, the woman fed the beggar a hearty meal and worked hard to serve and love her family until they were thoroughly satisfied. Then once again she prayed, "Heavenly Parent, is this enough?" Just then an angel took her by the hand, and they went up a hill. The angel said, "Here, look down this hill. How does your village look?" The village that the woman saw was heaven itself. The trees the woman had planted had become a beautiful forest; the poor people passing by praised her, and her family did not want to leave her embrace. There were lovable people and a beautiful garden before her.

You have heard the word "heaven" many times, haven't you? You probably have heard the phrase "died and gone to heaven" many times, too. What should one do to be able to get into such a place as heaven? Is heaven a place to go only after death? No, it is not. Unless heaven is attained on earth, it does not exist in the spirit world either.

If Adam and Eve, who were created in the image of Heavenly

Parent, had not fallen but instead had attained oneness with Heavenly Parent through love, the kingdom of heaven would have been established upon the earth. Heaven is a not a conceptual land of clouds that exists in a far-off place. When the love of Heavenly Parent is put into practice on earth, that moment of experiencing joy is the very moment that one experiences heaven. You probably have experienced true joy welling up from deep within when you have given love for the sake of others. That joy is not experienced by you alone but rather the joy is experienced together with Heavenly Parent. Have you ever experienced loving Heavenly Parent with all your heart, jeongseong and will, and showing love to your neighbors? Such actions transcend the realm of material things and include every aspect of your very being, time, talent, everything. If you experience enough moments of giving and receiving love, you can experience heaven while living on earth.

People who have experienced heaven on earth by living this way can live naturally in the kingdom of heaven when they go to the spirit world. The kingdom of heaven in spirit world is a world that connects to eternity by transcending time and space and the experience of heaven on earth. After shedding our earthly body and entering the spirit world, we will find that it is a world where we live and breathe in the air of true love. Those who have thoroughly felt the joy of true love by experiencing the heart of Heavenly Parent while on earth will be able to savor the air of true love in the spirit world and, intoxicated by such an aroma, will be able to enjoy eternal happiness and joy.

As you can see, the essence of Heaven is love. However, love cannot be achieved alone. Only when a subject partner and an object partner engage in give and take for the sake of the other can love be experienced for the first time. People live lives that consist of forming various types of relationships. In the family they form parent–child relationships, the husband–wife relationship, sibling relationships and, based on that, they form relationships in work, school and church. When we plant the love of Heavenly Parent in all relationships, and share that love and joy with others, Heaven slowly will reveal itself to us.

The meaning of the term "Cheon Il Guk" is right here; it means "a nation where two people have become one." Starting with the mineral, plant and animal kingdoms, the entire human world consists of pairs to sing the language of love of Heavenly Parent. The world where all such pairs become one through love is Cheon Il Guk. The source of love, Heavenly Parent, hopes to arrive safely in that kind of world of Cheon Il Guk and live together with us.

❋ Points for contemplation

1) If Cheon Il Guk is a world where two people become one, think about the meaning of "the two people." Then think about the meaning of "become one." Finally, contemplate the ways in which "two people can truly become one."
2) Let's think about what the following means: One must experience heaven on earth to be able to experience heaven in the spirit world.

7
Cheon Il Guk Is a World Where People Live for the Sake of Each Other

— The Ideals of Interdependence, Mutual Prosperity, and Universally Shared Values

True Parents' Words

Humanity desires a world of interdependence, mutual prosperity and universally shared values, which is a reflection of God's ideal kingdom. It is not a world where one can live alone; no individual can create such a world. Whenever we talk about "I," there also must be "my partner," whether it is my spouse or my family. This should not remain as a concept but should be applied in real life. The kingdom of God is the world where this concept is manifested in reality, on the stage of life. [CSG 10.4.1:5]

In an ideal society or nation, everyone will transcend nationality and skin color to engage in mutual cooperation, create harmony, and live in happiness. The community will be like an extended family. People will be conscious of being the sons and daughters of one God, a single brotherhood and sisterhood under the True Parents. That will be the place where blessed families, who have restored their lineage, right of ownership and realm of heart, will realize a world of freedom, peace and unity. It will be a world of True Parents' language and culture. People will be interdependent and prosperous, sharing universal values and God's culture, which is based on heart. As true owners, people will find ways to stop polluting the earth's environment and to love and protect all things. In that world, people will generate their livelihood in joyful service and act based on a heart that lives and loves for the sake of others. All of society's members will follow this standard of living. These ideals are impossible to achieve without the implementation of True Parents' thought, the thought that teaches that true love is living for the sake of others. [CSG 10.2.4:7]

Sharing Thoughts

Russian author Lev Tolstoy had the following three questions. First: When is the most important time? Second: Who is the most important person? Third: What is the most important thing to pursue? The following is Tolstoy's answers to these questions. "The most important time is now. The most important person is the person whom you are with, and the most important pursuit is making that person, the one standing at your side, happy. That alone is the pursuit of life. That is why you have to practice love and goodness with whomever you meet and wherever you go."

Tolstoy practiced these words religiously throughout his life. His words show us clearly the time, the person, and the pursuit we always must keep in mind. No one is able to live alone, devoid of human relationship. Whether we are aware of it or not, we live our daily lives while helping each other, either directly or indirectly. We receive help from our family members, our neighbors, the society, and even nature. We must realize that we can exist only because of others' efforts. That is why all humanity must live for the sake of the other. We will be able to live a truly happy life if we share not only our material blessings but also our spiritual blessings, and when we make an effort to look at the world from the viewpoint of others and multiply goodness.

Expanding this set of principles will create a world where people live for the sake of each other beyond national borders. That world, then, will be the utopia that humankind has been yearning for throughout history. The principle of living for the sake of Heavenly Parent can be used anywhere in the universe.

This is the reason why we have to spread the idea that we are the co-owners of all things in the universe created by Heavenly Parent. All created things are the priceless gifts that Heavenly Parent gave to human beings. We have to conserve the creation in the position of siblings while attending Heavenly Parent as our parent. The creation should not be hoarded by the few who look after only their own economic well-being. Those who are in the political realm, too, should refrain from advocating the interests of the few. Politicians should respect the people and try to reflect the people's opinions in their management of the nation. In the environmental field, any action that hurts nature for the benefit of the few should be halted immediately. Everyone on earth should work together to alleviate the detrimental effects of climate change and protect and develop the environment through sustainable means.

The heart of living for the sake of others and putting the objectives of the group before that of the individual will be imperative in establishing the world where everyone is prosperous. The fundamental essence of our creation is love and the heart of living for the sake of others. This is the reason we have to practice a life of sharing. The world in which this ideal is prevalent is called "a world of interdependence, mutual prosperity, and universally shared values." In other words, it is a world where everyone lives in harmony, prospers together, and lives with the heart of thinking of the whole before the individual. It is a world where people do not live for the sake of themselves but for the sake of others. It is a world of mutual prosperity.

Heavenly Parent's true love is at the foundation of such a world. Managing our economic, political, ethical, and social spheres based on the love of Heavenly Parent will ensure that Heavenly Parent can take part in them directly. Human beings are created in the image of Heavenly Parent. Our desire to live for the sake of others and practice love is stronger than our desire to be selfish. We can attain the true original value of being human when we live and practice this type of love.

One of True Parents' core messages, which they have preached for a very long time, is "live for the sake of others." We should practice this teaching and embody it in our everyday lives. Cheon Il Guk is a nation whose citizens live for the sake of others. Let us train ourselves to practice this teaching and invest our daily lives in giving happiness to others.

❋ Points for contemplation

1) Think about why people cannot live alone.
2) People who pursue selfish goals eventually come to a roadblock. Why is this? It is because human beings are relational beings and their happiness expands when they share. Which part of our life should we try to expand today?

8
Let Us Become True Parents, True Teachers, and True Owners!
– Three Great Subject Partners

True Parents' Words

God is the eternal True Parent, eternal True Teacher and eternal True Owner. To become a child of God, we first have to become a true parent like God. We have to go the way of a true teacher like God, and then the way of a true owner like God. This is the three-great-subject-partners principle. God is the ultimate exemplar. [CSG 1.2.1:26]

God is our True Parent and, at the same time, our True Teacher and True Owner. What kind of teacher is He? He is one who teaches us while caring for us, over and over again. What kind of owner is He? He does not try to possess everything and make it His. Rather, He gives us everything, even Himself. He tells us, "You will become the owner." If we were to sum this up in one sentence, that sentence would be: "I will give birth to you, raise you and make you an owner." In short, God gives us birth, nurtures us and establishes us as owners. So, it begins with God. Having created us, God's intention was to nurture us and elevate us to a position higher than His own, as children who would love on His behalf. As the Owner of the cosmos, His intention was to make us owners. [CSG 1.2.1:28]

God is the eternal True Parent, True Teacher and True Owner who always gives true love. All people are God's children, so, like God, they too have to go the way of the true parent, true teacher and true owner. Through these relationships these paths will lead to the completion of the ideal of love, the love that lives for the good of others. The right path of the law of heaven leads to self-realization through an altruistic life of true love. Through the harmony of the vertical parent–child relationship with the horizontal left-and-right husband–wife relationship and the horizontal front-and-back sibling relationship, the ideal family based on true love is realized. The completed family can be expanded to the completed nation, world and cosmos through the same principle and formula. The worldwide foundation that True Parents have achieved in the areas of education, media, art, and relief work comes through the investment of true love following the same formula to realize the ideal world. Ideally, true love education on how to realize the character of a true parent, true teacher and true owner should start in the family. [CBG 4.3.1:5]

Sharing Thoughts

In a small town in Massachusetts, there was a 14-year-old boy named William. He was a troubled boy with a very bad reputation. Even the school had forsaken him. He was also a bad influence on other students, and the school faculty was gravely concerned. Then one day, a new teacher came to William's school. After hearing about William, the new teacher wanted to see if he could help him. Many of the fellow teachers discouraged him. They said that his efforts would be in vain. However, the new teacher carefully observed William and analyzed his character and nature. He continued to show kindness and understanding to William, who had been branded by others to surely walk the path of delinquency. The teacher showed William the true meaning of love. He taught him to distinguish right from wrong. He gave him true courage and a sense of self-worth. He sowed his seeds with tears. After some time, these seeds began to sprout and take root. William started to do away with his old habits. He studied all night. He was accepted by a college and graduated at the top of his class. William pursued the study of law. In the end, he became an associate justice of the U.S. Supreme Court. William later became the governor of the state of New York, and even became the secretary of state. He was forsaken during his early years, but his life was completely changed by the efforts of a single teacher who saw the image of Heavenly Parent within him.

Heavenly Parent created human beings to realize His love. Love originates from the heart of living for the sake of others, not from a selfish heart. To love someone is to hope that that person becomes a better person. What is the highest position that is attainable by a human being who has inherited the love of Heavenly Parent? It is the position of true parents.

We can attain this position of true parents, who can be the ancestors and lords of love of future generations and all things in the universe, through uniting with and practicing the love of Heavenly Parent. Anyone in this position of true parents can inherit everything from Heavenly Parent. The parents in this position also raise their children from Heavenly Parent's perspective.

As they grow, children imitate everything that their parents do. They learn from what their parents say, what they do, and their parents' habits and character. Every moment such children spend with their parents who have attained the position of true parents will be educational. These children will grow up and become the true teachers who will lead the world with Heavenly Parent's love and truth. Everyone's first and best teachers are their parents.

Once they have attained the position of true parent and true teacher, they will want to protect nature, to live in harmony with their environment. When we say we become true owners, it means that we take great care of nature and invest a lot of love in this world. It means that we gain dominion over all created things in the universe while being united in heart with Heavenly Parent. That is why our ultimate objective should be to resemble Heavenly Parent, who is our True Parent, and become true parents, true teachers, and true owners. Essentially, it is to "give birth to and nurture our children and raise them to become owners."

Like this, we human beings have to experience the love of Heavenly Parent and become true parents, true teachers, and true owners during our lifetime. Moreover, we should guide our offspring on the path of becoming true parents, true teachers, and true owners. This world truly will become the original, ideal world envisioned by Heavenly Parent when His love continues to expand through the relationships of true parent and true child, true teacher and true student, and true owner and true object partner.

✻ Points for contemplation

1) What kind of person is a true teacher? A true teacher is more than someone who merely hands out knowledge. He is someone whose words and actions are united, who teaches while practicing and practices while teaching. Let us silently reflect on the characteristics that a true teacher should have.

2) Let us silently reflect on Heavenly Parent's heart to "give birth to and nurture our children and raise them to become owners." Let us experience Heavenly Parent's hopes and desires contained in that heart.

9
Toward the World of Unity, Peace, Happiness, and Freedom
— The Nature of Cheon Il Guk

True Parents' Words

Our family, the owner of Cheon Il Guk, pledges to build the universal family encompassing heaven and earth, which is God's ideal of creation, and perfect the world of freedom, peace, unity and happiness, by centering on true love. [*Family Pledge*, No. 4]

As the gap between the mind and body widens, the amount of distress increases. Suffering and tragedy take hold. Thus, we need to narrow the gap between our minds and bodies until they unite into one. If we cannot do that, this world will never know peace or happiness. Even if the global battle ends and we try to live in peace, we will not see hope, fulfillment or peace unless each of us ends our own internal battle. The problem is within me, within myself. I have to resolve my own fundamental issues. Once I do so, when I come upon ideal surroundings in the external world, peace and fulfillment will permeate my mind. In order to realize a free and happy kingdom of heaven, we need to connect with the world on that basis. No matter how well organized the environment may be, if our own problems have not been solved, we cannot blend into that happy environment. [CSG 10.2.2:31]

Where there is no unity, there can be no peace. Where there is no unity, there is no hope. Can you be happy when your mind and body are not united? Can you be happy when your mind and body are fighting? Can you be free? The two have to work well together. Peace requires a balance between the two. Have you found that balance? Do you get along well with your spouse? If you fight with your spouse in the morning, do you just go your own way, feeling happy the rest of the day? No. Freedom exists on the foundation of unity. If there is no unity, there is no happiness; if there is no unity, there is no peace; if there is no unity, there is no hope. [CSG 10.2.2:24]

Sharing Thoughts

"I spent my entire life visiting the lowest places on earth. I cultivated old forests and sowed seeds. I cut down trees to build schools for children and fed them with fish I caught. I met then-President Mikhail Gorbachev of the Soviet Union as part of my efforts to bring reconciliation between communism and

democracy, and I met then-President Kim Il Sung of North Korea for a serious discussion on how to bring peace to the Korean peninsula. I went to the United States, which was in moral decline, and played the role of a fireman responding to a call in an effort to reawaken its Puritan spirit. I dedicated myself to resolving various conflicts in the world. In my work for peace among Muslims and Jews, I was not deterred by rampant terror. As a result of my efforts, thousands have gathered for rallies and peace marches, with Jews, Muslims, and Christians all joining together. Sadly, however, the conflict continues. However, I continue to believe that, one day, the gate to a world of peace will open wide."
[*As a Peace-Loving Global Citizen*]

Have you ever thought about peace, freedom, unity and happiness in your everyday life? Which do you think is the one that needs to be attained first? It is unity that should be attained first. Only when unity is attained at the smaller level, can it be attained at bigger levels. Unity of mind and body can be attained at the individual level, then it can be attained between individuals, an individual and the family, group, society, nation, and the world. What opposes the idea of unity is boundaries. Boundaries exist between our mind and body. Starting from this, the existence of boundaries expands to individuals, groups, and nations. The very beginning point of unity is the mind and body of individuals. Then why is it that people hold on to their boundaries and fight among themselves? First, it is because the Fall turned us into contradictory beings. This means we are stuck in a system of conflict. Second, it is because we lost the purpose of our existence due to the Fall. Those without a clear objective are bound to find themselves lost. They are lost and conflicted.

There is no truth in their heart. Third, it is because our excessive desire puts individual interest before anything else, naturally creating boundaries that lead to conflict. In other words, people feel limitations when they are no longer able to pursue their excessive desires. Fourth, it is because we look sideways while pursuing our goals. People who pursue their own selfish interests rather than the good of the community tend to be affected by external elements.

What does it mean to attain unity? First, it means to have a clear self-identity and goals with no internal borders that create conflict and no shadow in the heart. A person can attain this state of unity when he finds himself completely centered upon Heavenly Parent. Second, it means to set aside selfish desires, aligning our goals for the sake of the world and walking the transparent path of joy and glory.

You may have experienced a change in your relationship with someone after quarreling with that person. For example, if a married couple fights, each of them may feel as though the air is so full of tension that it is difficult even to breathe. Their every action begins to feel unnatural, as if their body is entangled in chains. In this type of predicament, the whole family will lose its freedom and happiness. This also means that there is no peace without unity, and no happiness without peace. Things change completely when the couple reconciles its differences and witnesses the other's true intention. They will be free from the shackles that slowed them down, and peace and happiness will begin to flourish again in that family. In the end, the matters of peace, happiness, and freedom are closely related to the unity of heart between the husband and wife.

No matter the time and place in history, human beings always have pursued unity, peace, happiness, and freedom. True Parents teach us that these values are possible only upon the foundation of unity. At the very base, there is the unity of mind and body. The human mind originally is designed to pursue noble values such as truth, goodness, beauty, and love. The human body, however, always is trying to drag us in the opposite direction, toward clothing, food, shelter, and carnal desires. This has led humanity to experience endless internal fighting and struggles. Human beings were supposed to live a valuable life by having dominion over their bodies. Instead, however, people have been dominated by the desires of their flesh and living for their own sake. This conflict between mind and body materializes not only within individuals but also between the individual and society, and individuals and nature.

That is why True Parents have long taught us, "Attain mastery over yourself before seeking to master the things in the universe around you."

What should we do in order to unite our mind and body? The true world of goodness will emerge when all relationships center around Heavenly Parent's heart of living for the sake of others.

The true world of unity, peace, happiness, and freedom will come when we completely align with Heavenly Parent and eliminate all boundaries. That is the place where peace will settle. Peace is possible only when we start to place others first. In other words, it is the culture of living for the sake of others. Happiness then will follow naturally. Happiness expands, the more it is shared. Later, it will take the shape of a culture. This is how the true world of freedom, with unity, peace, and happiness, can emerge. The foundation of Heavenly Parent's culture of living for the sake of others is required before individuals and societies can enjoy their freedom.

❋ Points for contemplation

1) Let us silently reflect on the meaning of True Parents' teaching, "Attain mastery over yourself before seeking to master things in the universe around you."
2) How should we eliminate the borders between our mind and body? Let us examine what kinds of boundaries exist in our life and think about ways to eliminate them.
3) What are some of the things we can do to create a society where unification, peace, happiness, and freedom are realized in their truest sense?

10
One Family under Heavenly Parent

True Parents' Words

The unity of the world as a global family is essential for heavenly fortune to come. Astonishing developments in science and technology bind humanity together through a revolution of information, communication and transportation. Thus, international cooperation is needed and a shared commitment is necessary in order to protect the earth's fragile environment. But what can bring the power to change people's tendency toward selfishness and their attachment to a self-centered perspective of the world? What can fundamentally resolve the problem of nations competing to satisfy their own interests? Each one of us must find the answer in Heaven's law, and by means of a fundamental awareness of God, who is our origin and root. The nature of God's true love is to give and want to give more, to give and forget what He gave, and to love His object partner more than Himself. God's love is the only answer. We can get answers when we realize that all human beings are brothers and sisters under one set of True Parents. When all human beings form one family under God and True Parents, live for the sake of one another and are united, all problems can be resolved. Throughout my life I have practiced the way of true love and educated people about it. I have lived for the sake of others and created a worldwide foundation. I have raised young people in each nation to live unselfishly for the sake of others. Not only that, I have also conducted international Marriage Blessing ceremonies in order to establish ideal families of true love that are international, interracial and interreligious. This is the work that changes the history of human culture. Centered on true love, we have brought down national barriers and have gone beyond racial barriers to overcome hatred. We have fought to give birth to ideal families that live for the sake of one another. As a result, we are forming a new world culture. [CBG 4.1.1:12]

With the start of the new millennium, we are rapidly heading toward one world. We are leaving behind the era of "One Nation under God" and going toward "One Cosmos under God." The world of one great family and one global village, which I explained already, is emerging. However, there are two serious obstacles to realizing this ideal: racial discrimination and religious discord. In particular, conflicts among religions represent the most serious impediment to a peaceful world. God did not create denominations and sects. Religion itself is a byproduct of the Fall. The movement to break down all varieties of national boundaries and head to a world of peace, which I already clarified at the U.N., is rapidly developing. [*CBG* 11.2.2:14]

Sharing Thoughts

Peter was a mere fisherman when he became a disciple of Jesus Christ. He used to pray like this on his journey to spread Heavenly Parent's words: "Grant me the courage to mend the things that can be mended. Let me accept the things I can't mend, and give me the wisdom if there are things that can be mended in this world with others. The sins of my flesh have received your judgment, but I am grateful to you for guiding my spirit to live as Heavenly Parent does. We will resemble you and practice love more than anything, and this love covers all the sins. Let me serve others without reserve, and be the bearer of Heavenly Parent's endless grace, which I received. I will let my tongue speak the words of my Heavenly Parent and serve others through the power given to me by Heavenly Parent." We can see from Peter's short prayer his strong desire to realize love and prosperity for his neighbors.

People have been building barriers throughout history. These barriers have many names as well. Today we see barriers in national borders, language, race, culture, religion, gender, place of birth, and "haves" and "have-nots." These barriers affect not only our hearts but also the societies we live in.

How did these barriers come about, and why have we created them with our selfish hearts? That is because people have forgotten what it's like to be brothers and sisters, which comes from a concept of one family under Heavenly Parent. Since the Fall of Adam and Eve, humanity has been divided into Cain-type people and Abel-type people. This type of conflict still exists today. The human ancestors, who were like brothers, fell from their position and began to fight. If this is so, then they can unite only centering on their parents. This is because fights between brothers cannot be resolved within that realm of siblings. They can be solved only when their parents appear, embrace them, and help them to make unity. By uniting thanks to their parents, humanity can restore their status as one family under Heavenly Parent, as it was envisioned by Him in the first place.

We human beings are brothers and sisters with one common set of parents. Tracing the root of humankind leads to one absolute cause, the creator, our Heavenly Parent. We were created by Heavenly Parent and are all equal beings as brothers and sisters under Heavenly Parent. That is why we should never pass judgment lightly, based on other people's external conditions. We have to discover the essence of Heavenly Parent within others that makes us all equal.

We can slowly break down the barriers that surround us when we regard our neighbors and people around us as our own brothers and sisters. How can there be barriers and racial discrimination within the realm of heart that connects brothers and sisters? As we often say, "We will be able to establish a new world through demolishing barriers and overcoming conflicts with true love, creating a culture of living for the sake of others."

Some people say that today's world is a global village. This means more than just the fact that we can go anywhere in the world within one day, thanks to technological advances. It also should mean that humanity realizes that we are brothers and sisters of one family under Heavenly Parent. Based on this revelation, we should strive to create a world where people live for the sake of each other. When we can interact with this world with Heavenly Parent's viewpoint, we will be able to discover the visage of Heavenly Parent within each other's face and restore the heart of brothers and sisters.

❋ Points for contemplation

1) Reflect on your life and think if you have created barriers in the past. Think of what you can do to break those barriers.
2) Draw a picture in your heart of the world where everyone is "One Family under Heavenly Parent."

Chapter 3
Heavenly Parent

1
One Must Experience the Existing Heavenly Parent

— the Existence of Heavenly Parent

True Parents' Words

The phrase "God exists" is not an empty one. It is not that we deduce the necessity of God's existence by understanding the subject–object partner relationship through the Principle. It is that God existed before we came into existence, that He existed before we could think, and that He leads our senses and our whole being. This awareness is more important than anything else. The basic point is that awareness precedes knowledge, not the other way around. If we are cold, we feel cold before we know we are cold. Likewise, since God exists, we should be able to feel His existence in our very cells. Achieving that awareness is what matters. The issue is how we achieve that awareness, the ability to experience these things. The most serious issue in human life is to know whether or not God exists. If God really exists, the greatest of sinners is the one who denies His existence. For example, if a son denies his parents' existence when they are truly alive and well, we would call him an unfilial son. Then, what will happen to the person who denies God's existence, even though God exists? That person will come to ruin. Hence, there is no greater sin than the denial of God's existence. There are even those who say God is dead. There is no sin greater than the utterance of such words. We should not perceive the existence of God only vaguely and conceptually. It is impossible to understand the existence of God through logic alone. This is because God's existence, while within the realm of logic, also reaches beyond logic. Can a religious belief in which we know God only through logic guide our lives? Can such a belief perfect us as substantial beings of eternal life? There are many problems with that idea. With only that foundation, how can we expect to stand before God, our true Lord? Our coming to God has been the hope of humankind and also God's providential objective throughout history. [CSG 1.1.1:2–4]

Sharing Thoughts

A person approached a Christian and said the following: "Christians always speak of God. Where is that God? If you can tell me where He is, then I will also believe in that God." Though the Christian didn't like the person who asked this question so much, he still took him outside and, pointing to the sun, said the following, "Look straight at the sun." The person replied in anger, "Stop speaking gibberish! How can you look straight at the sun?"

"If you cannot look straight at the sun, which is only one out of the many creations made by God, then how can you look, with your eyes, at such a great God?"

This parable is conveyed within the Talmud. To say one cannot believe in that which cannot meet the eye can easily become a dogmatic and dangerous thought, as there are many things we cannot see that exist in our surroundings.

From ancient times, many philosophers, theologians, scientists, and others have passionately debated on the existence of the Creator, the Heavenly Parent. Diverse thoughts on this topic have emerged, including theism (the thought that recognizes the existence of a Heavenly Parent), atheism (the thought that denies it), and agnosticism (the thought that asserts people cannot know of the existence of such a being). However, as we can know from the story, there are limits to debating about what cannot be seen.

Love, for example, is an actual emotion; yet, we cannot see it. No matter how logical an argument for the existence of love would be, a person who has never experienced it could not clearly understand this emotion. Furthermore, such a person easily could define love as either an illusion or simply a temporary desire. Hence, what is needed is experience and not a debate on whether love exists or not.

The same applies to the wind. It would be meaningless for people in a room without windows to logically discuss whether the wind is blowing outside. If a person is in a place with windows, he or she can observe leaves or flags moving in the wind. A more effective method would be to open the window, put one's hand outside, and feel how much the wind is blowing. Therefore, instead of trying to logically prove whether the wind is blowing, a useful and certain method would be to visually observe a windy phenomenon or tactually sense it.

Likewise, the debate as to whether Heavenly Parent exists can be logically conducted, yet is limited, as Heavenly Parent cannot be seen directly with the naked eye. The most effective way to prove Heavenly Parent's existence is to directly experience Heavenly Parent's substantial being. Just as a person would put his or her hand outside a window to feel the wind or go out the door to feel it fully, an individual must pray and practice different forms of asceticism to experience Heavenly Parent's substantial existence.

True Parents teach that it is essential to experience Heavenly Parent's existence and to live with certainty in Heavenly Parent. That is because unwavering, firm faith is based on experience and certainty, and not vague hope and assumption. We all need to invest efforts in strengthening the foundation of our faith.

❈ Points for contemplation

1) Through what kind of phenomena can we verify the existence of Heavenly Parent?
2) What kinds of effort can we invest to experience Heavenly Parent?

3) Have you ever experienced Heavenly Parent's substantial being? If you have, can you describe it?

2
The Relationship between Heavenly Parent and Humankind Is That of a Parent and Child
– Heavenly Parent Who Is a Parent

True Parents' Words

What is the center of heaven and earth, and what is the root of the universe? When I entered a mystical state and prayed to God about this, He told me that it is the relationship between the Father and His sons and daughters, that is, the parent–child relationship. If you think this refers to the relationship between a physical father and mother and their sons and daughters, you do not understand it fully. I am talking about the relationship between God and human beings. God and human beings have a parent–child relationship. How do we come to this conclusion? When you enter a mystical state in your prayer and ask, "If human beings are the center of the created world, what is the center of the universe?" you will receive a simple answer: "It is the parent–child relationship." You may think that the parent–child relationship here refers to the relationship between your physical mother and father and yourself, that is, a relationship centered on human morals and ethics, but that is not what I am talking about. The parent–child relationship between God and human beings united in heart is multidimensional. It is that point that is the center of the universe. From the viewpoint of love, we are each the fruit of a mother's love, of a father's love and of God's love. Vertically we are the fruit of God's love; horizontally we are each the fruit of a mother and a father's love. Because we want to follow this love forever and unite with it, we can never betray it. We want to stay and live in that love forever. That is why, even though mothers and fathers are fallen, they still want to live with their children forever. [CSG 1.2.3:3–5]

Sharing Thoughts

Many tourists were enjoying Niagara Falls in the United States. They let out cries of exclamation as they looked at the magnificent waterfall, saying, "Such a majestic waterfall! Who could have created it? If it did have an owner, he or she would have earned so much money from tourism."

Then one confident-looking young man spoke to the tourists, saying, "Ladies and gentlemen! That waterfall belongs to my father, and I am his son!" The tourists looked at the triumphant young man with envy. One old man approached the young man and asked, "Who is your father?" Then the young man smiled and replied, "Yes. My father's name is God, who is the creator of the heavens and the earth."

This young man was none other than Robert Schuller, a world-renowned pastor from the United States. What kind of being is the God described in Christianity? (The Family Federation for World Peace and Unification has called God "Heavenly Parent" since Foundation Day in 2013.)

People in ancient times regarded God as a fearful being. Whenever unexplainable natural disasters happened, they regarded it as a curse from God and feared Him even more. Hence, God was regarded as not only the Creator but also as a being and king that rules the world. Judaism, which emerged before the birth of Christ, believed that God was omnipotent and perfect, and its adherents strictly kept His commandments.

Hence, the emergence of Jesus, who called God "Father," was a shock to the Jewish people. Jesus taught that God was not a law-centered, angry king but a father who loves humanity.

Despite such teachings by Jesus, many people could not think of God as their father. Jesus, who came as God's only begotten son, unlike regular people, could call God his Father. Others, however, could not call God their Father. Even when they were able to do so through the grace of Jesus, they connected the term "Father" to a Creator, a king, and a father ruling with patriarchal authority instead of a Father as in a loving parent.

The understanding of God as the king, lord, leader, judge, father, etc., is limited, as it leads people to connect His essence with domination and judgment. Many theologians today have questioned whether such an image of God is correct, and they are trying to understand God as a Being who stays by our side, instead of a God ruling us from above. In other words, they introduced God in a new image: that of a friend, companion, lover, etc. Our understanding of God therefore has changed from that of a vertical and authoritative God.

True Parents teach a fundamental change in regard to our understanding of God. God is not of one single gender. in other words, God is not just a father or just a mother. God is a true parent and, hence, the Heavenly Parent. True Parents revealed that our relationship with God is that of a parent and child. To a young child, his or her parents look perfect like Superman, and at times, they may seem fearful. When the child grows, he or she comes to understand his or her parents' heart. Likewise, our understanding of Heavenly Parent will deepen, depending on the degree by which our faith has matured.

Hence, our relationship with Heavenly Parent should be understood not as a one-directional relationship but as a reciprocal relationship of give and take. Furthermore, it is a relationship in which Heavenly Parent can come down into the human world and be with us in character, and it is a relationship in which we can experience His heart. The God who was joyful after creating humans, the God who was sorrowful after the Fall, and the God who led the providence to save humankind is not a God whom we can find only in history. Heavenly Parent created people as His children and, being their parent, never gave up on those children throughout the 6,000 years after the Fall, continuing the providence of salvation.

Understanding Heavenly Parent as the True Parents of humanity is the starting point of a mature faith. As children of Heavenly Parent, True Parents comforted Heavenly Parent's sorrowful heart and followed the path of true filial heart, or hyojeong, to realize the ideal of creation that Heavenly Parent envisioned at the time of creation. Hence, instead of having a young faith that simply desires to receive Heavenly Parent's love, it is necessary to have the heart of a true child that strives to realize Heavenly Parent's hope.

✻ Points for contemplation

1) Let us meditate on the meaning of Heavenly Parent being the parent of humanity.
2) You have realized that Heavenly Parent is your parent. What attitude and mindset should you have?
3) As a child of Heavenly Parent, how can I comfort the sorrowful heart of Heavenly Parent, who lost His children? What changes should there be in my life for me to advance toward Heavenly Parent?

3
Heavenly Parent Who Is the Eternal Owner of the Heart

— The Owner of Heart

True Parents' Words

God is the eternal Lord of our body and our heart. In the original world, if a husband and wife say that no matter how much they love each other, they love God even more, neither will feel resentful. The kingdom of heaven is the world in which we can rejoice that our spouse loves God more than us. God, who is in the position of subject partner transcending any kind of love and any circumstances, is the eternal Lord of our body. Therefore, if we are embraced in the bosom of God, who owns our body, and thus dwell in His garden, we will be happy even when we die. Today, with what heart do we venture out? With what eyes do we observe the world? With what senses do we feel? Before you think about this, you should pray, "God, as I lead my life, I am dealing with these kinds of sensations. Yet I want to lead my life understanding the heart of Adam and Eve toward You prior to the Fall, the heart they had at the time of the Fall, the heart You experienced when You had to expel Adam and Eve, the heart with which You toiled laboriously for the sake of humanity for 1,600 years until You called Noah, and Noah's heart as he worked for 120 years bearing ridicule and persecution, holding on to Heaven in order to build the ark on top of a mountain. I want to know Your heart throughout all the twists and turns of history and hold on to that heart." The question is how we empathize with God's feelings in our daily life. When you are alone, you should be able, without forethought, to call out to God, "Father!" Then you will feel God's reply, "Yes, I am here!" If you are one with God, that's how it will be. It seems that no one is around, but someone is leading and guiding you. If you live such a life, you never question God's existence. When you face difficulties, you know God will protect and guide you. Knowing this, you cannot desert Him. [CSG 1.2.1:3,7.8]

Sharing Thoughts

One night, I had a dream. I was walking along the beach with God. Across the sky flashed scenes from my life. For each scene, I noticed two sets of footprints in the sand. One set belonged to me and one to God.

When the last scene of my life flashed before me, I looked back at the footprints in the sand. I noticed that at many times along the path of my life, there was only one set of footprints. I also noticed that this happened at the very lowest and saddest times in my life. This really troubled me, so I asked God about it. "You said You'd walk with me all the way. However, when I needed You the most, You would leave me." Then God replied, "My beloved and precious child, I never left you. When you saw only one set of footprints in the sand, those were not your footprints; they were Mine. During your times of difficulties, distress and misery, it was then that I carried you."

This is a poem of an anonymous author that has been read by many at least once. How many footsteps are there on the sand that you have walked on until now? From a distance, humans look as though they all live the same life; yet when you look into each individual's life, each is unique, with its share of ordeals, ups and downs, and stories about how they overcame them.

When we look back on the path of our life that has passed by so suddenly, we can see that there were times that rushed by, when we did not understand even the hearts of our physical parents. Furthermore, even though Heavenly Parent is our parent, humankind has not given any thought to Heavenly Parent at all. If a person were not acknowledged as a parent, even by his children, and were living by himself in loneliness, and if that person were your own parent, what words of comfort would you want to offer? What would you like to say that you would do from then on? This parent is the one who has always spiritually, unseen to our eyes, come down into our lives, loved us and accompanied us always. This one and only parent is Heavenly Parent. At this very moment Heavenly Parent is next to us, with His hands reaching out to us.

He knows my mind when even I do not know. During those moments when I go through difficulties and shout out that I am alone, it is Heavenly Parent who invariably comes to me and comforts me. Please feel Heavenly Parent's love at this time. Being the source of the heart, Heavenly Parent knows more deeply about our heart than we do. If there is anyone who hasn't been able to experience this heart of Heavenly Parent yet, please try to open your heart at this moment. Please look into His warm eyes, which have always been looking at you in the most loving way in the world. However, because our hearts have been closed, until now we have not been able to feel Heavenly Parent's warm heart, and we could not be held in His embrace when He approached us with a feeling of love.

Opening one's heart wide to Heavenly Parent is not a grand or difficult task. When you wake up in the morning, greet Heavenly Parent first, saying, "Heavenly Parent, did You sleep well? Thank You for protecting me throughout the night. Please be with me throughout the day again today." When going out, you can say, "I am now leaving home. Please be with me so that whatever I am endeavoring to do goes well." In the evening, when you come back home after work, greet Heavenly Parent saying, "Thank You for protecting me throughout the day. How difficult it must have been." It is enough to greet Him. Through hoondokhae, you can envision the world that Heavenly Parent desires based on the Word, and if you put it into practice one step at a time, that is enough. Think that Heavenly Parent is with you in your daily life; once you begin doing so, you will be able to feel the presence of Heavenly Parent.

When you meet people who have prayed a lot and offer jeongseong, you will sense that their prayers are quite simple, without fancy, flowery words or an especially excited tone. They comfortably and honestly report about their life and heart, just as though they were reporting to their parents. When praying to Heavenly Parent, asking that He be with us, it is like a conversation between a parent and child. Those who pray like this experience the Heavenly Parent who is always together with us, the Parent who knows our heart better than we do, rather than an omniscient and omnipotent, holy and authoritative Heavenly Parent.

Heavenly Parent is the eternal owner of our heart, because He knows our joys and sorrows, our happiness and unhappiness, our loneliness and emptiness, and much more. Therefore, when we can feel we are living with our Heavenly Parent, our insecurities, fears, dread and agony can disappear. I pray that you will be able to make every single day one of attending Heavenly Parent.

❋ Points for contemplation

1) Have you ever felt that Heavenly Parent is with you? Let us share our experiences.
2) Let us reflect on how many times we pray to Heavenly Parent a day. What kind of changes did you experience while you were praying and after you prayed?

4
Heavenly Parent Is the Starting Point of True Love
– The Source of True Love

True Parents' Words

God is omniscient and omnipotent. He can obtain everything He desires and can do everything He wishes. It seems ideal and that there is nothing God could need. Nonetheless, there is still one thing that He needs: love. Even though He is absolute, even God cannot have love by Himself. This is because love can be had only in a mutual relationship. No matter how all-knowing and all-powerful God is, He cannot possess love on His own. Of course, He has love's attributes, but love's signals and love's stimulation can come only from another person, not from within oneself. Such is love. That is the power of love. For what purpose did God create us? He created us and established the standard for our perfection based on love. Hence, love is the standard. In other words, becoming a perfect person is based on God's love, not on our ability or level of leadership. Once we become a perfect person centering on God's love, we can unite with God in love, play with Him and enjoy everything together with Him forever. The perfect person, the one who meets the highest standard of God's desire, is the person who is one with God in love. True love began from God. Love started from Him, is sustained by Him, and must return to Him in the end. God is the King of kings. Since God is absolute, His love is eternal. Therefore, if you stand in the position of object partner to that absolute love, you are bound to have eternal life. This is what God intended from the very beginning of creation. It is for this reason that we want to live eternally. It is natural that we have such hope. [CSG 1.2.2:1.3]

Sharing Thoughts

One day, a person visited a jewelry shop run by a friend. His friend showed him many expensive and valuable jewels. Suddenly his friend lowered his voice and said, "I'll show you alone a very special, rare and precious jewel." He took out a small jewelry box from one corner of the display stand and opened the box.

But different from the man's great expectation, the jewel in the box was neither shiny nor transparent. "This doesn't look so precious." His friend smiled brightly. He gently grasped the jewel, placed it on the palm of his hand, closed his hand and then opened his hand again. The jewel on the palm of his hand was radiating the bright colors of the rainbow. "Wow! What happened? Oh my gosh! I've never seen such entrancing lights!"

"This gem is called an opal. It radiates these beautiful colors only when it comes in contact with human body temperature. We call this the gem that connects minds. Isn't that true between people too? When two people hold hands, their hearts connect; once their hearts are connected, a beautiful world is formed that cannot be compared to anything else."

Like the gem called an opal in the fable, we cannot shine by ourselves, but within a loving relationship we shine, and that warm love is true love. Within true love shared together, we can feel infinite happiness. Without a doubt, a partner for love is essential for relationships to be established, for love to act, multiply and expand. That is why people find the value of their existence in the process of giving and receiving love. The more people we have who are close to us, like family and friends, with whom we can give and receive true love, the more we experience happiness and long life.

We feel true happiness in loving relationships because we were created resembling Heavenly Parent. Heavenly Parent was almighty, but He also was alone. Wanting to have substantial beings with whom He could give and receive love, He began creation, investing all His love in it. Hence, His desire to give and receive love with a partner was His biggest motivation. Creation began from this strong motive.

All things of creation that were created through the motivation of Heavenly Parent's strong heart of true love possess this fundamental desire to give and receive love. The heart of wanting to become one with another through love is a heart that comes from our resemblance to Heavenly Parent. We were created as beings who can feel and meet Heavenly Parent through love. That is why the standard of true love is not based on me or on my partner. Human beings who take after our eternal Heavenly Parent think of their partner and give true love centered on Heavenly Parent as the standard of that love. Love that is centered on one's own mind and desires can easily become self-centered; while love that is centered on goodness, that fills the heart and the needs of the partner, and that matches itself to the other is always filled with abundance. Two people love one another through their hearts that think of Heavenly Parent. Even if people have several individuals with whom they need to give and receive love, if they match themselves to the object partner centered on goodness with the desire to unite, then true love will occur.

❋ Points for contemplation

1) Let's all think about the reason Heavenly Parent is the source of true love.
2) What methods are there for matching oneself to one's partner and sharing true love centered on goodness? Let's discuss it with other people.
3) What kinds of people are the object partners with whom I have a relationship? How can I best help them?

5
Heavenly Parent Invested Everything
— Heavenly Parent's Ideal of Creation

True Parents' Words

Creation entails the investment of energy. Every artist in the world desires to create the greatest of masterpieces. He or she invests everything—spirit, heart and soul—with the utmost jeongseong. It is not partial investment but total investment that gives birth to the perfect masterpiece. Perfection finally comes when the created object needs nothing more. Can you fully love an object of hope that you made while withholding something of yourself, withholding your flesh and blood? It is only when you have given everything—your bones, your flesh, your ideas and everything you possess—that you can bond with what you have created as the object of your hope. That is why I am saying that the beginning of the process of creation itself could have been possible only through investment. There has to be the investment of energy. Nothing can be made without the investment of energy. Committed to the principle that the perfect object partner is created from an infusion of all one's energy, God invested everything He had as the subject partner to create His object partner. God's work of creation was the beginning of His movement toward the state of existing not for Himself but for His object partner. In the world of physics, the input is greater than the output. But in the world of love, the input is less than the output. Because this principle applies on the horizontal plane, the universe exists forever. Consumption depletes everything. Thus, God's existence is perpetuated based on love. The universe maintains its existence eternally through this continuous circular motion. [CSG 1.3.1:18, 20]

Sharing Thoughts

A Christian astronomer named Johannes Kepler and an atheist friend talked together about the birth of the universe.

Kepler: This universe is Heavenly Parent's creation.

Friend: No. The universe just came into being when a star with the greatest power in a certain orbit began ruling over the other stars. The solar system was created through its own strength. It was not created by someone.

After some deliberation, Kepler created an accurate replica of the solar system at a ratio that reduced the real size, colored it nicely and connected all the pieces so that they could revolve around the sun.

Friend: Wow! It is really beautiful. Who created this marvelous model?

Kepler: No one created it. It just appeared through its own strength.

Friend: Stop talking nonsense and tell me. Was it you?

Kepler: Are you saying you are certain that this trivial toy could not have been created without involving somebody's input? Then, the last time we talked, how could you say that this vast universe was created on its own?

His friend could not say anything.

How would the universe have been created? As you walk on a path, do all the small pebbles that you kick randomly exist simply because they were in that place?

For as long as humans have existed, we have questioned how we were created and have been curious about where the origin of matter lay. We have divided the answer into two main points and researched them. First, in religion, we thought about the cause of creation. We studied about who is the causal being that started creation and why human beings were created. Scientists focused on the process of creation. This is because it was impossible to know why the universe was created, but with the development of science, it was possible to know what the origin of matter was and the process through which life evolved.

When many physicists see the process of the Big Bang and evolution, they say that the whole process cannot be the result of some coincidence. It is possible only through the investment of energy with a creative and high dimensional directivity. Ultimately, as they carry out scientific research, they will discover that the universe and human beings are not a combination resulting from coincidence; rather, they can't help but discover that there is a Heavenly Parent who exists who invested in every stage with a consistent direction.

Together with the development of science, religion has let go of literalism, and there is a wide understanding that the period of creation was not six literal days but rather that it signifies several stages of creation, and a wider understanding about the idea that people who received revelations had recorded everything they saw with their naked eyes. In the past, religion and science walked opposite paths, but we have come to an era in which science has developed, and we are reaching the time when religion and science meet as one. The result of this discovery is evidence that Heavenly Parent invested all His love and effort into creating the universe and human beings.

Heavenly Parent did not create the universe by proclaiming words without any effort. He put forth every ounce of Himself and invested all His energy into creating it. When we think about Heavenly Parent's love and dedication, we come to feel grateful for the world of creation that we live in. Because Heavenly Parent's sincere devotion is in every blade of grass and every drop of water, they are precious. With a heart of gratitude for Heavenly Parent's hard work, we should treasure His creation and give back to nature so that the cycle of life can continue vibrantly.

❊ Points for contemplation

1) Let us think about the process of creating the universe that Heavenly Parent went through.
2) What feelings do you have when you look at the world into whose creation Heavenly Parent, our Parent, invested all His energy for the sake of human beings? Seeing Heavenly Parent's creativity and absolute investment, what are some things that we could do, resembling His creativity, for the world of human beings and the world of all things?

6
The Realization of the Kingdom of Heaven That Attends Heavenly Parent
– The Created World of Heavenly Parent

True Parents' Words

God created us to become one in heart with Him, to share His value in true love, and to experience an inseparable parent–child bond with Him, enabling us to relate with Him in daily life through our strongest emotions. God's ideal of creation, which entails this perfection, comes with the perfection of human beings, who would be His partners in love as sons and daughters. This elevation is the accomplishment of the ideal of true love.

To summarize, God's purpose in creating the first human ancestors, Adam and Eve, was for them to establish a family of goodness that would fully ripen the fruit of God's true love, true life and true lineage. On the foundation of their family, Adam and Eve were to nurture the heart of children, the heart of siblings, the heart of husband and wife, and the heart of parents. In this process, as discrete manifestations of God's dual characteristics of masculinity and femininity, they were to proceed step by step to master the ability to express God's love, bringing it to perfection at a place of safe settlement.

If Adam's family had fulfilled the true love ideal in this manner, with God in the central position, it would have been the first family of the kingdom of heaven. Starting from this ideal family, with Adam and Eve as true parents, the kingdom of heaven naturally would have expanded in scope to produce tribes, peoples, nations and the world. The tradition of the family of true love would have become the tradition of the world. In this ideal world, the incarnate true parents would be at the single central position. They would resemble and inherit all the attributes of God, the spiritual absolute True Parent, absolute True Teacher and absolute True Owner. In the kingdom of heaven of true love, the incarnate true parents, who are united with God, would create the vertical axis. Keeping this axis at the center, all relationships between created entities, occupying positions such as upper and lower, left and right, front and back, and internal and external, would be in harmony. Thus, all of creation would dwell in freedom, peace, unity and happiness. When our life on earth in our physical body comes to an end, our spirit-self transitions into the spirit world, which is the ultimate world. It is an extension of our life on earth and also a place where we are to perfect the ideal of the kingdom of heaven. [*PHG* 1.14:173–174, 2002.12.27]

Sharing Thoughts

There were two families living as neighbors in the same area. One was an extended family which lived together with the parents-in-law, and the other was a happy home in which just a young couple lived together. But strangely, the extended family with the parents-in-law was always harmonious and full of laughter, and the family with just the young couple was always fighting. The couple, who saw that the neighboring house was always harmonious, couldn't help but wonder about it greatly. Why is it that with just the two of us living together, we fight every day, whereas the house next door has several people, but they are so harmonious? Therefore, one day the young couple bought a box of fruit and went to the neighboring house. After giving them the fruit, the young couple asked, "You have a large family, but you are always laughing. We are just the two of us, but we fight every day. Please tell us the key to how your family lives so harmoniously."

The homeowner replied, "Ah, yes! That is because you are both great people and our family is just a bunch of fools!" The couple who heard this asked, "What does that mean?" Then the homeowner said, "This happened this morning. I was on my way out to go to work when I spilled some water. So I apologized to my wife for spilling the water due to my carelessness and asked for her forgiveness. However, she replied, 'No,' saying that it was her fault for putting the water container in that place without giving it much thought, and she apologized. Right then, my mother, who was nearby, said, 'No, it is my fault, because I saw it there but did not do anything about it.' We cannot fight because we each become fools for the sake of the other."

This is just a short story, but through it we can see a beautiful family. As we live, we hope to meet a loving partner, have children and create a happy and enjoyable family. Within the family we can develop our character and expand our heart. It is important for a man and woman to become a couple and love, believe and rely on each other. This is because, although they are two different beings, the moment they share love, they can achieve oneness and experience the joy of becoming completely one. A child is conceived through the couple's love, and the couple develops into parents through love. For parents, giving birth to and raising a child that resembles them is like getting to live life twice. They love their child and get to experience the growth of the child together.

Transcending themselves and completely loving and caring for another being, their child, causes the parents' heart and character to expand. The world of heart that they experienced only through knowledge expands into the parental heart as they raise their child. It expands like the Big Bang that exploded and gave birth to the universe, and they come to encounter the heart of a parent like Heavenly Parent who has loved human beings.

When these parents see their grandchildren, who are born from their children, they come to experience something that they had not experienced before while raising their own children. When they were raising their own children, because of their responsibilities and duties to resolve practical things, they could not completely feel the joy and fulfillment that they now can feel through their grandchildren. By observing their grandchildren being born and growing up, they come to experience a new realm of heart as grandparents. The reason that the large family in the story above could live happily is they took care of each other and loved each other and learned and practiced true love with three generations living together.

When Heavenly Parent created human beings, He planned out our life course so that the human beings whom He created as His children would grow into men and women, become a couple, and develop and complete their character as parents and grandparents. He wanted to partake in that process and share love and joy with them. Heavenly Parent's ideal of creation was to see the realization of a society, nation and world based on the family centered on true love.

✶ Points for contemplation

1) Let's think about the hope that Heavenly Parent had when He was creating human beings,
2) What is the original hope that parents have for children?
3) Let's imagine what a family centered on true love would be like.

7
We Have to Experience the Sorrow of Heavenly Parent
— The Heavenly Parent of Sorrow

True Parents' Words

God's ideal of creation should have brought Him boundless joy and delight in the garden of love, based on His love and truth. But God's joy was frustrated because of the Fall of Adam and Eve, and He has had to toil in history for thousands of years. You need to experience the sorrowful heart of God, who suffers to this day even as He fights Satan to fulfill the ideal of creation, which Adam and Eve did not fulfill due to the Fall. You also must experience God's intense grief at the loss of Adam and Eve, when they betrayed Him and fell. Unless you first understand what God's love is all about and experience how much God loves human beings, you can never fathom the depth of His sorrow upon losing them. [CSG 1.4.1:3]

Sharing Thoughts

There was once a mother who lost her husband in the flower of his youth and raised her only son, whom she regarded as her life. With sacrificial maternal love, the mother took care of her son with far better treatment than anyone is worthy of, not realizing that her body was falling apart. The son met the mother's expectations and grew up to become a person envied by many.

To further his studies, the son left the mother and went to study in America, and he settled there. He thought of his mother back in his hometown and sent her money every month with a sincere heart. However, the mother was always starving. People in the hometown began to speak ill of the son, saying he was not filial for not looking after his mother.

A few years later, his mother became a grandmother, and then one day she passed away all alone without seeing her beloved son. Before the son arrived, the people of the village entered the mother's room to hold a funeral for her. The moment they entered, they looked at each other and felt their bodies go weak. This is because they realized that the mother's suffering was due to their lack of interest and care for her. The mother suffered and could not go to the hospital or eat properly because she didn't have money, yet up on the wall of her room were all the checks that the son had sent every month. The mother had thought that the checks were simply letters from her son. She had longed for her son as she looked at the checks.

As we can see in this story, we may live our lives thinking that we are being filial by sending money to our parents and buying them nice clothes and delicious food. This is because we do not understand or know well the hope of the parents for the children. Heavenly Parent also had a hope when He created human beings who are His children. He did not create them so that He could receive good clothes and good material things. What Heavenly Parent needed was a very small thing. It was for His lost children to return and call Him their parent, to realize a family according to His Will, to show Him their family leading a happy life, and to return the beauty of love.

However, the first ancestors of humankind, Adam and Eve, did not understand Heavenly Parent's Will, and they fell before growing into a mature man and woman. The Fall was an incident that crushed Heavenly Parent's ideal of creation and dream to pieces overnight. This was not just an incident involving two people. Adam and Eve were supposed to have become the substantial origin of true love, true life and true lineage, but they were tempted by Satan and became the origin of false love, false life and false lineage instead. Due to this, all of humankind fell into the worst abyss. How do you think Heavenly Parent felt? He must have felt pain and sorrow as if the whole world had come crashing down. Have you ever imagined the sorrow of a parent who has lost his child? From the Fall of Adam and Eve until now, Heavenly Parent had to live with sorrow and the loneliness of having lost His children. He could not complain to anyone and had to live with deep grief.

If Heavenly Parent could have punished Adam and Eve who did wrong and exterminated Satan immediately, the tragedy of the Fall could have ended. However, He could not just punish Satan without a condition. This is because Heavenly Parent created this world, according to the principle of creation, on the basis of goodness and love. If we look at the Bible, we see that over the course of six days, Heavenly Parent created one part of creation each day and said, "It is good." Therefore, Heavenly Parent created only good. He did not create evil.

Furthermore, if He had simply punished Satan, Satan could have attacked back, saying, "Aren't You the Heavenly Parent of love? Am I not also one of Your creations? No matter how wrong I am, You should embrace me with Your love. If You ignore Your own creation, that means You lose Your authority as the Lord of Creation."

How shocking this is! This is the reason that the Fall became an indescribable tragedy. Just as we saw in the words above, "Even though His beloved son and daughter were violated and the kingdom of heaven and earth was violated, He was slandered by Satan." This sums up the painful heart that Heavenly Parent had to endure.

Restoring the world after the Fall to its original state is a sorrowful process. Even though Satan seduced His beloved children and left Him with a heart of bitter sorrow, Heavenly Parent had to move Satan with amazing love and have him surrender voluntarily. This process was not easy. Despite carrying sorrow that felt like it would melt His bones, Heavenly Parent had to continue loving all humankind unreservedly. This can be compared to the heart of parents who have no choice but to accept their children back again, despite knowing their sins, despite their having left home and lived a dissipated life. After the Fall, human beings lived in ignorance, and there was no one who understood or comforted Heavenly Parent's heart.

Now is the time to put an end to this tragedy. We must become people who can feel the sorrowful heart of Heavenly Parent and comfort Him. As true sons and daughters who have received True Parents' Blessing, we must liberate Heavenly Parent's heart. Many people know Heavenly Parent only as an omnipotent and omniscient God, but not many know His true situation and heart. Therefore, to become global citizens who know Heavenly Parent properly and can return to His bosom, we must do our best to fulfill our responsibility as the children who have been called first.

✤ Points for contemplation

1) When Adam and Eve fell, Heavenly Parent searched for them and asked, "Adam, where are you?" Let us contemplate the heart of Heavenly Parent that is buried in those words.
2) Let us contemplate why we need to bring Satan to voluntary submission through love.

8
Heavenly Parent Has Worked to Save Humanity for Thousands of Years as If It Were Only a Day
— Path of Restoration

True Parents' Words

Due to the Fall, human beings fell into the realm devoid of the Principle. Angels are God's servants; in comparison to them, how far did human beings plummet? They plummeted into a realm lower than that of angels, lower than servants. They were to be princes and princesses and, as such, the lords of the angels, but they fell to a position lower than servants. Hence, they must climb back up. From the position of a servant of servants, they must climb to the positions of a servant, an adopted child, a stepchild, and a child of direct lineage; and then through the mother to reach the position of the father. This is restoration. The providence of salvation is to bring human beings back to the standard of health they enjoyed before they became sick. That is why the providence of salvation is the providence of restoration. The providence of restoration is not carried out at random. To recover the world defiled by the Fall, God has been leading the providence of salvation by building relationships with human beings through the angels that remained on His side. God has been pursuing the providence of salvation to once again relate to human beings, even though they betrayed the glorious God through the Fall and fell to such a miserable state, lower than the things of creation. Human beings are under Satan's dominion and subject to his accusation, yet God has worked to bridge the gap between Himself and us so that He might govern us. He has continued this work through the Old Testament Age and the New Testament Age, even to this day. Why has God endured a path of suffering through the many millennia of the providence of restoration? Is it simply because He has a kind heart? Why has God continued His providence of salvation for the tens of thousands of years of human history without becoming exhausted? It is not because He is all-knowing and almighty. It is because He is on the path of love, seeking His beloved sons and daughters. Love has the great power to triumph over all the tribulations in its way. With love, we feel as if a thousand years are but one day. [CSG 1.4.1:47.49]

Sharing Thoughts

This is an incident that occurred in a farmhouse in Scotland. One summer morning, a couple put their small child in a large basket after breakfast and went out to work in the fields. However, some time later, an eagle swooped down over the farmhouse and flew away with the basket held in its beak. Villagers who had witnessed this scene stamped their feet with frustration, but there was nothing they could do. After flying for a while, the eagle left that basket on top of an inestimably tall cliff and flew off and disappeared.

The bravest youth from the village was chosen to go and save the child. However, after climbing a small part of the cliff, the youth gave up because he could not climb anymore. Luckily, a soldier who had been passing by the village volunteered next, but he became worn out halfway to the top and had to come down. The villagers were filled with anxiety and disappointment and did not know what to do. At that very moment, an expert climber from the village was lastly brought in to rescue the child.

When the fully equipped climber started climbing the cliff surefootedly, everyone was confident that he would be the one to succeed. When he had climbed a third of the way, however, the climber could not go up anymore and so he pulled out. Now it seemed there was no hope of rescuing the child and everyone was about to give up when they saw someone climbing the cliff like a person possessed. Her hair was in complete disarray, her clothes were torn, and her hands and feet were bleeding, but she gave no thought to herself as she continued to climb to the top like a crazy person. When she finally reached the top of the cliff and strapped the baby to her back, people down below cheered. And when she finally reached the bottom of the cliff after hours of effort, her whole body covered with bleeding wounds, people once again clapped their hands to cheer her. She was none other than the child's mother.

This story tells us that the parents' love for their children is so strong and firm that it cannot be compared to anything else. The strong will and sacrifice of parents to save their children, not giving up until the end, regardless of how many others gave up midway, demonstrate the most precious and eternal love in thousands of years of history.

The heart of parents is such that, even when everyone else has given up and the child is as good as dead, they cannot give up. What, then, would the heart of Heavenly Parent, the origin of heart and the owner of true love, be like? Heavenly Parent cannot give up for even one second on human beings, who fell and lost the ideal of creation, and He has continued His endeavor to save them.

Parents can love, support and encourage their children, but they cannot live their children's lives for them. Heavenly Parent, too, can create the environment to save human beings and lead them, but it is the responsibility of human beings to respond to His salvation. Every time humanity fails to fulfill that responsibility and the dream of human salvation is shattered once again, Heavenly Parent feels even greater anguish and sorrow. And yet, He has never given up His love for humankind.

Heavenly Parent has never abandoned the dream of human salvation or stopped loving humanity, not even for one day. We need to think about the boundless love of Heavenly Parent, who has led the history of salvation for 6,000 years as if it were only a day. We should be able to hold onto the loving hand of Heavenly Parent and make His dream of human salvation come true.

✻ Points for contemplation

1) Let's try to feel the love of Heavenly Parent, who never abandoned fallen humanity.
2) What would the heart of Heavenly Parent have been like, as He led the 6,000-year history to save humanity?
3) Let's repent for the people of the past, who did not know about Heavenly Parent's heart and were unable to realize the providence of salvation.

9
The Providence of Restoration Is the History of Re-Creation

– Heavenly Parent's Re-Creation

True Parents' Words

We know that God's providence is the providence of restoration. What is the providence of restoration? It is taking actions to recover and reinstate what has been lost. In other words, it is the work of re-creating human beings through the Word. Because human beings, whom God created, completely lost the Word, they need to be created again. We fallen people lost the Word by which we can align our mind and body and experience constant joy in our heart. Hence, we must find the Word, namely, the truth. The Word is also called the truth. The truth is the principle that governs any system. At the same time, it is the root of Heaven's principles. That is why the world seeks the truth to this day. However, the true Word in all its fullness has not yet appeared. Since there has been no true Word, there has been no one who could embody true life. Since no one has embodied true life, there has been no one who could embody true love. Since no one has embodied true love, the true cosmos, the true heaven and earth, have not emerged.

God's providence of restoration is not guesswork. Since the providence of restoration is the work of re-creation, and it is the work of recovering what was lost, God must do it based on certain principles. God is carrying it out according to the principles of creation. Because God lost human beings as a result of the Fall, even though God created them, they are standing in the position as if God did not finish creating them. So God must bring them back to the conditional position of having created them again. The providence of salvation is the providence of restoration. The providence of restoration is the providence of re-creation. How is the providence of re-creation carried out? During the creation, what did God create first? He created the world of angels first. Then He made all things. Then He created Adam and Eve. These were the three stages of His creation. History likewise has developed to this day through this three-stage principle. That is because all of history has been within the realm of the work of re-creation. To save fallen human beings, God has had to pursue a course based on the work of re-creation. [CSG 1.4.1:66.68]

Sharing Thoughts

Because athletes are always prone to physical injuries, they remember the pain of rehabilitation training. When they are injured severely, sometimes doctors give the diagnosis "You may not be able to walk again" or "You may not be able to play the sport anymore." However, even after receiving such diagnoses, there are many athletes who undergo rehabilitation, because they have not given up hope of playing their sport again.

An American boxer, Vinny Pazienza, had been winning victory after victory in the ring when he was struck head-on by a car on the street and his neck and spine were broken. The doctor told him that he would not be able to box again, but nothing could daunt his resolve. Pazienza underwent rehabilitation, and three months later, he made a splendid comeback in the ring. The miraculous story of his life as a boxer was even made into a movie, *Bleed for This.*

Yuna Kim, who was praised for raising the artistry of figure skating to a whole new level, also was once given the diagnosis that she might not be able to walk again, due to an injury. However, after undergoing incessant rehabilitation, she was able to become a world-class figure skater.

The process of rehabilitation is the process of painful re-creation. Because not only the injured part but also the parts surrounding it must be re-created, the rehabilitation plan is drawn up utilizing every resource in science and medicine, and the process of recovery takes place in stages accordingly. Moreover, one should undergo rehabilitation only after meeting with a specialist, in addition to a regular doctor, in order to receive the most accurate diagnosis and follow the right plan for rehabilitation.

Two actions must be in accord. The first is the will of the person undergoing rehabilitation, and the second is complete faith in and unity with the rehabilitation plan drawn up by the specialist. When one can persevere through these painful processes and stages, one may be in even better condition at the end of the rehabilitation than before the injury. However, if one cannot endure such processes and stages, one may be unable even to lead a normal life, let alone play sports again.

However, the pain of rehabilitation is beyond imagination, and so, though many people attempt it, not everyone can be successful. Therefore, those athletes who successfully conclude their rehabilitation are applauded all the more, because they have overcome great pain in a situation of uncertainty and anxiety about the future, challenging themselves day after day with the mindset to create themselves anew.

Human beings are like injured athletes, because they have fallen and do not know their identity or purpose of life. When the physical body is injured, science and technology can be employed to restore it to its original state, and that process of recovery can be seen. However, in human beings it is the spirit that is injured, and because they do not know the method and process by which they can return to their original state, all they do is continue to wander and worry. For human beings to be rehabilitated, they firstly need to be resolved, and secondly they need to become completely one with the rehabilitation plan drawn up by True Parents, who have come to earth as the medical specialists to cure fallen people.

To save fallen humanity, who are in just such a state, Heavenly Parent has continued to carry out the work of human salvation. This path cannot be realized by vague resolutions or miracles, for it is the providence of re-creation in stages following the principles and processes of the providence of restoration. In the providence of restoration, Heavenly Parent has looked upon many human beings who gave up midway or failed because of unimaginable pain or anxiety about the unknowable future. However, He never gave up on humanity, and He continues to cherish the dream of restoring and re-creating human beings into people who befit the ideal of creation. To realize that dream, He is guiding the providence based on True Parents in accordance with the plan of the providence of restoration.

Heavenly Parent has sent the Lord of the Second Advent to open the way for humanity to be saved in accordance with the providence of restoration. We therefore should receive His love and heart and take part in the providence of restoration.

Points for contemplation

1) Let's think what the plan of Heavenly Parent and True Parents, who have led the providence of restoration, would be.
2) Let us consider the central figures in the providence of restoration

who achieved Heavenly Parent's Will. How were they able to fulfill the providence of restoration? (Abraham, Isaac, Joseph, etc.)
3) What is the goal of the providence of restoration that Heavenly Parent wishes for us to accomplish in this age?

Chapter 4

Seeking the True Self

1
The 6,000-Year Battle Within
— Our Contradictory Life

True Parents' Words

In our own hearts, the remnants of 6,000 years of war between good and evil continue to flare. The First World War was horrendous, as was the Second World War. Such wars, though, were relative skirmishes in a much larger conflict, and neither lasted more than six years. Yet the struggle between mind and body that goes on within each of us is the worst kind of war. It is a war that seemingly knows no end and whose inevitable result speeds us to ruin. Everyone feels the torment of this struggle in his or her own life. The confrontation between mind and body is a fierce battle of good versus evil, representing the prolonged struggle between God and Satan. Throughout the ages, our original minds have longed for peace, happiness and unity. The problem has always been our physical body, which is at war with the desires of the mind. Yet our flesh is the container that holds our mind, so we cannot just discard it as we wish. The important thing is how we govern this physical body, whose impulses and directions change minute by minute. As the apostle Paul laments in Romans 7:23–24, "I see in my members another law at war with the law of my mind, making me captive to the law of sin that dwells in my members. Wretched man that I am! Who will rescue me from this body of death?" When we look honestly within ourselves, we all can see elements of good and evil. Our mind or conscience is oriented toward good, and our body pulls in the opposite direction, toward evil. If we cannot resolve this conflict of mind and body, sin will indeed torment us for eternity. This was true even for so great a saint as Paul. [*PHG* 1.12:152–153]

Sharing Thoughts

This is something written by the Danish philosopher Soren Kierkegaard. On a very cold winter day, a noblewoman who was a devout Christian took her horseman and went to the theater. She left her horseman outside and went into the theater to watch the play. As the play began, the hero of the story appeared and a scene played out in which pitiful people were being ignored. The same woman who was in the audience began to shout all kinds of insults at the hero. She became agitated, as though she herself were an abused person, and told the hero that weak people who are treated poorly must be pitied. However, at the same time she was weeping and crying, her horseman was outside waiting, with his whole body shivering in the cold.

Through this story we can understand how contradictory people's minds and lives are. Why did humankind come to live in this kind of contradictory state? Were people originally ignorant? Did they not know what they were doing, what way they were going, and what the difference is between good and evil?

In the Principle taught by the Family Federation for World Peace and Unification, it is explained that this state of humankind came about with the Fall of the first two humans, who thus descended into ignorance; this led to their ruined state. If so, couldn't people cast out their desire for evil, control themselves, and pursue only the desire for good that comes from their original nature? To remove the contradictory nature that is in us, what kind of efforts must we continually make in our lives?

Unfortunately, even though we are looking for a way, we are in such a state of ignorance that we cannot distinguish between our desires for good and evil. Everyone tries earnestly to be happy and good, but we really do not know how to be happy, what goodness is, or what the evil is that is blocking our way. Furthermore, we don't know our identity in relation to what we are doing or whether our actions are contradictory. Therefore, while we are vaguely conscious of the people around us, we live thinking that it is enough if we don't cause loss to others. However, we put our children into the best schools and think that happiness is having an expensive car and living in the best house. In addition, we compare ourselves endlessly to other people and believe we can attain happiness if we pursue fashion and fame. This is our mindset as modern people.

Ultimately we cannot arrive at happiness or satisfaction by comparing ourselves with other people. If we satisfy a physical desire, we feel happiness for a moment, but soon feel dissatisfied because that happiness is just temporary. Even if we are at the crossroads where good and evil separate, if we focus on ourselves, on keeping the standard that we are just not causing trouble to others, we end up causing problems somewhere in the society, nation, or world.

Accordingly, for humankind to arrive at eternal happiness and joy, the following ultimate questions must be answered: Where did humankind come from? What is the purpose of life? Is there a world after death?

Following certain principles, a baby lives in its mother's womb for nine months, preparing for the future, bigger world where it will live. The eyes, nose, mouth, ears, and four limbs are not needed in the world of the womb. They are things needed for life on the earth. If a child is born who had not developed eyes while in the womb, what would result? Unhappily, that child would have to live in the world blind. In the same way, are the 100 years that people live on the earth really only for happiness on this earth? No. Those years are a process to prepare a person for eternal happiness in the spirit world after death. The earth is merely a space to stay momentarily in our physical bodies as we prepare for a greater eternal world.

Therefore, we need to know that happiness does not come about only on the earth; it is connected to life after death. Accordingly, what is called life must not be lived only for our time on earth. Furthermore, we must live a life that overcomes the contradiction of the two minds of good and evil that are within us. What kind of person was the original person before the Fall? To return to the original state and position before the Fall, what path must we take? What is the original mind, which desires good, and what is the origin of the opposing mind, which causes selfish desire? What is the one root cause of the self-destruction which created the contradictory natures of the original mind and the selfish mind? We must find answers to those questions and others. Therefore, to attain happiness, first we must know clearly what happiness feels like and, through that knowledge, cast away the desire for evil. Following our desire for goodness, we must live a life of goodness that the original mind is aiming for. Overcoming the ignorance of our mind, we must be able to distinguish between good and evil on our own.

This being so, we must meet genuine truth. If a patient who has caught a disease does not know he has it, he cannot be treated for it. Likewise, we must realize clearly the truth about our situation; our efforts to do so will draw a bright light which will guide us until we discover the truth.

If we catch even a cold, we go to the doctor and make efforts to get well, but we don't know that our mind is ill; we have neglected it for a long time. Always check the state of your mind; the effort you make to find the truth will brighten your original form, and you will find ultimate happiness.

❊ Points for contemplation

1) What is the state of my mind? Is it in a healthy state?
2) How can we overcome the conflict of the two minds and achieve eternal happiness?
3) How can we find our way to happiness and not lose our way again?

2
A World Trapped in a Materialistic Civilization
— The Fallen World

True Parents' Words

In the 1960s, when I first visited that land of opportunity, it seemed that the whole world wanted to be like America. We deeply admired the life depicted on television shows such as *Little House on the Prairie*. Come Sunday morning, the sounds of hymns were heard from all directions. Superman, a superhero of justice, was a symbol of the righteous American spirit, and city streets were thought to be spotless, in good order and beautiful. The whole world looked at America with respect in those days. Yet if we look at America today, 30 years later, what do we see? It is a nation in decay, strewn with difficult problems they cannot solve. In the midst of this, moral decadence and increase in crime demand our close attention. Numerous unimaginable acts, including murder, drug abuse, divorce, child molestation, gang violence and teenage pregnancy, emanate from America today. As a person who loves that nation, I feel deeply hurt by what I see. Yet this phenomenon is not limited to America. All the developed countries at the end of the twentieth century are struggling with many of the same problems. Having reached the summit of consumer wealth and technological sophistication, the developed world is caught in the trap of materialism. With our minds and spirits obsessed by material wealth, our true essence as human beings is enslaved by selfish desires. The result is a collapse of true love. Although there is an abundance of material wealth and our cities are crowded with skyscrapers, the human mind has become desolate and dried up like a desert, and the oasis of true love is not to be found. The absence of true love is the breeding ground for selfishness. The most helpless victim of this attitude is the world of nature. [PHG 1.7:98–99, 1995.08.23]

Sharing Thoughts

One day, three elderly men came to a young couple. One elderly man was named Wealth; the next elderly man was named Success, and the third elderly man was named Love. The couple wanted to invite the three elderly men into their house together, but they could invite only one of them.

The couple agonized about it. "Whom should we invite?" "How about inviting Wealth? Then we could become rich. Or let's invite the elderly man named Success. Then wouldn't we be able to have a successful life?" Then his wife said, "It would be good to invite the elderly gentleman named Love. Wouldn't our home be filled with love then?" So the couple invited the elderly man named Love into the house. As soon as they did that, the elderly men called Wealth and Success followed him in as well. "It is the law that we too are always where Love is."

It is a very short fable, but it resonates quietly with a deep place in our hearts. If it had been you, what choice would you have made? The gifts of wealth and success do not follow unless there is an internal spiritual foundation. However, our current society, in which culture and scientific technology have developed more than at any time in human history, tips the scales of balance towards the materialistic side of things.

The Agricultural and Industrial Revolutions of the 18th century transformed human life more rapidly than in any other century. The creation of the computer and the Internet in the 20th century brought us into an information-based society that could expand beyond time and space.

Ironically, despite these developments, it seems that human happiness has not been enhanced. More than at any time before, we can live comfortably and easily, yet depression and suicide rates are concurrently going up, people are not able to get along with others, and many increasingly are feeling isolated.

In the last century, those who realized that materialistic civilization did not bring ultimate happiness began to have concerns about the development of artificial intelligence robots, which represent the fourth industrial revolution. Now efforts must be made to answer essential questions concerning these issues so that we can find happiness.

What makes us happy? Science gives us a convenient environment, but we need to realize that it cannot give us spiritual happiness. Since people are beings of both mind and body, the calmness and happiness of the mind are as important as the body's comfort and health. Thus, mind and body together must be calm and happy for us to feel total joy. Accordingly, for essential happiness, we must be concerned about internal problems and not just external appearances.

Basically, for us to be happy in mind and body, we must harmonize both spiritual satisfaction and material abundance. We must grasp material abundance on the foundation of spiritual happiness.

❈ Points for contemplation

1) What was the gift of material civilization?
2) What is the problem of material civilization, and why can't people be happy?
3) What is the alternative that allows us to realize ultimate happiness?

3
The Culture of Pleasure That Has Lost Life's Compass
— The Crisis in the Family

True Parents' Words

It is the family's failure to realize true love that has led to phenomena associated with family breakdown, including individual breakdown, as well as countless problems on the national and worldwide levels. Of particular concern is the emotional instability of youth, which leads to diminishing life goals, spiritual aimlessness, and unhealthy, self-destructive lifestyles. World leaders who are concerned about the future have to be very serious in order to solve the real problems of young people avoiding marriage, rampant divorce, and so forth; trends that destroy the fundamental foundation of families. Having lost the first and second blessings, humankind does not understand the importance of completing one's individual growth, which is the foundation for sacred and eternal conjugal love. Most of our young people are not aware of the importance of keeping purity before marriage and reaching personal maturity through true love. This is why they do not understand the value of true love, which is the fundamental root of joy, happiness and all ideals. The tendency to make light of trust and fidelity between husband and wife and to ignore the sacredness of marriage is an internal cause of indescribable disasters and tragedies for humankind. True love has been driven out by the so-called free love culture, in which people seek only sexual release as the cardinal yet momentary pleasure. The rapid spread of HIV/AIDS and sexually transmitted diseases threatens the very existence of the human race. [*PHG* 1.10:133, 2001.10.29]

Sharing Thoughts

"Be it ever so humble, there's no place like home."

Those are lyrics from the world-famous song *Home Sweet Home*, which were written in 1822 by the American actor and author John Howard Payne. Although he left his homeland and traveled the world, it is said that his dying wish was "I don't have a family to return to, but please at least bury me in the public cemetery of my hometown." The place to which people ultimately must return is their family. Only in that place can we have a peaceful rest; but in our society, the value of the family is being lost. Its meaning is fading and degenerating. What is the true value and form of the family?

Our loving Heavenly Parent created humankind as His children to be the object partners of His love. Heavenly Parent hoped that His children would grow to become a perfect man and woman and a couple with true love at their center. Then Heavenly Parent wanted them to have children and become parents, experience parental love united with Heavenly Parent's heart, and become perfected people of love. Heavenly Parent's hope and dream was a happy world of true families that all people would accomplish as true children, true couples, and true parents sharing true love.

But Satan completely destroyed this hope of Heavenly Parent. Satan destroyed the root of true love, which is living for others, and prevented humankind from knowing the root of true love. He made them pursue his self-centered and egotistical desire and love. As a result, human beings want to become happy through love, but because they pursue egotistical love centered on themselves, the longer they live, the unhappier they become. They have ended up making this modern, tragic society, one which is increasingly lonely.

Why did humankind come under Satan's dominion, lose the culture of genuine love, and become addicted to a culture of pleasure? It is because of the Fall of humankind. Through the belief that material things are almighty, the standard of good and evil has been lost, and as a result people have fallen into contradiction. People do not know what ultimate happiness is or what should be pursued. In conclusion, we came under Satan's dominion because humankind lost Heavenly Parent's original purpose of creation.

In today's world, people are bought and sold; love is bought and sold. In a single decision, we can waste our lives in momentary pleasure; and in the end, happiness does not appear. Ultimate love is not discovered. The thing discovered at the end of pleasure is that only futility and a sense of shame remain. The actual presence of this kind of person is nothing more than a false image of a human being who became involved in temptation, misplaced their identity, and became confused.

We should live by dominating our personal and worldly desires and, centered on the world of heart, achieving a balance of the spiritual and physical. Our self-portrait today shows us having fallen into a pit, unable to control ourselves. The people in this category do not care whether the world is heading toward goodness, toward evil or is destroyed. They are blindly pursuing the pleasures of their body. Having lost their original direction in life and the purpose for which they were born, they are simply wandering through life. This is comparable to a TV remote control being used to balance a wobbly piano. Anything that exists has a purpose, and if we don't know the purpose, it ends up losing its value. What did Heavenly Parent have in mind when he created humankind?

Human beings were supposed to be born into a family that attended Heavenly Parent at the center; we were meant to grow as we experienced grandparents' love, parents' love, and brothers and sisters' love. A person born into a family overflowing with this kind of true love would be able to give the same love to their peers. If people have not experienced human relationships based on love, they cannot learn responsibility, sacrifice or other things that comply with loving and trusting others. Eventually they have difficulties forming give-and-take relationships; many have one-sided or destructive relationships. It has been determined that many criminals and most psychopathic criminals were not able to form a loving relationship with their parents during their childhood. That can be considered a natural result. In modern society the rising suicide rate of adolescents and their increasing violent crimes point to youth who could not experience secure love within the family.

The clearest and fastest method for members of a society to become happy is to restore the value of the family and return to a family centered on Heavenly Parent, based on true love.

❈ Points for contemplation

1) What problems exist within the sex culture of modern society?
2) Why are youth crimes increasing and becoming more brutal?
3) Is your family happy? If there is something missing, which part needs to be worked on to make it feel complete? How should the members of the family participate in achieving this?

4
Fallen Nature That Cannot Be Eliminated, No Matter the Effort
— Original Sin and Fallen Nature

True Parents' Words

It is never easy to remove fallen nature. Even when trying to overcome long-term habits such as smoking or drinking, we go back and forth repeatedly. Then how can it be easy to remove our deeply rooted fallen nature, passed through our bloodline for many thousands of years? It is impossible by human effort alone. Even if you make God the center of your life, attend Him with absolute faith, and struggle throughout your whole life, it is a difficult battle. There is no point in even attempting this unless you are ready to attend God as the True Parent, with absolute love greater than the love you have for your parents and children. [CSG 8.3.2:12]

We have fallen nature. What are the four main characteristics of fallen nature? They are arrogance, jealousy, anger and deceit. We have been fasting and offering other acts of jeongseong to remove this fallen nature. To succeed in this, what are we to do in the era of judgment in the course of restoration? We each need to arm ourselves with the Word and become embodiments of the Word. We must uproot our self-centered and individualistic mindset and the behavior that stems from it. This is the root of fallen nature and the cause of evil. This can be said not only of self-centered behavior on the individual level but also of selfish behavior of collectives in society. Self-centeredness is directly contrary to the spirit of true love's system of absolute values. Instead of sacrificing and living for the sake of others, self-centered people call for others to sacrifice for them. Self-centeredness causes people to be more concerned with their own interests than with the well-being of others. Self-centeredness was insidiously injected into humankind through the Fall. It induced the struggle between mind and body. Satan planted this poisonous mushroom in the human heart. Although embracing self-centeredness may result in a person appearing beautiful and gaining worldly fame and earthly comforts, it is a trap that, once sprung, will lead its victim to addiction and a life of suffering that is difficult to escape. [PHG 7.16:1101, 2004.07.23]

Sharing Thoughts

The following passage about faith was recorded in a believer's diary: "No matter what kind of problem there is, if you do not get angry, Satan has no strength and can do nothing."

Not losing our quiet, peaceful, trusting attitude is our ability. Contrary to this, Satan's ability is exhausting our energy by making us agitated and fearful. Each time that you are confused and sense the action of something different from your original mind, stop and ask yourself, "What is Satan trying to do?" We are people who already have practiced this kind of subjugation.

When something good happened to a friend of yours, were you sincerely happy? While comparing yourself to him, did you feel jealous? Probably while congratulating him, to a certain extent you also felt envious and, in spite of yourself, felt jealousy arise. This kind of heart is called fallen nature. We cannot deny that deep in our hearts this kind of fallen nature exists. Although we try to hide it, human fallen nature is something that cannot be hidden.

Fallen nature's most representative elements are comparison, envy and jealousy, displaced passion, arrogance, and deceit. Among these, the first one is comparison. Discontent and complaint arise when you compare the difference between what you have and what another person has; this can be a possession or a position, for example. Among the unlimited desires of humankind, comparing does not arise from a good desire. Looking at others this way from one's own perspective gave birth to egotism. Before the creation of Adam and Eve, the Archangel had no one to compare himself with; but after Adam and Eve were created, while comparing his situation with that of Adam and Eve, he came to have excessive desire. Thus, the fallen heart came into existence.

The second component of fallen nature is envy and jealousy. While we applaud the possessions, inheritance, outstanding individuality, etc., of others, we must be able to digest it with goodness. We must be able to be thankful for the blessings that others receive. Instead, people are often envious and jealous of what others have achieved, or even attained through good luck. Such hearts are very far from the original mind that human beings had at the time of creation.

How about passion that becomes focused in the wrong place? In a Korean dictionary, this word, *hyeolgi*, is explained as "vitality of the blood." The vitality of the blood of the original Heavenly Parent was good and considerate of others. More than pushing itself forward, it drew out the subconscious of the counterpart. On the contrary, fallen nature began from the easily turbulent situation of someone insisting that others satisfy him alone. Without considering right or wrong, the individual blames their own failure on others, lashing out many times in anger.

Arrogance is a word that combines showing off, boasting and being impudent. It means lack of humility, showing off, and boasting. If people think they are better than others, they become arrogant. If one has a very arrogant mind, eventually he loses people and goes more deeply into a life centered on himself. In the Bible, as well, arrogance is considered one of the greatest criminal acts, which denies Heavenly Parent's grace and help.

Deceit refers to situations in which one is blinded by greed, tells lies, or swindles others. There are many situations in life when it is difficult to distinguish what is deceit and what is truth. Instead, the widespread social atmosphere dictates that honest people will suffer rather than win. Thus, the present reality of fallen nature which seeks its own profit is dominating our minds.

This kind of comparison, jealousy, passion, arrogance and deceit have different forms, but they have one thing in common: They start with self-centeredness and are based on an egotistical foundation which puts its own profit first. Where would this kind of fallen nature have come from? It was born in the mind caused by the human Fall. The archangel knew Heavenly Parent's ideal of creation, but through Eve he wanted to receive more of Heavenly Parent's love, and due to that self-centered greed, he became the main instigator of the Fall. He sacrificed others for himself; it was a shameless act. This content entered the blood lineage and spread, with the name "fallen nature," to all human descendants.

It is very difficult to get rid of fallen nature overnight; its roots are tenacious, and the fruits have been passed down through the blood lineage for many thousands of years. Therefore, the apostle Paul, who cannot be ignored in the New Testament, says in Romans 7:24, "Wretched man that I am! Who will deliver me from this body of death?"

But if we attend our Heavenly Parent as the center and main body of goodness, and we arm ourselves and family with the message of the returning Christ and True Parents, we can realize a life of true love; it will not be impossible. In order to be freed from our fallen nature, more than anything we must determine our position to love Heavenly Parent most of all. We must establish goodness at the center, because good and evil must be separated. Heavenly Parent hopes that we all will remove our fallen nature; then with a clear and clean mind and body we can live together within Heavenly Parent's realm of heart.

❋ Points for contemplation

1) Look back on your life and check whether there was comparison, arrogance, jealousy, passion or deceit in your mind. Look back deeply on your fallen nature and take some time to repent.
2) Meditate deeply on why, in order to remove fallen nature, we first must stand in the position of loving Heavenly Parent the most.

5
The Fundamental Principle That We Must Live for the Sake of Others
— Original Value

True Parents' Words

The human desire to achieve the ideal of peace has been consistent throughout history. Yet eternal peace has never been manifested. This is the problem. Human beings have lived in ignorance, chaos, division and strife. To this day, we have been unable to establish an absolute value system that can be shared by all people. An absolute value system cannot arise from human beings who harbor internal conflicts and are always changing. The root of this system can be found only in God, the Absolute Being and the Creator. God, who is the essence of love, created human beings to be the recipient of His absolute love. One cannot claim for oneself the status of owner or master of love, and that is true even for God. Only one's partner grants that status. This is a fundamental principle. One needs to live for one's partner and neighbor. This absolute value system of love stands above any political ideal or principle of economics. It is the heavenly law that transcends all ages.

What kind of being is God, who created this universe and the heavenly laws? God has manifested Himself in the universe as the quintessence of living for the sake of others. Though He is the King of knowledge, He does not ask us to come to Him through knowledge. Though He is the Owner and King of power, authority, money and material, He does not view these as conditions to come before Him. God says that anyone can come to His side as long as they live for the sake of others. Only those who live for others can become the counterpart of the center and stand in the position of a central figure. God is not an egocentric dictator. Rather, God invests Himself for the sake of humankind. Thus, for tens of thousands of years our original minds have sought to follow God. All beings must exist for the sake of other beings in order to maintain their place in this universe, as governed by the laws of Heaven. The principle of living for the sake of others has been valid throughout all ages and in all nations. An egocentric and self-centered way of life will bring about evil, while a life of living for the greater good will bring prosperity. [*PHG* 1.16:187–188, 2004.09.16]

Sharing Thoughts

"One bright summer morning in 1989, I woke up in Gunsbach. It was the day of Pentecost. I thought that I should not take this happiness for granted but that I also should give something. While I was wrestling with my thoughts, there were birds singing outside. I got up from where I sat and, after thinking silently, I decided in my heart that until the age of 30, I would live for the sake of study and the arts but after that I would volunteer directly for the sake of humankind."

These are the words of Albert Schweitzer, known as "the jungle saint." He grew up in a wealthy family with a father who was a Lutheran pastor. He was intelligent, and later became distinguished in philosophy and theology. He also had talent for playing the organ, and from the age of 18 began building a reputation as an organist. He lived a successful life and envied no one. However, one day he confessed that he thought that maybe he was living a selfish life.

The following year he received his doctorate in philosophy and at 28 became a professor of theology. However, he did not forget his determination. Ultimately, Schweitzer resigned from his secure job, and at the age of 30, he entered medical school, determined to help sick people in Africa. He had heard many stories during his father's sermons about poor people there and thought that he should help them. His success brought him joy, but he felt guilty knowing that many people were too poor to receive any education or medical attention.

Schweitzer is not unique. Across the world and throughout the ages, people who have been respected are those who began their careers by thinking about those less fortunate than themselves. Rather than think about their own safety, success or stability, they sacrificed for the sake of the community, nation and world. The True Parents, who lead the Family Federation for World Peace and Unification, devoted their lives to loving humanity. They worked to save and connect us, who are all lost and confused orphans after the human Fall, with our Heavenly Parent. That is why people worldwide attend, respect, and love Rev. Sun Myung Moon and Dr. Hak Ja Han Moon as the True Parents of humankind.

We were not created to live selfish lives; we were created to live for the sake of others. However, in this world it is "normal" to think only of ourselves or to love only our own family. It is easy to think that living beyond the family, for the sake of the neighborhood and society, is only for special or great people or those with amazing abilities.

Many people think that it is tiring to live for the sake of others, so they simply avoid hurting them; they think it's enough to love their own family and take care of them. Of course, it is a great thing to love and look after yourself and your family. However, we also need to love neighboring families as our own, think of them as having value equal to that of our family, and expand our perspective further to include the society, nation, and world.

The family is the smallest unit that expands outwardly; thus, the way that it connects to the society and nation is important. This makes the values and philosophy that the family adopts very influential. Therefore, if you seek to live only for the sake of your own family, the society and nation will fall into darkness. We call this false family-centeredness as egocentric. We need to realize the nature of our original value as human beings; we were created to live for a greater purpose and therefore must make an effort to return to our original selves.

❋ Points for contemplation
1) What do great people have in common?
2) What is the problem with family egocentrism?
3) What is the value of original human beings and families?

6
Before You Seek to Master the Universe, First Attain Mastery over Yourself
– Mastery over Yourself

True Parents' Words

The issue is not World War II or today's Russia and America. The issue is how to end the war inside myself, which could continue for eternity, and bring peace. You need to understand how extremely important this is. If it does not happen, then even if the world becomes a peaceful place, it will seem like hell. When I started on this path, my first motto was "Before you seek to master the universe, first attain mastery over yourself." People who cannot conquer themselves can never conquer the world. Jesus said, "The kingdom of God is within you." The kingdom of God is in your mind. However, God cannot dwell in your mind unless it is united with your body, because the kingdom of God is one world. Therefore, what the Unification Church emphasizes is not the unification of the world. Before the world can be united,

a nation needs to be united. Before a nation can be united, a united people, tribe, and family are needed. Before a family can be united, an individual must be united. This means you need to attain unity within yourself, with your mind at the center. Your mind is your fundamental starting point. The way to achieve unity is simple. All you need to do is to unite your mind and body. When someone who has attained mind–body unity becomes one with his or her family, there is peace in that family. When a family that is united in this way becomes one with its society, that family will be so happy that its members will not envy anyone in society. When a society united in this way becomes one with its nation, it will develop a realm of unity that is so strong that no one in the nation will deny it; everyone will respect it. Furthermore, when such a nation becomes one with all the world's people, the kingdom of God will be realized on earth.
[CSG 10.2.1:8, 10.11]

Sharing Thoughts

"When I was young and free, my imagination had no limits; I dreamed I could change the world. As I grew older and wiser, I realized the world would not change. And I decided to shorten my sights somewhat and change only my country. But it seemed immovable. As I entered my twilight years, in one last desperate attempt, I sought to change only my family, those closest to me;

but alas they would have none of it. And now here I lie in my deathbed and realize, perhaps for the first time, that if only I had changed myself first, then, by example, I may have influenced my family and, with their encouragement and support, I may have bettered my country, and who knows, I may have changed the world."

These are words carved on a tombstone in the underground cemetery of Westminster Cathedral in London, England. It is the story of a person who had a big dream when he was young but wasn't able to realize anything. In the end he realized too late that he should have started by changing himself.

Throughout history, many philosophers and religious people have advised that, in order to achieve true happiness, we first should cultivate our own heart. They say it is most important to recognize our root or foundation, then make it a principle to practice this understanding in our daily life. Inscribed at the Temple of Apollo at Delphi, Greece, there is a wise phrase. It says, "Know yourself." This has become the trusted advice of the temple for those who have come seeking answers to their troubles.

The idea that one should "Cultivate yourself, govern your family, rule the nation, and then the kingdom" is said to be the most fundamental enlightenment in the Orient. Before seeking to harmonize your family, rule your country, or make peace in the world, you first should look at yourself. These things cannot be done all at once. There is a structure by which cultivating your own morals is the starting point, and that has to develop until you rule the kingdom. That is why someone who has not cultivated their own morals cannot be of help to their family, nation or kingdom. Furthermore, the goal of education in the East starts with character education; we need to develop proper character.

Unfortunately, education today focuses on intelligence and technology, passing on knowledge and skills rather than character.

Academic achievement is emphasized through competition. In a nuclear family with few siblings, children cannot learn fully how to give and receive love and grow their hearts.

Rather than teaching about what kind of person you want to become, with what kind of heart, education focuses on what kind of person you want to become in functional terms. Mastery over yourself means that first, your mind and body are united and you live a balanced life. When you have control over your appetite, sexual desires, earthly desires, sleep, desire for power, and patience, you attain the standard of being able to rule your family, society and nation. Second, rather than focus on your own benefit, you take care of other people; what is important is how you raise people who can uphold the standards of interdependence, mutual prosperity and universally shared values.

That is why True Parents said, "Attain mastery over yourself before seeking to master things in the universe around you" and emphasized a lifestyle in which you know and control your desires centering on your own heart. To have a strong heart that can control your desires, you must experience God's heart and first think about the heart of the parents. This means living a life of practicing true love. Through this kind of lifestyle, you can come to have a true character, and when you clearly know yourself, you will come to have a character of unwavering self-dominion in actual situations. Then you can experience ultimate happiness.

❈ Points for contemplation
1) What does mastery over yourself mean?
2) Think about what is most difficult for you to master or have dominion over?
3) In the part of you that is difficult to master, think about how you can let go of the obstacle that blocks you.

7
Desires Should Be Denied, Centering on the Conscience
– The Way Back

True Parents' Words

What has religion been teaching? It has been teaching us to save the soul and conquer the body. Therefore, religions exhort us to sacrifice in the service of others. Religions also teach us, as we sacrifice to serve others, to go the way of penance, to fast, to inflict pain on the body. Unless we walk this path, we cannot enter Heaven. This is the Principle. Religion does not begin with approval or affirmation; it begins with denial. We live in an evil world, and if we support evil, we become evil. We each need to begin by judging ourselves. Each of us needs to deny him or herself. Self-denial does not mean targeting the evil society. Even though we need to reform this evil society, we need to begin with self-abnegation. The mind and body are fighting each other, and we need to chastise the body into submission. But what does it mean to chastise and subjugate the body? It means to do what is righteous. When we are asked what sets the criteria by which we subjugate the body, we should reply that it is our conscience.

Therefore, we must deny our sexual urges, appetite for food and other instinctive bodily cravings. We thus need to pray and fast as well as offer vigils. The various religions established value systems. Why have they collapsed? It is because the religions forsook their original missions, and this resulted in constant disputes and divisions. Thus, they lost their power to guide real life. The established religions do not teach clearly about life and the universe. They cannot distinguish clearly between good and evil or righteousness and unrighteousness. In particular, they cannot answer clearly regarding the nature of God and His existence. As the ability of religion to guide people faded, material possessions turned from a means to an end in life. Chasing pleasure became the norm. Sensual desires and material cravings dehumanize the world. In such tainted soil it is impossible for love, service, righteousness, holiness and other traditional values to flourish. [CSG 8.2.5:11, 13.14]

Sharing Thoughts

One densely foggy night, a navy admiral out at sea suddenly received a report that an unknown small dot had appeared on the radar. He commanded, "Radio that boat, and tell it to change its course by 15 degrees." Then he received the response, "You should change your course by 15 degrees."

The admiral shouted, "Radio that boat again, and say that we are a navy fleet and it should change its course by 15 degrees." However, the voice on the radio once again repeated, "You should change your course by 15 degrees." The furious admiral took hold of the microphone and shouted loudly, "I am a navy admiral. I command you to change your course at once!" Then the other side responded immediately, "This is the lighthouse!"

In the course of our lives, we come across problems of all sizes. When we are in a difficult situation, instead of trying to change ourselves, we try to change others first. Sometimes we hold onto things that cannot be changed, no matter how much effort we make, even though the struggles make our lives so much harder and more exhausting.

At times like this, if there were a standard and guidepost in our lives that could set the course for us, we would be able to head toward and reach our final destination, no matter how severe the storms we met were. Heavenly Parent and True Parents can be the lighthouse and compass for our lives. However, there is something within us that can take our mind and body by the hand: our conscience, which is still within us as an attribute of Heavenly Parent, despite the human Fall. Our conscience constantly guides our lost self to return to the essence. In our normal, everyday lives, we need to make efforts to live according to our conscience at all times; we can develop it through such methods as prayer, meditation and hoondokhae.

Mother Teresa, the Roman Catholic nun who founded the Missionaries of Charity order and was called "the mother of the poor and the orphaned," said, "We all need to take time for silence and meditation, especially those people who live in big cities where everything changes so quickly. I feel that the cities of the world need more silence and meditation. I always begin my prayer in silence, for it is in the silence of the heart that God speaks. God is the friend of silence, so we need to listen to Him." The life of Mother Teresa, who said that the fruit of silence is prayer, the fruit of prayer is love, and the fruit of love is service, began in silence and prayer.

True Parents said, "If you want to pray, you have to do so before beginning your daily activities. Hence, the most important time is daybreak. This is the time that determines the outcome of your day. The time for studying True Parents' words is the time in which you can bring your mind under control and set your zero point. It is not a time for thinking about your past or worrying about your future. When you empty yourself and focus solely on the words of Heavenly Parent and meditate upon them, you will find the direction that you need to follow from those words." Therefore, in order to return to the essence, we should not neglect meditating through prayer and hoondokhae.

When you submerge your heart in silence and focus your mind, you can hear the voice that resonates from deep within your heart. In particular, hoondokhae, through which you can set the standard of your mind and life, based on Heavenly Parent, in the silent hours as you begin your day, will serve as your life compass.

❇ Points for contemplation

1) When did you pray most fervently?
2) Let's reflect on our experiences of receiving answers to our prayers.
3) What problems will arise if you lead a life separated from religion?

8
Seeking the Vertical Parent and Connecting to Love

— Seeking Love in the Family

True Parents' Words

Due to the Fall, humankind became severed from God's love, life and lineage, and joined Satan's love, life and lineage. When we say that the human ancestors fell, we mean that Adam and Eve joined with the false parent, Satan, inherited his lineage, and bore his fruit. The question now is how to turn this around and change our false lineage back to God's lineage. To do this, we must change totally, 180 degrees. [CSG 4.3.2:7]

The Fall occurred at the completion level of the growth stage, and we must reverse its course to be restored to the original state. Adam and Eve fell through the misuse of love. In the course of our restoration as well, when we reach the stage in which Adam and Eve fell, we also must overcome this problem of love. Up to the present, people have been receiving love from the false parent, Satan. To overcome this problem of Satan's love, there is no other way but to connect to True Parents' love, which is centered on God. Therefore, human beings, who have inherited the fallen parents' lineage in the realm of the Fall, must meet True Parents and unite vertically with them to find their way along the path that leads beyond the realm of the Fall. The Divine Principle teaches that we must take that position. However, it cannot be fulfilled alone; it requires that men and women be paired as couples. This is the Blessing conducted by Family Federation for World Peace and Unification. The Blessing cannot be performed any way you want to do it. It must be done centered on God, the vertical center. [CSG 4.2.3:13]

Sharing Thoughts

Some animals on a farm were talking together. The hen said first, "I serve my master by laying eggs." Then the cow quickly said, "I serve my master by giving milk every day." The pig then said, "I give my master all of my meat," and the sheep said, "I give my master my milk, my meat, and even my fleece." Then the dog that had been sitting beside them yawned and spoke.

"I don't give my master anything, but I receive the most love." At its words, all the other animals looked at the dog. They realized that the dog really did not give anything when compared to them, but it monopolized the master's love despite that. The angry animals complained all together, "That is so unfair!" "It makes no sense!" "We are being mistreated!" Then the dog smiled and said:

"Though I don't give anything material to my master, when he comes back from an outing, I run to him and wag my tail to tell him, 'I love you,' and offer him all of my heart. So, to be loved, you need to offer your heart before anything else. Do you understand?"

All human beings want and yearn for love, no matter who they are. Not only is love the purpose of human life, it is also the purpose of all beings that exist in this world, including plants and animals. This is because love is the reason and hope with which Heavenly Parent created humankind and all creation. Heavenly Parent created all things in the world and humankind with love.

However, though love is the reason and purpose of existence for all beings, they may get hurt or suffer pain due to wrongful love. This is because, just like the farm animals from the story, they mistake false love for true love. That is where all problems arise. Because most people are yet to be equipped with the character to love, we often end up hurting each other. Therefore, our awareness of love must be changed.

First, we need to change our awareness to understand that love is not about receiving but about accommodating others. Love is something you give first, not receive first, and it is important to know how you should give that love to others. Just like the dog from the story, you need to first think about the person to whom you want to give love and give the love he or she needs. Giving love based on your own decision and complaining that you have not received love in return is the wrong way to love. Therefore, you should think about your object partner first and give love at his or her level.

Second, love is not about shackling or possessing your object partner but rather the process by which you can discover yourself and make your character more mature by giving love to him or her. Within the family, parents grow more mature by giving love to their children. Therefore, parents should be grateful to and respect their children, for their children help them perfect their position as parents. The place where human beings can perfect their position as parents is the place where Heavenly Parent and True Parents come together as parents who love humankind and are trying to save them.

True Parents tell us that the correct way to love is to right the wrongful order of love. We must give love, matching the viewpoint of our object partner with the desire to live for his or her sake, while taking his or her situation into consideration. True Parents have allowed us to meet our object partner through the Blessing and to experience the happiness of achieving self-perfection through our spouse. A husband and wife who have received the Marriage Blessing should endeavor to give true love to each other, so that they can firmly establish the Blessing in their family, centered on Heavenly Parent.

❋ Points for contemplation

1) What are the problems that arise due to the wrong order of love in the fallen world?
2) To right the wrong order of love, where should we establish the center within our families, and what should we practice in our lives?
3) To establish the true order of love, how should we educate the secular families around us?

Chapter 5

Humankind Needs True Parents

1
History of the Struggle between Cain and Abel

– Division of Good and Evil

True Parents' Words

Originally Adam and Eve should have ruled over the angels with God as their center, but this was reversed, and the angel came to control Adam and Eve. This is why indemnity is carried out through the second son, who represents the side of Adam or God, by having him win over Cain, who represents the side of the archangel or Satan. Because Abel stood in such a position, God accepted his sacrifice gladly. Knowing that Abel had returned joy to God, Cain should not have felt sorry that God did not accept his sacrifice. He should have loved Abel and approached the presence of God through Abel. If he had done so, the foothold for the providence of salvation would have been established right then and there. Cain, however, felt overwhelming resentment at Abel's receiving love from God and beat his brother to death. In the end, just as the archangel dominated Adam, so Cain, who stood in the position of the archangel on Satan's side, struck and killed Abel, who stood in the position of Adam on Heaven's side. Here we can see the fruits of both spiritual and physical sin manifested. [CSG 7.2.3:5]

The world has inherited the tradition of Adam's family, in which Cain killed his own brother, Abel. The outcome for us, the descendants of false love, is the unhappiness, sin and ruin manifested in family breakdown, the moral degradation of youth, and diseases such as AIDS. Consider the world's situation. The acute crises of the modern age are manifested in struggles between our mind and body, the confusion of values, criminal activities, drug abuse, the breakdown of the family that holds humanity's future in the balance, destruction of the environment, conflict and hatred, terror and war, and even conflict among religions and civilizations. With each passing day, these crises turn more serious, more complex and more pervasive. We no longer can stand by and do nothing as the world careens along this course. There is no time left. [PHG 1.14:174, 2002.12.27]

Sharing Thoughts

This is an actual incident that happened in the United States. A young man was sentenced to death for murder. His elder brother, however, was a prominent figure who had done many wonderful things during the long years he had served the public. He could not just stand by and watch his brother die, so he went to see the governor. He begged the governor to use his authority to pardon his brother, who he said had only been involved in an unfortunate accident. In consideration of the elder brother's many good deeds and love for his brother, the governor decided to pardon his brother's grave crime. With the letter of pardon in the breast pocket of his jacket, the elder brother went to see his younger brother in prison right away. He asked his brother, "If you are pardoned and you can walk out of this place alive, what will you do?" Then with a dark look the younger brother answered unhesitatingly.

"First, I'll seek out and kill the bastard judge who sentenced me to death, and second, I will seek out the witness who testified against me in court and shoot him dead!" The elder brother realized that his younger brother would not be swayed in his resolve. Unable to say anything to that, he stood up quietly and left the prison visiting room in silence. The governor's letter of pardon was still in his bosom, for he had not given it to his brother.

Just like the above story, we too may receive a letter of pardon from Heavenly Parent, thanks to the good deeds of True Parents, but those who do not know that and do not undo their sins can never be pardoned.

What is the fundamental cause of the various crimes, disputes and conflicts taking place in all parts of the world today? What is the origin of the extreme selfishness, wrongful sexual desires, hatred and other feelings harbored in human beings? To find the answer, let us trace back to the origin of human history, since the model of wrongful human relationships established by the human ancestors Adam and Eve and their children Cain and Abel is incorporated in every problem of today's world.

Originally, Adam and Eve were supposed to attend Heavenly Parent as their parent, experience the heart of children, grow up properly while becoming mature in their hearts as brother and sister, and then become husband and wife centering on Heavenly Parent. However, Eve involved herself in a wrongful relationship of love with the archangel Lucifer and fell spiritually. After that, without approval she formed a relationship of love with Adam, in her desire to return to Heavenly Parent, and thus both Adam and Eve fell physically. Therefore, the elder son Cain symbolizes the fruit of the spiritual fall of the archangel Lucifer and Eve, and the younger son Abel symbolizes the fruit of the physical fall of Adam and Eve. Because Cain was the fruit of the incident "caused by the premature greed for something before its time" [Gen. 3:5], he became the "manifestation of evil," whereas Abel could be considered the "manifestation of goodness" because he was the fruit of the incident "caused by the heartfelt desire to return to Heavenly Parent's side once again." In light of this, what should Cain and Abel have done to be saved, that is, to be restored to the time before they went wrong?

Cain in the position of the manifestation of evil should have helped Abel in the position of the manifestation of goodness and won recognition from him. Thereupon, Abel should have embraced Cain with love and humility and testified about him so that Cain could stand in front of Heavenly Parent. As can be seen, the first key to human salvation depended on the reconciliation of Cain and Abel. In other words, they should have united as loving brothers to restore the fraternal realm. Unfortunately, however, the Bible tells us that Cain became jealous of Abel because Heavenly Parent accepted only Abel's offering and not his own, and he killed Abel. Consequently, the reconciliation of Cain and Abel did not take place and remained a problem that humanity had to resolve.

What would Heavenly Parent's heart have been like as He looked upon Cain and Abel? And why did Heavenly Parent hurt Cain's heart by not accepting his offering? Though they were both His children, Heavenly Parent could not directly receive the offering of Cain, who was established as the manifestation of evil. This is because Heavenly Parent created only goodness, and if He were to involve Himself with an object partner of evil, He would have become a Heavenly Parent who created evil. The heart of Heavenly Parent who could not accept that offering would have hurt much more than that of Cain. Moreover, when Cain murdered Abel, Heavenly Parent would have experienced so much pain that it would have seemed as if all of heaven and earth were crumbling down around Him. This history of struggle between Cain and Abel has been expanded worldwide and repeated over and over again until now. Because Heavenly Parent lost His children and is restricted by limitations, even though He wishes to save them, the bitter sorrow in His heart must be fathomless. For us to fundamentally resolve the many problems in all parts of the world today, we first need to know about this sorrowful heart of our Heavenly Parent. Only when all humanity can deeply comprehend the heart of Heavenly Parent can true reconciliation between Cain and Abel take place, through which the chains of sin can be undone.

At present, are we Cain or Abel? Abel is a person who has been restored as Heavenly Parent's child and whose heart is close to His, and Cain is a person who does not yet know of his or her true nature and is yet to be restored. Therefore, we may be Cain or Abel, depending on our relationships. To become closer to Heavenly Parent, the important thing is for us to become wise people who can always listen to the person standing in the position of Abel and attend him or her with heartfelt sincerity, so that we can go before Heaven. To do so, we need to have a heart that is always awake and pure and innocent, like that of a child. More than anything else, instead of being swayed by the power, status or pride we have built up over the years, we need to find Abel who possesses the heart of Heavenly Parent and report and discuss our lives with him or her, thereby gradually eliminating the fallen nature embedded deep in our hearts.

❋ Points for contemplation

1) Think about the reason why Heavenly Parent did not accept Cain's offering. Let us try to experience spiritually what Heavenly Parent's heart must have been like at that time by offering deep prayers.

2) Let us contemplate the attitude we should assume and the actions we should take when we meet an Abel figure. In addition, let us think about how we can guide Cain to Heavenly Parent when we are in the position of Abel.

2
Foundation of Faith and Foundation of Substance to Receive the Messiah
— Formula of the Providence of Restoration

True Parents' Words

To go the way of restoration, you first need to establish a foundation of faith. The foundation of faith is necessary to create a solid foundation upon which you can secure your place and stand in the subject partner position. This will enable you to pursue Heaven's goals by yourself; however, that is not enough. You still must establish the foundation of substance. The foundation of substance is the foundation that makes Cain surrender to Abel. Cain is the son of the enemy, Satan. It was by the hand of Cain that struggles in history came about. Through him evil took root and waves of death swept through history. To block these evil actions and stop the evil side, a person in the Abel position, that is, a person on God's side, must win over a person in the Cain position. [CSG 4.3.2:4]

> The mission Abel must fulfill is more important than anything else in the course of restoration. The figure of Abel was set up within the Will because of the Fall. Had there been no Fall, there would have been no need to set up the position of Abel. Abel cannot be Abel by himself. There is no Abel without Cain. Furthermore, to be chosen as Abel, a person needs to go through a period of preparation. In other words, he or she needs to go through a period of time to show that he or she stands on Heaven's side. The Unification Principle terms this the period to establish the foundation of faith. It is the period when the sacrifice is offered. Abel offers the sacrifice so that God and human beings, who have been separated, can again form a bond of heart. Then Abel also can form an external bond of heart. [CSG 9.3.6:4]

Sharing Thoughts

Due to the Fall of the human ancestors, humanity fell to a midway position where they can relate with both Heavenly Parent and Satan. Human beings, however, are beings who should never serve two masters. Just as there is only one Heavenly Parent, human beings who were created in His image should live attending only Heavenly Parent as their parent.

For Abel to attain his right as Abel, that is, the right to become a person on Heaven's side, he needs to build the foundation of faith. The way to establish the foundation of faith is to offer your life to

Heavenly Parent as an offering, thereby walking the path of training to rid yourself of the fallen nature that remains in you. It means that you need to repent of your life lived centered on the flesh and create yourself as a being who can live centering on the heart. To do so, you need to follow a path in which your heart can rejoice, such as fasting to discipline your physical body, doing the penance of witnessing to show your love for the Cain realm, or carrying out volunteer work through which you can establish the standard of having loved other people. When your heart is thus able to control your physical body, you can recover the connection of heart to Heavenly Parent.

Once Abel has thus fulfilled the standard of having become one in heart with Heavenly Parent through the foundation of faith, the next thing he needs to do is to find Cain to carry out the restoration of the realm of siblings (restoration of the authority of the elder son). In other words, Abel cannot restore his elder brother, Cain, by brute force. He must make Cain walk that path by embracing him with love. Abel must embrace Cain with true love that springs from Heavenly Parent's heart. Abel must also introduce Cain to Heavenly Parent and make Cain realize that he needs to detach himself from Satan and find his way to Heavenly Parent, the original parent. Such efforts should make Cain stand in the position where, of his own accord, he desires to belong to Heavenly Parent.

By going through this process, Cain, who is physically in the position of the elder brother, can come to understand that Abel stands in the position of the elder brother spiritually, even though he is actually in the position of the younger brother. In this way,

Cain can be induced to show his younger brother respect and love, and the two brothers can stand in front of Heavenly Parent hand in hand. Thus, the two brothers Cain and Abel can unite as one, rid themselves of fallen nature, attend Heavenly Parent, and walk the path of the providence. That position establishes the foundation of substance for the first time.

What is the reason for establishing the foundation of faith and foundation of substance in this manner? By so doing, ultimately the foundation can be laid to receive True Parents, who are coming in place of Heavenly Parent with the mission of human salvation. What is the foundation to receive the Messiah? As has been explained above, it is the providence by which the brothers who were divided into Cain and Abel and antagonistic toward each other can achieve the restoration of the realm of siblings and recover the lost original parent based on their unity.

Among the Aesop's fables so well known to us, there is one titled "The Wind and the Sun." The wind and the sun made a bet to see who could make a traveler take his coat off first. The wind tried first by blowing strongly enough to raise a storm to make the traveler take his coat off by force, but it failed. On the other hand, the only thing the sun did was to shine brightly, but it made the traveler so warm that he took his coat off voluntarily, and it thus succeeded.

The traveler taking his coat off voluntarily due to the warmth of the sun can be compared to Cain of his own accord respecting and following Abel, who was spiritually established first. The more fiercely the wind blows, the closer the traveler holds his coat, but when he is subjected to warmth, he takes his coat off voluntarily. Similarly, for Abel to become one with Cain, Abel needs to make Cain disarm himself of his own accord by letting him feel the warmth of true love. In other words, Abel must thaw Cain's frozen heart through the warmth of love and embrace him.

The foundation of faith and foundation of substance are not stories that apply only to other people, such as the central figures of the providence of restoration. Each of us in our own life has the responsibility to practice and experience them. Therefore, we should never neglect our efforts to deepen our connection of heart with Heavenly Parent by leading a life of faith. In other words, our attitude toward life should stand upright on the foundation of faith. However, what is more difficult to establish than the foundation of faith is the foundation of substance. The foundation of faith can be established when we do well in our one-to-one relationship with Heavenly Parent, but we cannot establish the foundation of substance by ourselves, for it can be established only when we form a relationship of unity with other people through love. The solution is to practice love silently based on Heavenly Parent's heart. Just like the sun, if we continue to convey the warmth of Heavenly Parent's love to those around us, our foundation of substance naturally will expand and grow.

❋ Points for contemplation

1) On the path of faith, everyone starts out as Cain and then walks the path of Abel. Taking into consideration what it is like to stand in the position of Cain and in the position of Abel, let us think about the meaning of Cain's attitude and Abel's attitude.

2) Let us contemplate ways by which we can establish the foundation of faith and foundation of substance in our lives.

3
The Ultimate Purpose of Human History Is the Manifestation of True Parents
— Foundation for the Messiah

True Parents' Words

Salvation means returning to one's original state. Then, there should be some standard that determines what it means to be restored to one's original state. What is that standard? Humanity is made up of both men and women. Therefore, the first standard of restoration is not only to become a son or daughter of God but also, after going through the role of a child, to form a husband-wife relationship and become true parents so that we can establish a new lineage. This is the purpose for which God created us and the standard from which our history can begin anew. Therefore, the problem is not one nation, people or tribe. The problem is also not a specific son or daughter. The problem is that we absolutely need True Parents. The greatest problem for God is to find and establish the True Parents, who are the manifestation of God in the flesh. The greatest problem and purpose for humanity is how to meet the True Parents whom God establishes. [CSG 2.2.1:23]

The True Parents represent the greatest hope and the greatest foundation of victory in history. As they are the central point of hope in history, all people must seek them. The place of historical hope is neither a nation nor the world. Outwardly it may appear to be a nation or the world, but you cannot solve the external world's problems by working through the external world alone. The purpose of God's providence is to save the world, and to do so, He must send good parents to the earth to create a perfect foundation. Without that foundation there is no way to create a perfect nation or to save the world. Therefore, the overall hope of history is neither a nation nor the world; it is the True Parents. [CSG 2.2.1:9]

What is the purpose of the Second Advent? It is the coming of the True Parents. The returning Lord and his bride are the True Parents. The Messiah means the True Parents, who are the final destination of human history. One united world can come about only when all people, who are wandering about like orphans without a nation, come to the True Parents. That is how the world becomes one home. In this world of True Parents there is no devil. This is the viewpoint of the Principle. When the True Parents appear, Satan ultimately will have to withdraw. God wants the True Parents to appear on earth and defeat Satan. God wants to lay that foundation. [CSG 2.1.1:25]

Sharing Thoughts

What is the ultimate purpose of human history? To this question, the words in the main text give us the simplest and yet the most profound answer: We need True Parents, who are absolutely necessary to humanity and through whom Heavenly Parent can be manifested in the flesh. In the long course of history, an uncountable number of people have been born and have died. Innumerable tribes, peoples and nations have risen and perished, and countless religions have come into existence and disappeared. What is the reason and purpose for this continued struggle in human history? The process of history is not a meaningless product of coincidences. The core purpose and direction that pierce the very center of history have definitely existed. This is because there was the Will of Heavenly Parent, who wished for the manifestation of the True Parents. The sorrowful Will of Heavenly Parent to restore humanity through the appearance of True Parents has been incorporated in all of human history.

The parable of the vineyard owner and tenant farmers in the Bible clearly illustrates this point to us. A landowner planted a vineyard with much care and leased it to tenant farmers. One day, he sent his slave to collect some of the fruit harvested in the vineyard. However, the farmers beat him, insulted him and sent him back. The owner sent another slave, but the farmers killed him. Lastly, the owner sent his beloved son, but the farmers murdered that son in their greed to own the vineyard as their own. This is truly an unbelievable story. However, it is actually an account of the sad details of the providence of restoration. The owner in the parable refers to Heavenly Parent, his slaves the prophets, his son Jesus, and the tenant farmers fallen humanity. To save fallen humanity, Heavenly Parent sent many prophets and even His own son, but the result was horrendous. Humankind did not follow Heavenly Parent's Will and instead severely persecuted and oppressed the prophets again and again.

As can be seen, Heavenly Parent has had to make many sacrifices in the course of the providence of restoration. However, He never gave up His Will. Even when humanity repeated actions like those of the farmers, He clutched His anguished heart and never gave up His Will to save humanity. And in the end, He found the path by which He could send His son and daughter who could become the True Parents of humanity.

We need to realize that these stories of the sorrowful heart of Heavenly Parent have continued incessantly throughout human history until the appearance of the True Parents. Those of us living today must never repeat the mistake committed by the farmers. Engrave these words deep in your heart: "True Parents are the greatest beings of hope in human history." True Parents have finally appeared, and we need to become people and form families who can attend them with all our hearts.

❈ Points for contemplation

1) Human history is the providence of salvation and the providence of restoration. Let us contemplate together what the appearance of True Parents, who have come to restore fallen humanity, means to us.

2) Heavenly Parent sent the True Parents to save humankind. How should we attend and follow our True Parents?

4
World Religions Have Continued to Enlighten the Human Spirit and Intellect

— The Role of Religion

True Parents' Words

There are many religions throughout the world. What are these religions supposed to teach? The first priority for any religion is to teach people properly about God. A religion that teaches about God in a vague or ambiguous way leaves us uncertain. If God truly exists, and He does, then a true religion must teach what kind of being God is, what His love is like, and so on. [CBG 11.1.1:1]

When looking at all the cultures of the world and their histories, we find that behind them and supporting them is religion. Human history and religion are connected and share a common destiny. In different eras, religions sometimes have gotten ahead of history and sometimes have fallen behind it; yet religions have continued to exist. This is because religion is the foundation upon which God can achieve the ideal world and His ideal of the kingdom of heaven. The key teaching of religion is God and His love. That is why religions teach human beings to love God. The original mind of human beings wants to seek and find God, who created them and the cosmos. That is why religion must teach principles by which human beings can love God and receive His love. In Korean, the word for religion is *jong-gyo*. The first Chinese character, *jong* (宗), means "wooden floor." The second character, *gyo* (教), means "teaching." Hence, what we call religion is the teaching that helps human beings become a platform, or even the pillar that supports from beneath. If this is the case, what could be more important than teaching about God's love? Is there any teaching greater than this? Human beings' most ardent desire is to possess the love of God. Religion teaches us how to reach that summit. That is why the more it emphasizes God and the more it teaches His love, leading us to stand in awe of the absolute Creator of the universe, the higher a religion it is. [*CBG* 11.1.1:5]

The role of religion is to re-create human beings. How does it do that? It guides us to resolve the seemingly endless conflict between mind and body and reach a state of peace where forevermore there is no struggle. [*CBG* 11.1.1:11]

Sharing Thoughts

An old Buddhist monk was returning from an outing when it started to rain just as he was crossing the threshold of the temple. A missionary, who had been out on the street arguing about the superiority of his religion, had slouched down under the eaves of the temple when it started to rain to avoid getting wet. The monk asked him, "Why are you standing there?" and the missionary answered, "Can't you tell? I'm taking shelter from the rain." The monk then said, "Ha ha, is that so? As you can see, I arrived here without getting wet even in this rain." The missionary asked with a puzzled face, "Do you have a secret to staying dry?" The monk answered, "Do as I tell you. On a rainy day, look up at the sky without an umbrella over your head. Then you will receive a revelation." On the day after it had rained, however, the missionary appeared again, seething with anger. "I looked up at the sky like you said and got soaked in the rain, but instead of receiving a revelation, all I felt was that I had been made a fool. How will you explain that?" The old monk answered him, "Oh, really? You received a truly wonderful revelation on your first try. If you can realize your own foolishness by yourself, wouldn't that indeed be a great revelation from Heavenly Parent?"

It would not be an exaggeration to say that human history is the history of religion, for human life and religion are linked together by an inseparable connection. Not only global religions like Christianity,

Buddhism, Islam and Judaism, but other great and small religions have arisen and perished repeatedly, all the while fundamentally influencing the shaping of human culture. Even in today's secularized world, the number of people who answer that they have a religion amounts to 85 percent of the total world population. In other words, almost nine people out of ten recognize themselves as being religious believers. This is something we can easily perceive when we look around us in our living environment. The entire world looks like a religious exhibition, with churches, temples and chapels filling up every nook and cranny. Humankind is sometimes referred to as *Homo Religiosus*, expressing the belief that human beings were born with an innate desire to pursue religion.

Then why do human beings pursue religion? What is the ultimate purpose of religion? According to the words of the above text, the answer is simple. The ultimate purpose of religion is to teach humanity correctly about their parent, Heavenly Parent, and His love. The Chinese characters for religion (*jong-gyo*: 宗教) literally mean the teaching that serves as the basis, whose core content is none other than Heavenly Parent's existence and love. A religion that can teach in detail about Heavenly Parent's existence and His love based on the heart can become a mature religion of a higher order. In addition, a religion can also be said to be like a "repair shop" where fallen human beings are fixed. The Fall of the human ancestors planted the seeds of discord and conflict in human life. The origin of such conflicts begins in the mind and body of individual human beings and expands to become conflicts between individual people, groups, societies, nations and throughout the world. Therefore, because the various problems in the world cannot be resolved fundamentally unless the mind and body are united, religion must take on the role of repairing the broken human mind and body by arousing Heavenly Parent's absolute love in the hearts of human beings.

In short, religion can be said to give the fundamental teachings about why Heavenly Parent created humankind and how human beings should lead true lives. Human beings should believe in religion because, by learning and practicing those teachings, they can learn to care for others, to love them, to harmonize with them, to respect them and to live for their sake. They also need to realize that humanity is one great family.

Religion was not created by accident in the course of history. Heavenly Parent exists in the background behind every religion. He has given rise to various religions so that they can enlighten the human spirit and intellect in ways befitting the era and the characteristics of the different localities. Therefore, though every religion has a founder, the true founder of all religions can be said to be just the one being, Heavenly Parent. To save all humankind, He has continued to develop religions suitable to the ages and cultural realms. He has also unceasingly continued to enlighten the human spirit and intellect and to lead the providence of restoration in order to become one with humanity, His children.

Therefore, nothing could be more meaningless than the fights breaking out between religions due to doctrinal differences. In various parts of the world, wars are still being fought endlessly because of religious conflict. When we look upon such phenomena, we feel ashamed as fellow religious believers, and we even begin to question whether religion is really necessary. Such conflicts arise because we do not really know the true meaning of religion and we do not have a clear understanding of Heavenly Parent's heart. All religious believers should realize the true meaning of religion, which stems from the same root and has the same purpose. With one heart and one will, we need to unite as one and focus on our common destination, Heavenly Parent. We must go beyond the superficial differences between religions and discover Heavenly Parent's heart, which exists in the center of them all.

❊ Points for contemplation

1) Let us deeply contemplate the fundamental purpose for the existence of religions.
2) For religions to cooperate and harmonize with one another, what kind of attitude should religious believers adopt?

5
The Only Begotten Son and Only Begotten Daughter Were Finally Manifested
— Birth of the True Parents, the Messiah

True Parents' Words

True Parents must emerge in history. The one who carries out this historic mission is the Savior and the Messiah. What does he save? Not our physical bodies by making them last forever. Rather, he enables us to fulfill our hope for ideal love. To achieve this, the Messiah must come as the True Parents. Christianity teaches that Jesus is the Messiah and Savior. What does he need to do to come as the True Parents? We know he cannot do it alone. He comes as a man representing the true father. This is why Jesus said that he was the only begotten son of God. When the only begotten son comes, it will not suffice if he is alone. There has to be the only begotten daughter. He finds the only begotten daughter, and they must marry from the position where they like each other with God at their center. Upon their marriage, God, as the vertical Parent, would rejoice, and the True Parents as the horizontal parents must create the position of the Bride and Bridegroom who can rejoice. Then they must give birth to children on earth. [CSG 2.1.1:26]

Human history is the history of the providence of restoration in which God worked to establish one central figure. Two thousand years ago God established Jesus as the only begotten son of Heaven, but due to the Israelites' disbelief, he was nailed to the cross. Therefore, Heaven's providence was prolonged to the time of the Second Advent. Now we are ushering in the blessed age in which the Lord of the Second Advent has come to this earth and has found the bride of heaven, the only begotten daughter. Together they have manifested as True Parents. Humankind needs to meet, attend and follow True Parents, who are the representatives of our God. Only then can we rid ourselves of the original sin which has been passed down through us for 6,000 years. Then we can be reborn as people full of love and wisdom, fulfilling God's original purpose of creation. [CBG 13.4.3:14]

Sharing Thoughts

Three students, who met one another when they came to study abroad and who believed in different religions, were sharing the same room on the 24th floor of a tall building. One day, the three students returned after an outing together to find that there was a power failure and the elevator was not working at all. One of the students suggested that they take the stairs, saying that they were young and strong and walking up 24 floors would be easy. The other students agreed to do so.

The three started walking up, and one of the students said that they should slow down and talk about something, since their legs were starting to hurt. That student began talking about the greatness of the god he believed in, Allah. When they had reached the sixth floor, another student who believed in Buddhism started talking about the mercy and love of Buddha and the Buddhist salvation. The students had already climbed to the 13th floor. Lastly, the student from India who was a Sikh began to explain Nanak, the founder of Sikhism. He also talked proudly about the greatness of the religion in which he believed. By then the number in the stairwell told them that they had reached the 18th floor. They remained silent the rest of the way until they reached their room on the 24th floor. Though they had talked proudly of their own religions and the founders, in their hearts the students felt a sense of kinship with what their other friends had told them about their own religions. They gained a vast understanding of viewpoints other than their own. Upon reaching the 24th floor, they were about to open the door and go in, when they realized that not one of them had collected the room key from the guard office.

Many religious people believe that they have found the ultimate truth in their own way through their religion. And they climb the stairs of their religion all their lives with much effort, but when they reach the gates to the kingdom of heaven, they may find that they have not brought the key they need to get in. They may never be able to open those gates to the kingdom of heaven. Even living for 70 or 80 years in this world, all the while offering devout prayers, may be in vain. If you do not have that key, you may have to go all the way down to the first floor and climb all the way back, stair after stair, with the essential key in your hand.

In the course of history, many religions have earnestly yearned for a special being to appear who can save this world, which has been moaning and wallowing in the anguish of sin. For instance, Christianity and Judaism have waited for the Messiah, Confucianism for the "true man," and Buddhism for Maitreya. Though the attributes of this being may be different for different religions, they all have been waiting for the Messiah. What they have in common is the fact that the Messiah" is the being who can change this world filled with sin and anguish to the ideal world.

The Family Federation for World Peace and Unification has revealed that the essence of this messianic being is True Parents. Humanity has been degraded to become the children of Satan due to the Fall of the human ancestors, and as long as human beings are languishing under the influence of Satan, no ideal world of any kind can be realized. Therefore, the most important key in opening the ideal world is to convert the lineage of fallen humanity to the lineage of Heavenly Parent, and the beings who can perform this role are the True Parents.

That is why a father alone or a mother alone is not enough for human beings to be born again. For a life to be conceived, both the father and mother are necessary. The same is true for giving rebirth to fallen humanity as the children of Heavenly Parent. Therefore, the True Parents, who are the key that can open the true ideal world desired by Heavenly Parent by converting humanity's lineage, should be a man and a woman who have been manifested on this earth as Heavenly Parent's true son and true daughter. In other words, the son and daughter of Heavenly Parent born without original sin must be manifested together to become husband and wife and stand in front of humanity as their True Parents. For this reason, the essence of the Messiah is not just one person as we have believed until now, but a couple, the True Parents.

In the beginning, Adam and Eve were born as the son and daughter "who can exclusively receive Heavenly Parent's love," that is, His only begotten son and only begotten daughter. This is also the case for the True Parents, the Messiah, who come again as the second Adam and Eve. They must be manifested on this earth as the only begotten son and the only begotten daughter. Just as the purpose of creation was to create Adam and Eve and have them start their life together as husband and wife, restoring fallen humanity can be carried out only when they appear together as husband and wife and start their life as True Parents. In conclusion, the Messiah for whom humanity has waited for a very long time is the Messiah who comes as True Parents.

January 6, 1920, and January 6, 1943, are blessed days that will go down in history for all eternity because they are the birthdays of Heavenly Parent's only begotten son, Rev. Sun Myung Moon, and Heavenly Parent's only begotten daughter, Dr. Hak Ja Han Moon, respectively. We need to profoundly realize the value of their birthdays. We need to know the heart of Heavenly Parent, who endured sorrow and pain for 6,000 years, waiting with anticipation for this one day on which the salvation of humanity could begin.

Now we who have received the teachings of True Parents also need to follow the path of becoming unfallen parents. On the foundation of true love, true life and true lineage established by Heavenly Parent and True Parents, the Messiah, we need to be reborn as Heavenly Parent's true sons and daughters.

❈ Points for contemplation

1) Let us deeply contemplate the meaning of the words that the Messiah must come as True Parents.
2) Let us think about the common religious values that we need to pursue of our own accord, and ponder ways by which humans, who have been divided due to the Fall, are brothers and sisters who are walking different paths and can live together centering on one value.

6
A New Horizon in History, the Marriage Supper of the Lamb
- Holy Wedding of True Parents, the Messiah

True Parents' Words

On the day when two human beings, a filial son of God and a filial daughter of God, can stand before God as the Bridegroom and Bride for the first time since the creation of heaven and earth, God will say to them, "You have worked so hard to come here, seeking heaven's heart and the heart of the God, even amid all the adversity on earth!" He then will give His blessing to this couple and install them as the True Parents who represent the incorporeal God in physical form. Such is the cosmic banquet, the Marriage Supper of the Lamb. The Marriage Supper of the Lamb is offered based on the Bridegroom and Bride having become a true filial son and daughter, with the true Bride having pledged herself to the Will and having understood the Will. From the day they receive the Blessing, they become the True

Parents of humankind who represent the incorporeal God in substantial form. [CBG 1.2.1:10]

The original human beings were not supposed to fall. They were supposed to receive God's blessing at the right time and, within the right environment, become the true ancestors of humankind. But they failed to do so; instead they became the fallen ancestors. Thus, the good ancestor, free from the Fall, should appear in front of all humankind. He is the one who can become the True Father to all in the spiritual world and the physical world. Christianity calls this person the Lord of the Second Advent. The Marriage Supper of the Lamb is the banquet to which the returning Jesus comes as the True Father to bring forth a woman as the True Mother. This is the core truth of Christianity. The center of Christianity is Jesus, and the center of Jesus is love. The center of the Bible is also love. The center of love is the Bride and Bridegroom, and the center of the Bride and Bridegroom is the Marriage Supper of the Lamb. The paramount significance of the Marriage Supper of the Lamb is that the Returning Lord and his Bride receive the marriage Blessing at the time of God's choosing and in the right environment, whereby they become the true ancestors of humankind who can inherit heaven and earth. [CBG 1.2.1:6]

One Father and one Mother must appear on earth. The Marriage of the Lamb is the moment when we finally can start building on earth our lost original home. To build that home, we must have the Parents and we must have brothers and sisters. Upon this foundation we can propagate children, and from them will unfold the original tribe, people, nation and world. Then, finally, the existing evil world will be vanquished. This is how the providence of restoration progresses toward the world of goodness. [CSG 1.4.1:46]

Sharing Thoughts

Eve, born as Heavenly Parent's only begotten daughter, was seduced by the snake to eat the forbidden fruit, "the fruit of the tree of the knowledge of good and evil," and fell. After she fell, she realized that her originally intended husband was Adam, and she made him eat the forbidden fruit, too. In the end, Adam and Eve were caught in Satan's trap and lost their position as children given to them by Heavenly Parent, as well as the right of true parents by which they would have governed the created world when they reached maturity. Therefore, humanity has lived waiting for the unfallen only begotten son and only begotten daughter to appear who can save them from the Fall and perform the Marriage Supper of the Lamb and become True Parents.

The Book of Revelations in the Christian Bible allegorizes the kingdom of heaven realized through the Lord of the Second Advent as the Marriage Supper of the Lamb. Given that the Book of Revelations is full of many parables and symbols, the Marriage Supper has been interpreted to mean various things, but most Christians today understand it to mean that Jesus is the bridegroom and the community (church) of his followers is the bride. In short, they understand the essence of the Marriage Supper of the Lamb to be the spiritual union of Jesus and the church.

However, restoration refers to what Adam and Eve originally should have done, that is, become husband and wife and the true parents of humanity. Hence, the Marriage Supper of the Lamb begins when the only begotten son and only begotten daughter, who come in place of Adam and Eve from lineages that have not fallen, come to earth, become husband and wife and start multiplying the lineage of goodness. Therefore, Jesus, who came as Heaven's only begotten son, should have found the prepared bride of heaven at that time and established a true family in which Heavenly Parent's love could bear fruit. However, due to the distrust of the people who should have attended and followed Jesus, he had no choice but to end his life nailed to the cross before he could realize that will.

After the fall of Adam and Eve, Jesus' death on the cross was the time when the heart of Heavenly Parent collapsed horribly once again. In the end, the Will to find and establish Jesus' bride had to be postponed to the age of the Second Advent. Christianity should have fulfilled its responsibility of preparing the foundation on which the bride of the Lord of the Second Advent could be born, thereby creating the environment in which the ideal of true parents could be realized once again.

The Marriage Supper of the Lamb signifies the holy ceremony by which the only begotten son and only begotten daughter, who are born as Heavenly Parent's true son and daughter without original sin, get married to each other and finally become the True Parents of humanity. It is the Holy Wedding Ceremony of the True Parents who can put an end to the history of sin that has continued since the time of Adam and Eve's Fall and give new birth to humanity as Heavenly Parent's sons and daughters. The ultimate purpose of the history of fallen human beings until now has been to prepare for the manifestation of the original, unfallen true parents who can save them, and to fulfill the mission of preparing for the Marriage Supper of the Lamb.

However, in the future, history will be a historical record of heavenly humanity, newly born after receiving the Blessing of the True Parents who are already manifest on earth as the True Parents and have performed the Marriage Supper of the Lamb. In other words, it will be the history of the substantial realization of the world of the original ideal of creation. As can be seen, the Marriage Supper of the Lamb is the day that marks the transition point at which human history can be begun anew once again. Therefore, historians of the coming generations will be able to assess human history as being either before or after the Marriage Supper of the Lamb.

April 11, 1960, was the day this new horizon was opened in history. It was the day of the greatest feast for humanity, on which the only begotten son, Rev. Sun Myung Moon, and the only begotten daughter, Dr. Hak Ja Han Moon, became manifest on this earth, performed the Holy Wedding Ceremony after overcoming innumerable difficulties, and were thus enthroned as the True Parents of humanity. Only a small number of people were gathered at the time to celebrate this Marriage Supper of the Lamb, because the prepared foundation of Christianity had failed to fulfill its responsibility at the time. From now on we should celebrate the Holy Wedding Ceremony of True Parents every year as the greatest holiday and propagate the meaning of this day to all parts of the world. More than anything else, we ourselves should be reborn as the hopeful fruits of the Marriage Supper of the Lamb. We will need to continue to practice our way of life as heavenly tribal messiahs, so that the blessing of Heaven bestowed through True Parents' Holy Wedding Ceremony can shine more brightly through the continuous birth of more and more blessed families.

❋ Points for contemplation

1) Let us deeply contemplate the meaning of True Parents' Holy Wedding Ceremony, which is the Marriage Supper of the Lamb, and its relation to our lives today.
2) Let us think about ways by which we can expand the meaning and value of the Marriage Supper of the Lamb in our lives.

7
From Wild Olive Tree to True Olive Tree
— The Need for a Change of Lineage

True Parents' Words

Our bondage to the lineage of Satan has caused so much suffering throughout history. Humanity must step forward boldly to sever that tie and be engrafted onto the root of True Parents' lineage. Why should we foolishly continue to live and die as wild olive trees? A wild olive tree, even if it lives 1,000 years, will only continue producing the seeds of more wild olive trees. Where can we find the path to escape this vicious cycle? It is through the Holy Blessing. The Blessing ceremony offers the grace of being engrafted onto the true olive tree, the True Parents, who bring God's true lineage to humankind. It is necessary because you cannot change your seed without changing your lineage. [CSG 13.1.1:18]

The True Parents are the Lords who correct the lineage. They know the secret of how to do that. When the first parents fell, they became the false parents, but the True Parents know how to deal with this problem and revive them by giving them an injection of life, that is, by establishing the standard of true love, true life and true lineage, and then connecting that standard to them, replacing the false love, life and lineage. Thus, they turn from false back into true. In reversing the situation, however, True Parents cannot give rebirth to all families at once. They will engraft themselves to those families branch by branch. In order to engraft to a wild olive tree family, there needs to be a model true olive tree family. When a shoot from the model olive tree family is engrafted and three years have passed, each wild olive tree family can bear the fruits of a true family. I am saying that I will engraft a shoot of the True Parents to the mothers and fathers from false, wild olive tree families and transform them into families of True Parents' sons and daughters. [CSG 2.2.3:10]

True Parents are the Adam and Eve who did not fall. God is the first generation, True Parents are the second generation, and blessed families are engrafted into the realm of the third generation. Now that you wild olive trees have received grafts from the true olive tree, you need to make much effort to become true olive trees. Your most urgent priority and responsibility are to purify yourselves internally and externally in order to cultivate true love, true life and true lineage. You must feel that the True

Parents are your own parents and that you are their direct lineage. By fulfilling your duties, you must become completely one with True Parents, attending them as their filial sons and daughters. Then you must serve the nation, and also heaven and earth, as patriots, saints and divine sons and daughters. [CSG 2.3.2:21]

Sharing Thoughts

There is a Korean proverb that says, "Where you plant soy beans, beans sprout up, and where you plant red beans, red beans sprout up." Actually, this saying is too obvious. You would not see red beans sprouting where you planted soy beans, nor would you see soy beans sprouting where you planted red beans. Nevertheless, if you were to accept the meaning of this proverb, it would also mean that fallen humanity can only continue to give birth to fallen human beings, and that we would have to continue living our lives repeating that vicious cycle. However, could there be any parents who would just let their children continue to inherit the lineage of Satan? Heavenly Parent has sent to the earth the True Parents who are able to remedy this defiled bloodline.

Then how can this defiled bloodline be remedied? We can learn the answer to this question by studying the natural process applied by a farmer who grows fruit trees. When a farmer grafts a wild olive tree to a true olive tree, he begins by cutting off all branches of the wild olive tree except a few central branches. Then he cuts off a scion, a small piece for grafting from a true olive tree prepared in advance, and after removing the bark from the remaining branches of the wild olive tree, he grafts the scion to the exposed surface and binds them together. A while after this process is completed, the scion of the true olive tree settles onto the branch of the wild olive tree. After the branch has grown for a certain period of time, it sprouts the buds of a true olive tree, and later it also bears the flowers and fruits of the true olive tree. In this illustration, fallen humanity is the wild olive tree and the true olive tree is True Parents, who have come to save humanity. Therefore, fallen humanity must receive grafts from True Parents, who have come as the true olive tree. The process and the pain involved in being converted from a wild olive tree to a true olive tree are not easy at all. To do so, we need to completely sever ourselves from the habits and wrongful elements of a wild olive tree which are still flowing inside our old selves.

The people who have led ugly lives may have to experience pain that is almost as severe as losing their lives. However, if we do not sever ourselves from our past way of life of self-centered egoism, we cannot be reborn.

We need to make the effort to correct the mistakes we committed unknowingly in our past relationships with the opposite sex and sever ourselves from the attributes of Satan. We need to focus all the nutrients in our body so that only the scion of the true olive tree can grow on us. Even when the new scion has settled on the branch and asserted its identity, when spring comes again the next year, buds of the wild olive tree also will continue to sprout around, it because the trunk of the wild olive tree has not yet become completely converted into a true olive tree.

At this point in time, the farmer needs to lend a helping hand. We also need a helping hand in the form of True Parents' words. We need to cut away those new wild olive tree branches mercilessly. What that means is that, even after receiving the Blessing, we still may have passion, anger and self-centered thoughts because we were accustomed to having them in the past. If we cannot completely eliminate them by diligently studying True Parents' words, those self-centered assertions will continue in us. Therefore, we need to engraft the scion of the true olive tree to us through the Blessing ceremony, and even after receiving the Blessing, we need to be able to control our self-centered thoughts through True Parents' words. In other words, we need to continue leading a life of rebirth so that the traditions and culture of Heaven can be firmly established.

In this analogy of the olive trees, True Parents paid attention to the value of the true olive tree. They considered the true olive tree to be the source of the true lineage of Heavenly Parent. And they allegorized fallen humanity who inherited the lineage of Satan to be in the position of the wild olive tree. A wild olive tree by itself will always remain a wild olive tree. It cannot change its essence of its own accord. In short, "a wild olive tree will only be able to produce the seeds of a wild olive tree even if it lives for 1,000 years, and this vicious cycle is repeated again and again." That is the situation human beings are in at present as the descendants of the Fall. To put it another way, fallen human beings cannot escape from their origin as wild olive trees, no matter how much effort they make on their own.

Hence, fallen human beings, who are like the wild olive tree, need the true olive tree to pass the lineage of Heaven on to them. The people who came as the substantial true olive tree are True Parents. True Parents are manifest on this earth without original sin, and they must be engrafted on to human beings through the Blessing ceremony to eradicate the sinful lineage so that fallen humans can be reborn as the true sons and daughters of Heavenly Parent. Herein lies the fundamental reason why we need to receive the marriage Blessing from True Parents. Through the grafting ceremony that is the marriage Blessing, we wild olive trees can be born anew as true olive trees. During the conversion from the wild olive tree to the true olive tree, we need to climb the hill on which those who seek to die will live and those who seek to live will die. Only when you have the determination to risk even death, can you make your way to the place of new life.

When we have filled the place we have thus emptied in ourselves with nothing but the words and love of True Parents, we can receive the graft of true love, true life and true lineage from True Parents. After being grafted to them, we will experience true joy, the likes of which we have never experienced before. The greatest happiness that human beings can enjoy is finally realized when they are reborn as true sons and daughters of Heavenly Parent and are able to enjoy His love 100 percent.

At present, are you wild olive trees or true olive trees? If it has been only a short while since you were engrafted, you will need to make a lot of effort and offer much jeongseong to make the loving life force of the true olive tree envelop your entire life. May you manage every day of your life well, so that the true olive tree in your heart can flourish!

❋ Points for contemplation

1) What must fallen human beings, who are the wild olive trees, do to eradicate their past lives and lead new lives?
2) Let us deeply contemplate the value of True Parents, who have come as the substantial true olive tree.

8
Life of Blessed Families Living in Attendance to True Parents
— Children's Portion of Responsibility

True Parents' Words

Even if Father goes to bed late, he rises early in the morning and prays seriously. Even if the wind is blowing or if it is raining, night and day he is praying for you, the children of the Unification Church. When I see the face of Father meditating deeply on how to fulfill God's Will, I think he is someone whom God cannot help but love. I hope that you empower yourselves as much as you can with the Divine Principle. I hope that you can be unchanging in a world of heart that is firmly connected, not in a master–servant relationship, but in a father–son relationship. When you are suffering, please think about True Father. [CBG 13.4.4:25]

Our hope is a world of freedom, peace, unity and happiness. God also wants this. It has taken this long because throughout thousands of years of history the perfect True Parents, those who could complete the providence of restoration through indemnity, did not appear. Now, having attended True Parents, we have entered a new era, but is this enough to make us happy? Isn't our goal to open a happy kingdom of heaven on earth and in heaven and attend True Parents and our God together with our neighbors, our nations and the world? To achieve this, you must stand in the position of proud filial sons and daughters, loyal patriots and divine sons and daughters. Please pray that you will become blessed families that will accomplish your entire responsibility in this era by proudly informing the whole world about True Parents. [*CBG* 13.4.2:2]

You should now set up the hoondokhae study tradition in your family, in which three generations of a family start each day by reading Heaven's Word and lead a life practicing what they read with a new heart. Let's create a world where people in the spirit world and the earthly world attend True Parents at the same time and read the words about the heavenly path together. Once this happens, no matter how hard Satan may try to worm his way in and infest your lineage, when he encounters the hoondokhae tradition, he will have no room to move. If the blessing of God does not come to the family that is living the standard of high noon, where no shadow is cast, then who could possibly receive it? When such heavenly families fill the earth, the world automatically will become the heavenly kingdom on earth and in the

eternal spirit world, fulfilling the vision of one family under God.
[CSG 13.4.2:12]

Sharing Thoughts

What is a home?

What makes a home is not the kitchen or the dining table with flowers on it, but the mother's smile filled with devotion and love.

What makes a home is not cars or family members coming in and going out, but the excitement caused by seeing the father crossing the threshold to give love.

What makes a home is not green grass or flowering plants, but the laughter of children that breaks out on that green lawn.

What makes a home is not sleeping, waking, going out and coming back, but when a meeting of affectionate whispers and understanding is realized.

A happy home is not a place where you are judged on what you are good or bad at, but a place where everything about you is embraced and where you receive help, comfort and love.

A blessed home is a home that attends Heavenly Parent and True Parents.

It is the place where the original parents' love exists and where you learn about unity, peace, happiness and freedom.

It is a place where a father's love that is as wide as the sea and a mother's love that embraces everything like the earth can be found.

A home is a garden where forgiveness, rather than criticism, and understanding and magnanimity, rather than contention, have priority and where you always can hear laughter.

The total number of people in the world today is estimated to be over seven billion. That is an awe-inspiring number, but if we were to take into consideration all the people who lived on this planet ever since the first appearance of humanity, that number would be incalculably large. The entire human history has been a preparation period in anticipation of the appearance of the True Parents, the Messiah. An unimaginably large number of people were born on this earth, lived their lives in their own way, and died in the end, and until the last few decades there was not one person who personally witnessed and received the manifestation of True Parents, who are the ultimate purpose of humanity.

In light of this, we should acutely realize the great benefit of the age we are enjoying today, for we have been given the opportunity to live in the same age as the True Parents and to attend them. The saints and martyrs of the past would have paid all the money in the world if they could have met the True Parents, the Messiah, for even one second. Such is the preciousness of the opportunity given to us. We need to know how precious our lives are to be living in the same age as the True Parents, and we need to realize that they are so valuable that we should not waste even one minute or one second of our lives doing something else.

We are people who have received the Blessing from the True

Parents. As the main text tells us, "having attended True Parents, we have entered a new era." Now, we have two great responsibilities. One is to profoundly comprehend the value of the Blessing given to us by True Parents and form true families overflowing with love.

Centering on the love of Heavenly Parent and True Parents, parents and children, husbands and wives, and brothers and sisters in every family should live for one another's sake and endeavor to realize the original family. To do so, it is more important than anything else to value and uphold the tradition of hoondokhae.

Why is hoondokhae important? The love that should bloom in our families can be perfected only on the standard of having achieved oneness with the heart of True Parents. That love can be grasped only by diligently studying True Parents' words. Therefore, all members of the family need to read and study True Parents' words every day and endeavor with one heart to spiritually experience and understand the love and the Principle contained in those words on a deeper level. To do so, we need to establish hoondokhae as a family tradition that must be upheld always.

Our other responsibility is to spread the Blessing we received from True Parents to our surroundings. True Parents' love must fill up and overflow in our homes until it can flow out to our surrounding neighbors, society and the world. That is the core of the heavenly tribal messiah mission. We need to play the role of the bridge, through which the light of true love, true life and true lineage that we have inherited through True Parents' Blessing can spread out evenly throughout the world. By so doing, just as our families were transformed into true families through True Parents, we need to guide our neighborhood families to receive that benefit of love. Our neighbors who are still living behind the veil of spiritual ignorance are waiting for True Parents' words. By conveying the heart of True Parents to them, we must make the entire world work together to establish Cheon Il Guk where the "ideal of one family under Heavenly Parent" can be realized.

❋ Points for contemplation

1) "Is it all right if we alone are happy? Isn't our goal to open the happy kingdom of heaven on earth and in heaven and attend True Parents and our Heavenly Parent together with our neighbors, our nations and the world?" Let us deeply contemplate together the heart reflected in these words of True Parents.

2) Let us think about the reason True Parents so strongly emphasized the tradition of hoondokhae.

Chapter 6

The Meaning of the Marriage Blessing

1
The International Marriage Blessing and the Salvation of Humankind

— Family Peace and World Peace

True Parents' Words

The literal meaning of our word for the Blessing, *chukbok*, is "praying for blessings." If you analyze the word *chukbok*, *chuk* means to pray or wish for something. When you are praying for blessings, what is most precious? The blessing of love is most precious. The core starting point of the universe's promise is a man and a woman creating harmony. So, the Blessing is the most wonderful thing. Because the Blessing is the greatest blessing you can receive, the Unification Church refers to the wedding ceremony as "the Blessing." The most precious Blessing is one that is officiated by the True Parents. [CSG 5.2.2:1]

The Marriage Blessing is for the sake of God and the world. With the Blessing you can love the world and, as the representative of the world, love the person who is closest to you. A woman should love her husband as the representative of her father, husband, older brother and younger brother. A man should love his wife as the representative of his mother, wife, older sister and younger sister. In representing these four positions, we love the person in the position closest to us, respecting each other and stimulating each other to love the world. The husband–wife relationship is the most basic embodiment of the world-level give-and-receive action of love. Therefore, when you get married, you should love your wife in place of your mother, older sister and younger sister; love your husband in place of your father, older brother and younger brother. Furthermore, you should love your spouse even more than you love the members of your family. This is the formula by which a husband and wife love each other and realize the ideal of reciprocal partnership. [CBG 4.1.1:21]

Sharing Thoughts

In 1988, a well-educated Korean young man who had joined our church wanted to get married and sought to be matched. He was matched with a Japanese woman. The father of this young man reacted very negatively to the match. He said, "Of all the women in the world, you have to marry a Japanese?" During the Japanese occupation, his father had been one of the Koreans conscripted into forced labor and taken to a coal mine in Iwate Prefecture in northwestern Japan. He risked his life to escape the mine and walked for well over a month to Shimonoseki, where he was able to board a ship back to Korea. He harbored a tremendous hatred for Japan.

Every time the relatives would gather for a major holiday, the father-in-law would have his daughter-in-law sit near him, and he would tell her all the things that were done to him in the Iwate coal mine. Each time, the daughter-in-law responded by saying, "Father, I apologize to you on behalf of Japan. I am sorry." She would shed tears and ask for his forgiveness. While he continued to vent his anger at her, she listened to him tell the same tedious stories over and over until he was finished, and she endlessly bowed down her head.

Only after this had gone on for about ten years, the father-in-law stopped his persecution of his daughter-in-law. The surprised relatives noticed that his cold attitude toward his daughter-in-law had become much warmer and that he even seemed to like her. So, they asked him, "Why are you behaving so kindly toward your daughter-in-law. She's a Japanese woman. Don't you hate her?" "I don't hate her anymore," he answered. "All the hatred that had accumulated in my heart has gone away. I never hated her," he added. "I was just venting at her all the hatred that was in me for having been conscripted to work in the mine. Because of her, that hatred has all disappeared. From now on, I'm going to be kind to her because she's my daughter-in-law." The daughter-in-law paid for the sins of the Japanese. This is an example of the path of redemption that will lead humankind into a world of peace. [*As a Peace-Loving Global Citizen*, pp. 221–222]

This is an excerpt from True Father's autobiography. Through the Marriage Blessing of two people from former enemy nations, the resentment and grief that had piled up could be mended and the two countries could go forward on the path of reconciliation and peace.

True Parents restored the first True Family, realized a peaceful world and have been carrying out the providence of salvation to transform hell into the kingdom of heaven on earth and in heaven. Through their engagement ceremony on March 1, 1960, by the lunar calendar and their Holy Wedding Ceremony on April 11, 1960, they manifested the model of the true couple, true parents and true family that attend Heavenly Parent. They came to the earth as the only begotten son and only begotten daughter and realized the ideal of the True Parents. Furthermore, they saved fallen humankind, and, as the original children of Heavenly Parent, they stood in the position to give the Blessing.

Only when the family is peaceful can the society be peaceful. World peace can be achieved through marriage. True Parents always regarded blessed families who were reborn through the international Marriage Blessing to be the central figures in realizing world peace. When we can offer up and sacrifice everything we have to our enemies through true love, then a united path for true forgiveness and reconciliation can be opened. Because the first human ancestors fell in the family, the family became the frontline of the providence of restoration.

Blessed families should follow the order established by True Parents and sacrifice and devote themselves with love in the family and devote themselves for the sake of the society, nation and world. They practice greater love and are building a peaceful world. All humankind must inherit the tradition of the Marriage Blessing and become true couples and true parents who can realize an ideal world of peace. This is the shortcut to making our regions and nations peaceful.

❈ Points for contemplation

1) What will happen if a man and woman from enemy nations marry? How will their conjugal relationship develop?
2) The Marriage Blessing is not simply a marriage centered on the love between a man and a woman. It is the foundation for the settlement of a peaceful world by attending Heavenly Parent and living for the sake of the tribe, people, nation and world. Let us contemplate this.

2
Absolute Sex and True Love
— Chastity Before Marriage and Marital Fidelity

True Parents' Words

This standard you must keep is absolute sex. The first stage is to maintain absolute sexual purity prior to getting married. We absolutely must fulfill one requirement, which is to maintain our purity, adhering to the model of absolute sex. God gave us this responsibility as the means to fulfill the ideal of creation. This heavenly path is the way to perfect conjugal love. [CSG 13.1.3:4–5]

The second stage is the perfection of love between husband and wife. More precious than life is the heavenly law of absolute fidelity. Husband and wife are eternal partners, given to each other by Heaven. Through having children, they become co-creators of true love, true life and true lineage, and the origin of that which is absolute, unique, unchanging and eternal. It is a heavenly principle that one person alone can never give birth to a child, even in 1,000 years. If two people had preserved their purity before marriage and were bound together in marriage by God, how could they ever go astray and deviate from the way of Heaven? People are different from animals; if they understand God's purpose in creating them as His children, they will realize that deviating from heavenly law constitutes an unimaginable betrayal and defiance of the Creator. It is a path of self-destruction on which they dig their own graves. [CSG 13.1.3:7]

The absoluteness of conjugal love is the greatest blessing that Heaven has bestowed on humanity. Without adherence to the principle of absolute sex, the path to the perfection of one's character and spiritual maturity is inaccessible. Furthermore, unless Heaven implants the principles of absolute sex within a true family of perfected individuals, it is impossible for God to appear with dignity as the God of substance and personality. Only in a family that is rooted in the principles of absolute sex is it possible to create ideal relationships in accordance with the original ideal. This affects the three generations represented by grandparents, parents, children and grandchildren. Please understand clearly that God's eternal life and our eternal lives depend on this foundation. [CSG 13.1.3:8]

Sharing Thoughts

There is a story about the beautiful love of a lady called Margaret in France. She loved a man named Gaspard who lived in the same village.

Because they both lost their parents at an early age, they depended on each other and eventually became engaged. However, Gaspard, the soon-to-be husband, became disabled after being injured while working in the quarry. Gaspard was very sad.

One day, he met his fiancée and told her, with tears in his eyes, "I was born with an unhappy fate, and that is why I have become disabled. Since this has happened and I no longer have a body able to marry you, I have no choice but to break up with you. Please find another man and live happily." When she heard this, she burst into tears and said with a weeping voice:

"Where would I go, leaving you behind? I already decided long ago that you would be my husband! When I hear you say these words, doesn't it mean that if I were in your position and were the one to become disabled, that you would leave me?" She spoke as though scolding him. At these words, Gaspard lost his temper.

"What are you talking about? How could I ever think like that? I made a pledge with Heavenly Parent as my witness, and I would not have left you," he said while looking up to heaven. In this way the two were married, and despite living a difficult life, they loved each other and lived happily.

The Blessing of a man and a woman getting married under Heavenly Parent is the most glorious, greatest ceremony and promise. When the couple together can push through adversity and hardships during their married life, they can realize a stronger love. That is why True Parents gave guidelines that couples who have received the Marriage Blessing must absolutely follow. First, you should attend Heavenly Parent at the center of the family and not be self-centered. Second, there should be mutual trust and love between husband and wife. Third, you should not hurt each other's hearts. Fourth, teach your second generation and third generation children to keep purity properly. Fifth, the members of the family should cooperate and live for the sake of each other to realize a true, ideal family.

When giving these guidelines, True Parents emphasized two most important points. The first is sexual purity before marriage. Human beings resemble Heavenly Parent and must become people who can attend the absolute, unique, unchanging and eternal Heavenly Parent within themselves. There are organs of the mind and body that especially attend Heavenly Parent; these are the reproductive organs. They are like the palace where Heavenly Parent resides. These precious organs are the place where the lineage of Heaven is passed on. That is why indulging in false love and having sexual relations with someone who was not chosen for you by Heaven is an act of breaking the moral laws.

The second is to maintain absolute fidelity with your spouse after marriage. Fidelity is a moral standard that needs to be kept between husband and wife and is even more precious than life. The act of love between husband and wife should be a sacred act that gives birth to children who resemble Heavenly Parent and create true love, true life and true lineage. However, if you leave the eternal partner chosen for you by heaven to have sexual relations with another partner, you will lose the palace where you can attend Heavenly Parent and will not inherit true love, true life and true lineage.

As time passes, we see the breakdown of families, and the reality is that people are avoiding marriage and are reluctant to have children. There is an increase in the number of people who want to remain single and pursue their own desires. However, there is no future for a world filled with these kinds of people. Blessed families who have received the Marriage Blessing must keep absolute purity and absolute fidelity and do their best to show the world the model of innocent, true love. These efforts can make the world beautiful and peaceful. You also must do your best and offer sincere jeongseong so that your children can maintain purity in mind and body and realize true love.

❋ Points for contemplation

1) Let us contemplate the Pure Love Movement that can heal the problems of our society today which has lost purity before marriage and fidelity in marriage.

2) Let us discuss how a blessed couple can do their best in mind and body together with their children so that they can attend Heavenly Parent and realize true love. Let us also discuss purity and fidelity.

3
Blessed Families and Three Spiritual Children
— The Responsibility of Blessed Families

True Parents' Words

You will receive the Blessing and give birth to children. When you conceive a blessed child, you must establish the standard of having three spiritual children who are completely united with the blessed child in your womb. In this way, babies born of parents who have received the Blessing must be protected and cared for by the spiritual children so that they do not fall before getting married after turning 21. This is similar to the mission of the three archangels who should have protected and cared for Adam and Eve during their growth and until they became an ideal couple. Blessed children, who were physically born to the same people who are their spiritual parents, are like Adam and Eve who received their form from God. God's bitter grief is that the archangel caused Adam and Eve to fall. Without attending the blessed child, there is no path of restoration for the three spiritual children who are standing in the position of the archangel. The spiritual parents who have received the Blessing and the spiritual children should develop a relationship of attendance centering on the blessed child. It is only by centering on the blessed child that the parent can stand in the position of the restored parent. Just as fallen Adam and Eve were to have been restored through Abel, parents who have received the Blessing also can become completed through the second generation. You absolutely must establish three spiritual children before receiving the Blessing. To you, this is as important as meeting the Messiah. In order for you to stand in a position of receiving love from God, you must stand in the position of Abel. The position of Abel is a position in place of Adam, so there must be three archangels before him. Only when these three archangels establish a foundation of completely obeying Adam can they be restored to the position of the unfallen and perfected Adam. [Blessed Families and the Ideal Kingdom of Heaven II, 165]

Sharing Thoughts

After receiving the Blessing, blessed families must restore (witness) to three spiritual children before starting their family. When Heavenly Parent created Adam and Eve, He created three archangels: Gabriel, Michael and Lucifer. These three archangels were supposed to have protected and cared for Adam and Eve, establishing a relationship of attendance. Heavenly Parent's bitter grief is that the archangel Lucifer caused the Fall of Adam and Eve, and therefore blessed families must restore through indemnity three spiritual children who are in the position of the archangel. Traditionally, blessed families of the Family Federation for World Peace and Unification were not qualified to attend the Marriage Blessing ceremony if they had not restored three spiritual children before the Blessing ceremony. This is because without having three spiritual children, they could not give birth to biological children who had the lineage of Heavenly Parent and were free from Satan's attacks.

True Father said that if you do not restore three spiritual children, then as a couple you do not have the qualification to start your family life and live together as a blessed couple, and you do not have the qualification to love the child that you give birth to. To restore and raise three spiritual children, you first must invest completely and love them so that you can hear them call you their parent. When that standard is established, you must ensure that your spiritual children can completely attend your biological son or daughter from the time they are in the womb. Through this process, the fall can be reversed and restoration centered on the blessed family can take place. Satan cannot interfere with blessed families who have established this kind of standard, and that means that in terms of lineage, they can completely sever the lineage of Satan.

Furthermore, blessed families who receive the Blessing as restored first generation members must follow this same tradition and do their best to fulfill the responsibility to restore three spiritual children. They must find and establish three spiritual children before having their own children and create a realm of protection that cannot be attacked by Satan.

Before their Holy Wedding Ceremony, True Parents carried out the engagement ceremony of three spiritual children who were in the position of three children. After their own Holy Wedding Ceremony, they held a holy wedding for those three couples and started off with eight church members centered on Heavenly Parent.

Blessed families must establish the standard of having loved their spiritual children more than their own children. Through your doing that, your spiritual children will feel that they have received greater love than your biological children, and to return that grace, they will protect your children. By doing this, the parents and children of blessed families establish with their spiritual children the foundation of a family relationship of true love that will never change.

It begins from loving and living for the sake of the spiritual children who are in the position of Cain. It is only when they feel moved and touched by the love received from the blessed families and they return love for the sake of the children of the blessed families that a tradition of the principle of group love (the principle that began by feeling love for others) can be established.

❋ Points for contemplation

1) Let us contemplate how we as a blessed family can find and establish three spiritual children who meet the standard before heaven.
2) If you already have spiritual children, then let us contemplate how to establish the standard of loving our spiritual children more than our own children and have them become one with our children.

4
Holy Wine Ceremony and Change of Lineage
– Cleansing the Bloodline to Join Heavenly Parent's Lineage

True Parents' Words

Because we received Satan's blood, we must have a ceremony to cut it off. That ceremony is the Holy Wine Ceremony. From a principled viewpoint, it is absolutely impossible for us to receive the Blessing from God if we allow any stains from the blood of Satan's world to remain in us. We must eliminate not only all the blood that we received from Satan's world but also all the sins that occurred up until now. There are many kinds of sin, such as hereditary, historical and individual sins, but the one thing that makes a condition to settle all of them is the Holy Wine Ceremony. The Holy Wine includes 21 different substances. Each of them has been sanctified. Each of them was established through victorious conditions set during my confrontations with the spirit world, with Satan and with God. It may seem that drinking a cup of Holy Wine is a trivial gesture, but that is not the case. On the day you drink that cup with faith, you will stand on the foundation of True Parents' victorious conditions, cut off from the blood of Satan's world, and cut off from all the ties you have with the sins of your ancestors and from all the tangled connections your ancestors wove. [CSG 5.2.3:16]

Sharing Thoughts

One believer dreamed that he had passed away and was standing in front of the judge of history. In his dream he heard a voice: "Were you always good?" It was Heavenly Parent's voice. He looked back on his life, and, realizing that he had not been good, he said in a shaking voice, "No."

Heavenly Parent continued, asking, "Were you always righteous?" This too he had not been. "No." "Did you always keep your purity?" Again, he had not. He answered, "No." He barely answered and was holding his breath, wondering what kind of punishment he would receive, when suddenly he felt a bright light embrace his entire body. He opened his eyes in surprise and found himself standing in front of Heavenly Parent. "Drink this, confess your past sins, and from now on, for the rest of your life, stand on My side and live a good, righteous and pure life."

Today, Satan's culture is dominating our society. Especially the culture of free sex that came into existence after the Fall of Adam and Eve has developed into a culture in which teenagers and youth take delight in and enjoy false love to the fullest. On a worldwide scale, prostitution has been increasing exponentially, and through mass media such as pornography sites, sexual promiscuity is reaching extremes. The family and society are breaking down and collapsing. Members who will be receiving the Blessing in this kind of environment first must separate their stained selves from the false love centered on Satan.

In the environment in which we have grown up, we have seen friends and neighbors who have committed sexual sins. Sometimes we have participated in them and sometimes acted on our own. Only when we repent and change, can we stand properly as candidates for the Blessing. Furthermore, through the Blessing ceremony we must cleanse our lineage with the love of Heavenly Parent and be able to reproduce the love of the parents within ourselves. That is why it is necessary to have a ceremony to separate from all the fallen things since Adam and Eve.

The procedure of the Holy Wine Ceremony is as follows. The participants offer a bow to True Parents (or the couple that has been anointed with their authority). A restored senior blessed couple (in the position of the archangel) passes the Holy Wine glass to True Mother. True Mother then passes the Holy Wine glass to True Father. True Father passes the Holy Wine glass to the wife of the couple that is to be reborn. The wife bows, receives the Holy Wine glass and drinks half of it. The husband then bows to the wife, receives the Holy Wine glass and drinks the rest of it. The husband bows to the wife and returns the empty glass to her. The wife bows and returns the empty glass to True Father. True Father then returns the empty glass to True Mother. True Mother returns the empty glass back to the restored senior blessed couple (in the position of the restored archangel). After the „ True Parents offer the benediction.

During the benediction, there is a special placement of the hands. The groom's right hand should be open with the palm facing up and the bride's right palm should cover his hand from the top. And then the groom places his left palm face down onto the back of the bride's right hand. The bride places her left palm face down onto the back of the groom's left hand. True Mother (wife of the officiator) supports the back of the groom's right hand with her left palm, and True Father (officiator) places his right palm to cover the back of the bride's left hand.

In the Holy Wine Ceremony, True Parents first must give birth spiritually to the woman. Through this woman, the man also is born again spiritually. Adam should have become the husband and Eve should have become the wife, and they should have loved each other. However, Eve reversed dominion with Adam, centering on Satan, so their fallen state must be restored to a perfected state. Through the officiators, True Parents, they can receive the new bloodline of Heavenly Parent, cleanse their sins and cleanse their bloodline. The Holy Wine Ceremony is the breaking-off point of good and evil and the line that separates life from death.

After the Holy Wine Ceremony, we should not commit sexual

acts that will cause us to become stained. As a body that can attend Heavenly Parent, we must be reborn as people who can keep the absolute purity of true love and fidelity without lies. After the Holy Wine Ceremony, do not ask about any past acts (because they have been separated), become a blessed couple and realize a family that can bring about the settlement of Heavenly Parent's true love on this earth. The Holy Wine Ceremony is the grace of salvation and blessing from Heavenly Parent. This is because the Holy Wine Ceremony is the love of Heavenly Parent that can cleanse our bloodline internally so that fallen human beings can be reborn as Heavenly Parent's children. We must be grateful for the special grace of the Holy Wine Ceremony and must be able to participate in the Blessing ceremony as disciples who will become heavenly tribal messiahs.

❋ Points for contemplation

1) Let us remember that the Holy Wine symbolizes the lineage of Heavenly Parent and True Parents, and let us pray that we can cleanse our fallen lineage through the Holy Wine Ceremony.
2) Let us write down in our journal our resolution and determination after the Holy Wine Ceremony to become a blessed family that attends Heavenly Parent and practices unchanging, true love.

5
Indemnity Stick Ceremony and Change of Lineage

– The Blessing and the Indemnity Stick Ceremony

True Parents' Words

What is the Indemnity Stick Ceremony for? Adam and Eve fell by misusing their lower parts. During the Indemnity Stick Ceremony, both wife and husband strike each other's buttocks as hard as they can, saying they will never fall again. We do this so that they will never again misuse that part of the body. Likewise, when the Israelites made a pledge, they placed a hand under their thigh. They also conducted circumcision. When a son was born, his male part was bled on the eighth day after birth. This ritual was instituted because the male reproductive organ had been misused. Because the seed had been damaged, the ritual of circumcision was established to change the seed. All these are conditions to determine ownership. [CSG 11.3.1:24]

Why do we have the Indemnity Stick Ceremony? When we read the Bible, we learn about circumcision, which is a condition of indemnity. Adam's family broke apart because of wrongly directed love.

What is baptism? It refers to the time of Noah. The reproductive organs had been defiled, and Noah's time was when they were indemnified. At the time of Noah, these organs were subjected to judgment by water. In short, they were washed. However, the washing was incomplete. They had to be "baptized," but that was only a condition. Once those defiled bodies were washed and the defiled spot indemnified, the time of Jacob was to have been the time of settlement. For this purpose, Jacob had to live a life that would restore love. He had to begin the change of lineage, change of ownership, and change of the realm of heart. The chosen people got their start when their lineage was transformed. [CSG 11.3.1:26]

Sharing Thoughts

The plant called Nepenthes on the island of Borneo is known as the master of catching and eating insects. The Nepenthes plant gives bloom to beautiful flowers to lure insects. The moment that the insect, drunk with the beauty of the flower, enters the mouth of the flower, it is the end of its life. The plant emits a special digestive juice that melts the insects.

There is no guarantee that even in our world where people live there are no Nepenthes. From the outside, they seem alluring, and the fragrance is out of this world. However, if you fall for that temptation, there is no way out.

Especially today, the easiest temptation that people fall for is sexual indulgence. The spirits of people who fall for lewd temptation drift further away from Heavenly Parent. Their bodies become slaves to sexual desire and eventually face death. Immoral acts kill the spirit, paralyze rationality and cause the physical body to fall. That is why Heavenly Parent told Adam and Eve that they could eat all the fruits in the garden of Eden but warned against eating the fruit of the knowledge of good and evil. He told them that the day they ate that fruit, they would die. However, Adam and Eve, the first human ancestors, fell for the fragrance of that attractive and appetizing fruit and faced death. The death that we speak of here is a spiritual death more than a physical death. In other words, immoral acts mean death. If we look back at the cause of the destruction of the palace where Heavenly Parent's bloodline and life are born. we can see that it means the reproduction of Satan's lineage.

In order to have Jacob raise up the people of Israel, Heavenly Parent had an angel hit his hip bone first before blessing him. When the people of Israel make an important pledge, they put their hands on their hip bone. They are pursuing the path of returning to the original state by confirming to Heavenly Parent and human beings that they no longer will commit sinful acts as a result of their lower parts.

True Parents established the Indemnity Stick Ceremony so that first generation blessed couples, after receiving the Blessing, can establish a condition to restore the sin that the first ancestors committed as a result of the lower parts. The husband and wife, each in the position representing Heavenly Parent, hit their partner. Through this ritual, all the sins of the past committed by that person can be indemnified. There may be cases of men and women who before the Blessing ceremony have engaged in acts of love with another partner with their mind or body. As true ideal partners who attend Heavenly Parent, in order to have a new start of pure and innocent love with their partner, it is very important to do this Indemnity Stick Ceremony so that all the past wrongdoings can be cleansed, forgiven and indemnified.

Blessed couples indemnify not only the wrongdoings of Adam and Eve but their own past wrongdoings as well. Pledging that they will create harmony as an eternal couple, they partake in the Indemnity Stick Ceremony before Heavenly Parent, True Parents and senior blessed families. The program for the ceremony begins with the couple coming forth and offering a bow to Heavenly Parent and True Parents, and then offering a bow to each other. Next, the husband hits the wife's lower parts (buttocks) three times. Following that, the wife hits the husband's lower parts three times. When they do this, they should be careful not to hit the small of the back or other bones and cause damage to the body. If they hit weakly or without sincerity, and the leader there does not approve it, they must hit again. After that, they offer another bow to True Parents and to each other to conclude the ceremony. Before and after the

Indemnity Stick Ceremony, the officiators should guide the participants through a report prayer, a sermon and a benediction so that they can properly understand the significance of the event.

Hitting three times during the Indemnity Stick Ceremony signifies indemnifying the three stages of formation, growth and completion of life's course. It also signifies indemnifying the three stages of the Old Testament Age, New Testament Age and Completed Testament Age of the vertical providential history.

Blessed couples who participate in the Indemnity Stick Ceremony indemnify not only their own individual lives but also the sinful acts committed in mind and body throughout the historical era of the providence. The couple give and receive true love centering on Heavenly Parent and True Parents, separate from Satan, get rid of their fallen nature and go on living their lives, realizing the ideal of a true family. There is a need for an external separation ritual for blessed families to be reborn as children before our parent, Heavenly Parent. Blessed families should not forget the spirit of the Indemnity Stick Ceremony. Even after the Blessing, there are many sexual temptations between men and women, but they should attend Heavenly Parent and stand firm on their determination that they will become absolutely one with their spouse through love. Whether you are at work or in society, you should remember the pain and suffering of the indemnity that you experienced through the Indemnity Stick Ceremony and keep absolute purity. You must do your best so that you do not do anything in mind or body that goes against the order of love.

❋ Points for contemplation

1) Let us contemplate the Pure Love Movement that can heal the issues in our society, where purity before marriage and fidelity within marriage have been lost.
2) Let us discuss about how a couple who have received the Blessing can do their best in mind and body, together with their children, to attend Heavenly Parent and practice true love. Let us discuss ways to keep purity and fidelity.

6
Three-Day Ceremony and First Love
– The Substantial Restoration Ceremony of the Blessing

True Parents' Words

If you do not go through the Three-Day Ceremony, you will have nothing to do with True Parents' lineage. You will be nothing but a spectator who has come within the fenced area. Only after you complete the Three-Day Ceremony can you dress in holy robes and be included in True Parents' lineage. Otherwise, although you may have eaten a piece of the wedding cake, watched the celebration from beginning to end, and enjoyed yourself with your friends, you will end up being apart. You will not become one with True Parents' lineage. [CSG 11.3.1:28]

Through True Parents, the wives of the blessed couples are endowed again with Mother's mission. What this means is that we must go through a ceremony to be born again in three stages.

We were born through love, so to establish that kind of condition, we must make love in a way that is opposite to what we have been doing until now. The woman is on top and the husband is underneath. You must do this well when making love. When you do the Three-Day Ceremony, the woman prays first. In order to give birth to Adam of the formation stage, there must be a blessing. Next, the same ceremony must be carried out as a condition, "Please bestow the blessing of giving birth to the second Adam in the position of Jesus." When you get him to be born again twice, then he can pass onto the stage of the completed position. Then the next step is for the man to be restored to being on top. So, the third time they make love, the man is on top. After finishing making love in this way, you can pray as an eternal couple of God and as an eternal family that has received the inheritance of Heaven that you now belong to God's authority. Then you can enter life as a couple. When you do this, you can proudly enter the heavenly nation as a family that has been completely restored through indemnity. [*Sermons*, 90-134]

Sharing Thoughts

In his book, *The Turning Point of My Thoughts* (2007), Kim Hakjung wrote, "A person's life changes depending on how he thinks. That is right. 'Do not miss the chance, the turning point.' You should not hesitate when a new beginning point of life appears. When you have to make a spiritual decision or go a new path in life, you must learn to drive on the highway and not just the ordinary roads of the past. If you think you are happy, then happiness will find you. Try proclaiming that if you go this path, you will become happy. Then a greater happiness will come to you."

First-generation blessed couples who are planning to start family life after the Blessing ceremony will go through a 40-day separation period. The separation period is a period of no conjugal relations, in which the focus is to attend Heavenly Parent and True Parents and become one in heart. During this time, so that the wife can find and establish the position of the restored Eve, she must establish the ideal of oneness of heart with Heavenly Parent that fallen Eve lost. The husband, in the position of the restored Archangel, must fulfill the mission of the separation by cooperating so that the wife can faithfully follow the Will appropriately during this separation period. These days, the second-generation couples also go through a 40-day separation period. The significance of the Three-Day Ceremony is for the couple to inherit the vertical love of True Parents and become one before starting their horizontal love as a couple.

After having completed the separation period, the blessed couple, under the guidance of the pastor, participate in the substantial restoration ceremony in which they are born again through True Parents. True Parents have named this the Three-Day Ceremony. The couple who received the Blessing can be born again through this ceremony of first love. The Holy Wine Ceremony is internal; it is a spiritual ceremony to restore the lineage, but the Three-Day Ceremony is the ceremony to substantially change the lineage and to restore the order of dominion.

The Three-Day Ceremony restores the failures of the Old Testament and New Testament and realizes the will of the Completed Testament. It is the day that a true couple begin attending Heavenly Parent and share their first lovemaking on the way to becoming a true family. It is the day that each vows together with their partner, who resembles Heavenly Parent, to share absolute, unique, unchanging and eternal true love with each other and to bring about the settlement of the tradition and culture of love which was the ideal of creation. It is because of the Three-Day Ceremony that blessed families can restore through indemnity the fall of Adam and Eve and become a family that attends Heavenly Parent. The tradition and culture of true love which start from this ceremony should be passed on to the second, third and fourth generations and make possible the realization of a pure, true family and peaceful world.

After the Three-Day Ceremony, blessed couples should truly care for each other, protecting and loving each other as ideal partners. The husband should attend the wife as the queen of Heaven and fulfill her needs, and the wife should attend the husband as the king of Heaven. In this way they become one and move forward. As a substantial couple that come to attend Heavenly Parent through the Three-Day Ceremony, they must practice the morality of love absolutely.

❋ Points for contemplation

1) Through the Three-Day Ceremony, first-generation blessed couples can sever the fallen lineage. Let us contemplate how they can be born again through the works of rebirth centering on Heavenly Parent.
2) Let us contemplate the precious sexual organs which are the couple's organs of love and the settlement place of true love, where their lives become intertwined as one.

7
Conjugal Love in Blessed Couples

― Couples' Love as the Most Perfect Love

True Parents' Words

In order to have conjugal love, you need to inherit the love of your parents and then go through the stages of filial love and sibling love. To become a true couple, the husband and wife first must experience these three stages of love. A person who does not pass through the stages of filial love and sibling love cannot succeed in loving as a couple. Only after passing through these three stages of love, that is, only by inheriting your parents' love and then growing in filial love and sibling love, can you achieve conjugal love as a true couple. Only after a man and woman each has fulfilled the duties of children and siblings, can they join as a true couple. Then they reach the stage to love each other as husband and wife. After learning filial love and sibling love, they should become one in heart and body as husband and wife. This is marriage. The purpose of marriage is for the man to occupy the world of women, and both to occupy the world of God. Why must we occupy God? It is so we can stand in the position of creators in the Creator's stead. If we are to multiply God's children, there is no alternative but to occupy God. This teaching is based on the principle of creation. [CSG 12.2.3:30]

God is vertical, while Adam and Eve are relating horizontally. A settlement can be established only when the vertical God and horizontal Adam and Eve become one. That is, God can fully settle only when, centering on His original internal character, Adam and Eve as His horizontal embodiments can come into union to manifest His original external form. That is when His settlement takes place. Yet, because of the Fall, that did not happen. The universe has no center today, because they did not become one in accord with Heaven's textbook and did not settle in the ideal realm of perfect love. Hence, the new settlement of true love is needed. It will begin only after God, who is vertical, attains a virtuous union with Adam and Eve, who are horizontal. [CSG 12.2.3:32]

Sharing Thoughts

I have never raised my voice toward my wife. This is not because of my character, but because my wife has never given me cause to do so. Throughout our life together, she has labored to care for me with complete, loving devotion. She is even the one to care for my hair. So, this great saint of world affairs is also the best barber in the world. Now that I am old, I make many new demands on her, and she always responds. If I ask her to cut my toenails, she will do it cheerfully. My toenails are mine, but I can't see them very well. She sees them perfectly well, though. It's a strange thing. The older I become, the more precious my wife is to me. [*As a Peace-Loving Global Citizen*, p. 206]

There are four types of love. There is children's love, sibling's love, conjugal love and parent's love. The representative love among them is conjugal love. In a blessed family, the husband first represents the men in the family; second, he represents all the men of humankind; third, he represents the yang that is half of the universe; and fourth, he represents the yang that is one of Heavenly Parent's natures. The wife in a blessed family first represents the women in the family; second, she represents all the women of humankind; third, she represents the yin that is half of the universe; and fourth, she represents the yin that is one of Heavenly Parent's natures.

The ideal of creation is realized at the place where a husband and wife become one through love. Centering on the love of a couple aligned with Heavenly Parent, the power to have dominion over the entire universe is created.

In conclusion, the love of a couple is love that represents Heavenly Parent. The two of them are the manifestations of the incorporeal

Heavenly Parent's masculinity and femininity in substantial form as husband and wife. Therefore, as the substantial manifestation of Heavenly Parent's yang and yin, the couple have to perfect give and take with each other and love each other. Only when this unshakeable conjugal love exists, can the four great loves (parental, conjugal, sibling and children's loves) be completed and, centering on that couple, the ideal of the kingdom of heaven that Heavenly Parent desires can appear. Therefore, the conjugal love of a blessed couple is influenced greatly by the vertical love of Heavenly Parent. This kind of love relationship in which Heavenly Parent and the couple are one influences the relationships of love between the parents, their children, their descendants, and so forth.

The model of excellent child education is created when a couple first attend Heavenly Parent and realize the ideal of love. True Parents said, "The husband and wife must love each other more than a mother loves her son or daughter. The true love of a couple is the conclusion of life."

Usually couples spend more time and dedication in loving their children than on the love between husband and wife. Especially when the child is small, the parents focus on raising and nurturing the child. There are also quite a few couples who on their own initiative sacrifice one side of their love for the sake of their child. (They have to live apart because their child is studying overseas, for example.) It may seem like this would have a good impact on the child, but it makes the child unable to experience the ideal conjugal love of true parents. In the end, the husband and wife end up living as strangers, even though they are a couple, and some may even end up divorcing. The last stage of life before you go to the spirit world is to perfect conjugal love completely and become one as husband and wife. You attend Heavenly Parent and go the path of ultimate oneness.

Couples must achieve beautiful harmony like a rainbow in their varied activities as a couple through their loving hearts, the conversations they share, the hobbies and activities in which they can become one, and through making love. When couples truly love each other, their love can have a positive influence on the children of the future generation. The result would be that the daughter in the family would say that she wants to marry a man like her father. And if it's a son, he would say that he wants to marry a woman like his mother. The unity of a couple in which Heavenly Parent's vertical love is present will expand and develop through their children on the earth.

❊ Points for contemplation

1) Let us contemplate what kind of husband or wife we should become with the perspective that our couple are the substantial manifestation of the incorporeal Heavenly Parent on earth.
2) Let us think about whether the love between my spouse and me is carried out through various conversations, experiences or relationships that can attend Heavenly Parent.

3) Let us contemplate the fact that our conjugal love is the representative of the four great loves, including "children's love, sibling's love and parental love," in the family.

8
Blessed Couple and Blessed Children
– Ideal Parent–Child Relationship

True Parents' Words

Parents who have given birth to and raised children understand the desire to receive blessings and feel happiness through their beloved sons and daughters. If they can establish a foundation of happiness and blessings, they want to bequeath it to their offspring for eternity. Even fallen parents hope that their children will grow up as fine people whom all nations can follow, revere and praise eternally. The parent's heart seeks to protect children from harm and is anxious about them day and night. Even fallen parents have this heart. A mother accepts the smell of her baby's urine and feces. While nursing her child, she whispers and sings lullabies, while continually wishing for the child's success in life. Every parent has such a heart. If a child is incompetent or lacking, or suffers from a disability, the parents' hearts suffer to the point of breaking. If this situation is then resolved, their relief and joy go beyond the pain they had felt. [CSG 5.3.2:11]

What is the limit of parents' love for their children? Parents love their children beyond their childhood years, through adulthood, and even into eternity. If a relationship is established between a parent and child, through which both feel increasing worth and value, then infinite strength and infinite stimulation—something infinite and new—will arise within that relationship. [CSG 5.3.2:17]

Children should be able to say, "My mother and father are the best in the world! They are representatives of God." When children see their parents' unchanging hearts and minds, they should think, "We must emulate our parents' love and unite with each other." When they can say that, the ideal family is right there. Our mind and heart seek an object partner with whom to unite. If this unity does not occur in a marriage, we lose everything. Thinking seriously about and striving hard to achieve this oneness is the proper way for both men and women. For this reason, we need to build families in which the father and mother are united with God's heart and love, and in which the children resemble their parents in their unity with God's heart and love. [CSG 5.3.2:20]

Sharing Thoughts

We had a stretch of rain for one period, and we couldn't work for 20 consecutive days. When the rain cleared and we went out to start the work again, we found that some kind of waterfowl had created a nest where there were some water weeds. It was a place not more than a few meters from where the prisoners would walk for exercise. At first, we didn't even realize that the bird was there. Its camouflage was so perfect that the bird's feathers could easily be mistaken for the water weeds. Once the bird laid its eggs, though, we could see there was a bird in among the grass. The bird was sitting on some eggs that looked like pieces of black gravel. Once the chicks hatched, the mother would go find some food, bring it back to the nest, and put it in the beaks of the chicks. When the mother was returning to the nest with food, however, she never flew directly to the nest. She would land a little distance from the nest and then walk the rest of the way. Each time, she approached the nest from a different direction. This was her wisdom to make it more difficult for others to find out the location of the nest where the chicks were.

The chicks ate the food their mother brought them and grew larger. Sometimes, when a prisoner would walk near the nest, the mother would fly out and chase him away with her sharp beak. She was afraid the prisoner might harm her chicks. The waterbird understood the true love of parents. True love is willing to give up its own life, and there is no calculation there. The heart of the bird that was willing to sacrifice its life, if necessary, to protect its offspring was true love. Parents go the path of love, no matter how difficult it becomes. A parent is prepared, if needed, to bury his life for the sake of love, and this is true love. [*As a Peace-Loving Global Citizen*, p. 213–214]

What is family? The word "family" comes from the Latin word *familia*. It was a word that referred to a group consisting of parents, children and servants. Therefore, the family is a community. This community is always creative. When a man and woman love each other and become a couple, the children who are born from that become siblings. Even if they are different in age, generation or gender, they do not discriminate against each other but blend together and realize harmony. And the family is a place where the people love deeply with the center of their hearts, live together, and help each other. In the family, children grow up learning about their duties as human beings. Humankind would not exist without the family.

It is said that in one nation, the educators gathered and held an essay contest on what the family is. The following is the conclusion that came out on the beautiful value of the family.

"First, the family is a world without war and a world filled with love.

"Second, it is a place where the small person is big and the big person seems small.

"Third, it is the kingdom of the father and mother and the children's kingdom of heaven.

"Fourth, there are the most complaints within the family, but following that, it is the place where they are treated the best.

"Fifth, the family is the central place of love, and it is the place where our heart's utmost desire lies.

"Sixth, the family gives three meals a day to the stomach, but it is also the place that feeds the heart 1,000 times every day.

"Seventh, the family is the place on earth that hides human beings' faults and failures."

These days, the family in our society has become ill. There are many families in which the family members pursue only their individual desires, hurt the others and make difficulties rather than living for the sake of each other. We must be able to restore and heal the wounds and pain that arise from selfishness and mistrust. To change into a family that receives Heavenly Parent's love, the relationship between parent and child must be restored to one of love.

The love of true parents begins from the conjugal love of a couple who are united centered on Heavenly Parent. The parental love in which Heavenly Parent's vertical love and the couple's horizontal love become one manifests as a force of unconditional love for the children. From now on, within your families you must restore the ideal family of the ideal of creation that Heavenly Parent longs for.

Heavenly Parent experienced deep sorrow and pain in the position of a parent who lost His children due to the Fall of Adam and Eve. True Parents have shown us the path of becoming ideal blessed families that can heal the bitter pain of Heavenly Parent.

They taught that following this model, the ideal of love must settle in the family. As parents, we give true love to our children, and children who see this exemplary true love of the parents resonate with it and return filial piety. In that kind of family, the love of children, love of siblings, conjugal love and parental love can mature, and that family can fulfill their duty of filial piety before heaven to become a harmonious and mature family.

❋ Points for contemplation

1) What is the difference between the love of parent and child that Heavenly Parent fundamentally yearns for and the general love that parents and children in today's world pursue? Let us contemplate it together.
2) As parents of blessed families, let us contemplate ways in which we can give love to our children.

Chapter 7

The Basic Building Block of the Ideal World of Creation:
Blessed Central Families

1
What Is Family?

— Understanding the Meaning of Family

True Parents' Words

When we study the meaning of the word "family," *gajeong* in Korean, the second character, *jeong* (庭), stands for garden. Parents and siblings in a family are like the colorful variety of lovely flowers in a garden. The family should be a place where each member can be joyful, singing and dancing. If family members fight each other, the garden will become a wilderness. When a flower hears harmonious music, it grows well, but if it hears discordant music, it cannot. The same goes for a family. When its members hear the melody of love, they can grow wonderfully. What makes them do so is the heart of love. [CSG 5.1.1:1]

It is not mere words that unite the members of a family. It is not money that draws them together, nor the necessity of living and eating together. Sharing the same house does not guarantee that family members will get along well. Overcoming and going beyond highs and lows, they should become one with mutual affection at the center. They should become one with love at the center. Within a family—through not only the love of the mother and father, the love of the husband and wife, and the love of the brothers and sisters, but also the love of the grandparents and grandchildren at the center—all these relationships are harmonized, vertical and horizontal, left and right, and front and back. The family with love as its core has the foundation upon which each of its members bonds with others, moves and acts. A family is made with love at its center. [CSG 5.1.1.2]

Sharing Thoughts

There could never be a word that inspires emotion as much as the word "family," because in a family there are affectionate mothers and fathers and brothers and sisters, too. The family is the nest and the foundation of our lives. If we lose our family or leave home, our lives become difficult and arduous from that very moment.

A painter wanted to paint the most beautiful picture in the world, so he left home with his painting gear and went on a journey. Once he was on his way, the painter started looking for what the most beautiful thing was. A pastor told him that the most beautiful thing in the world was faith, and a woman told him it was love, and a soldier who had just returned from a war told him it was peace.

Based on those answers, he traveled to various places to find what he should paint in order to paint a picture with faith, love and peace in it, but he could not find a subject for that picture anywhere. By then, most of his money was gone, and he could not even afford to eat decent meals or ride in cars. Both his mind and body were exhausted, and he had not yet painted even one painting.

The painter then thought of his home. He decided to return home, rest a while and then go out to look some more. He headed home and arrived after several days of traveling. He reached the front door when it was starting to get dark and rang the doorbell. His children's voices asked, "Who is it?" When the children heard their father's voice, they all cried out, "It's Daddy!" and opened the door for him.

Seeing their father after such a long time, the children hugged their father and rubbed their faces against his and held onto him. It was dinnertime, and the table was set with rice and side dishes. His wife said to him, "You are finally home! Aren't you hungry? Hurry and sit down at the table." It was only then that the painter finally became aware, and he started his painting. He painted his family and gave the painting the title, "The Most Beautiful Picture in the World."

Since the home is a place where love overflows, centering on the family's love for one another, it embraces everything. As True Parents have told us, the family does not unite for money, honor or power. They do not unite solely because they eat and live together.

What's more, higher or lower statuses are unnecessary within a family. A happy family is formed only when the family unites centering on love and heartfelt affection.

In addition, the family is where every kind of love—parents' love for their children, love between husband and wife, love between siblings, grandparents' love flowing down to their grandchildren, and grandchildren's love flowing up to their grandparents—is harmonized as one. In this way, the entire family unites and moves as one, with affection at its core.

Family members encourage, forgive and help one another, instead of trying to determine who is right or wrong. It is said, "Praise makes even whales dance," and a family whose members embrace and encourage one another can overcome any difficulty and be more energetic, for such embraces and encouragements are more effective than any restorative herbal medicine.

❋ Points for contemplation

1) What do you think family is? Let us each say one thing we can do to make our family happy.
2) For our family to live attending Heavenly Parent, what kinds of changes and preparations should we make?

2
Introduction to the Family Pledge
— Providential Value of the Family Pledge and
Understanding Cheon Il Guk

True Parents' Words

The fact that we now have the Family Pledge is truly the greatest of all blessings. It came from Heaven as a gift to all humanity on May 1, 1994, the day when the Family Federation for World Peace and Unification (FFWPU) was inaugurated. The Family Pledge was given when the Completed Testament Age, which brings to fulfillment the Old Testament Age and the New Testament Age, was proclaimed. It is to serve as a milestone and guiding principle, piercing through the darkness of the age before the coming of heaven, and opening a new heaven and earth in the era after the coming of heaven. It is also the blueprint for the building of God's kingdom of peace and unity in heaven and on earth in the era of the creation of a new heaven and earth.

Father and Mother Moon, the True Parents of humankind,

emerged victorious from the battles they had fought throughout their long course of indemnity that lasted 40 years after Father Moon founded the Holy Spirit Association for the Unification of World Christianity (HSA-UWC) in 1954. On that foundation, we were no longer required to recite My Pledge as individuals. We were to recite and practice the Family Pledge together as true families, the basic units of triumphal entry into the kingdom of heaven.

This Family Pledge is filled with the pain and suffering of God and True Parents, and it should not be recited without tears. It is something that people should recite forever, long after they discard the mask of religion in the fallen world and attain liberation. This is because the family is the basic unit of the kingdom of heaven.

Ladies and gentlemen, have you ever heard of the phrase "Family Pledge" anywhere in the world? It has appeared for the first time in human history. In the beginning, God lost the true family through the Fall of the first man and woman. He had created them to be His children and the first ancestors of humankind. Consequently, as God has the providential mandate to fulfill His ideal for the creation to an absolute standard, He instituted and proclaimed the Family Pledge. It is God's blessing to human beings that they would establish the prototype of all true families—of ideal families on earth—and return eternal joy to God. It is an essential tool for building the kingdom of heaven on earth and in heaven, in which your families can live while directly serving and attending God. The precondition to properly recite the Family Pledge is first and foremost to attain a state of complete mind–body unity, which is the state of "one heart, one body, one outlook and one harmony." This means that we must reach the standard of perfecting our character through absolute faith, absolute love and absolute obedience. Our body should fully obey the orders of our conscience, which was given to us as our first parent, teacher and owner. ["The Value and Significance of the Family Pledge," *Pyeong Hwa Shin Gyeong*, 250–252]

Sharing Thoughts

The method of swearing in a witness in court differs from country to country. In England and Ireland, after the witness listens to the oath recited by the bailiff, he or she kisses the four Gospels to express assent. In Scotland, the witness repeats the words spoken by the judge and, while standing and holding up his or her right hand, pledges to the omnipotent Heavenly Parent to answer the questions as he or she would answer the questions asked by Him on the Day of Judgment. Jewish people place their hands on the Pentateuch with the Jewish cap on their heads and pledge, "Jehovah, please watch over me!" Muslims are sworn in with their hands on the Quran. Chinese people are sworn in by kneeling and striking a china plate against the witness box and breaking it.

However, the mere method of how the witness is sworn in is not important. No matter what method it may be, the witness makes the pledge in the way that holds the most binding power over his or her conscience. The essential thing is that the witness's oath includes his or her god and what may happen in the future. Furthermore, he or she even recognizes the binding power that comes from his or her faith.

The Family Pledge starts with the phrase "Our family, the owner of Cheon Il Guk." Then what does Cheon Il Guk refer to? First, Cheon Il Guk means the nation where the spiritual and physical worlds are united as one in peace.

Second, the core of Cheon Il Guk is *cheon*, meaning "heaven" (天); this Chinese character is the combination of the characters for "number two" (二) and "human being" (人). That is why Cheon Il Guk also signifies the nation where two people are united as one. Those two people refer to (1) Heavenly Parent and humankind. In other words, it means that Cheon Il Guk is the nation that should have been achieved through the unity of Heavenly Parent and Adam and Eve. Secondly, they refer to (2) the unity of mind and body. That is to say, Cheon Il Guk signifies the nation that should have been constructed by the unfallen human ancestors whose mind and body are united as one. Lastly, the two people refer to (3) Adam and Eve, who were created as the first ancestors of humanity and as husband and wife. Adam and Eve should have united as one and formed a peaceful family. Based on that, they should have gone on to realize the ideal tribe, ideal people, and ideal nation, Cheon Il Guk.

True Parents have fulfilled the above three meanings of Cheon Il Guk. And they have blessed us so that we too can become true parents and be eligible to live in this Cheon Il Guk. Family is not something one can realize on one's own. It is the most basic building block of happiness that husband and wife must cultivate together throughout their lives with heartfelt affection. The same is also true for Cheon Il Guk. It cannot be realized without the unity of Heavenly Parent and humankind, the unity of mind and body, and the unity of Adam and Eve.

❈ Points for contemplation

1) (Applicable to unmarried members) Am I endeavoring to achieve the unity of mind and body centering on Heavenly Parent's love that realizes an internal Cheon Il Guk within myself?

2) (Applicable to couples who have been blessed) Are you and your spouse endeavoring to unite as one as a blessed central couple centering on Heavenly Parent's love, and are you working to create the culture of Cheon Il Guk?

3
Restoration of the Original Homeland Centered on True Love

— My Family, Central Figures in the Construction of the Kingdom of Heaven on Earth and in Heaven

True Parents' Words

Family Pledge #1:

Our family, the owner of Cheon Il Guk, pledges to seek our original homeland and build the kingdom of God on earth and in heaven, the original ideal of creation, by centering on true love.

The ideal of creation is to build the kingdom of God on earth and in heaven. However, since that ideal could not be fulfilled due to the Fall, we must achieve it through restoration. This means that we must build the kingdom of God on earth and in heaven, the original ideal of creation, by seeking our original homeland. Here we say "build." Why do we use that word? It is because we must create God's kingdom. It will not come about by itself. We must build it ourselves. This current world is already hell on earth, and it is connected to hell in the spirit world. We must re-create this world and turn it around 180 degrees. Because the family was lost due to the Fall, we must now build God's family. This is not an individual's task. It is rather the task of our families, the owners of Cheon Il Guk. Centering on true love, our families must "seek our original homeland and build the kingdom of God on earth and in heaven, the original ideal of creation." The "original homeland" referred to here is the original homeland centered on families. That is why all of you must go back to your own hometown and establish God's kingdom on earth and in heaven. Once you restore your hometown, your nation and the world will be unified naturally. Then, there will be nothing further for you to worry about. People who have lived on earth in a unified family centering on God's true love, where the kingdom of God on earth and the kingdom of God in heaven are one, will become a family of the heavenly kingdom. We no longer live in the age of individual salvation. Religions, and Christianity in particular, talk about the salvation of the individual, but that will not suffice. God's Will is for the salvation of the family. Restoration must occur in the family because the Fall destroyed the ideal for the family. That time has now come. In all of history, this has never before happened on earth. Finally the family has entered the era of settlement. It is through families that we must build the kingdom of God on earth and in heaven, the original ideal of God's creation. Because we lost the family, our families must restore that kingdom. The original homeland is centered on families, not on a nation. That is why I am saying that you must return to your hometown. If you still have a family there, you must go back to your hometown and build God's kingdom on earth and in heaven.

["The Value and Significance of the Family Pledge," *Pyeong Hwa Shin Gyeong*, 255.256]

Sharing Thoughts

There is a beautiful English word, "family." If you divide up the word "family" and use each letter as the first letter of a word, you can make the following words: "father" from the first letter, "f," "and" from "a," "mother" from "m," "I" from "i," "love" from "l," and "you" from "y." As can be seen, the word "family" can be said to be the acronym of the sentence "Father and Mother, I love you!"

We human beings are the owners of Cheon Il Guk. That signifies the time when two people (Heavenly Parent and humankind, mind and body, Adam and Eve) have returned to their original state and position as the son and daughter of Heavenly Parent. It means reaching the standard at which Heavenly Parent can give human beings, Adam and Eve, the right of dominion over the world He has created. When restored blessed families reach that stage, they come to be centered on true love. The center of true love refers to the mind and body being in a state of unity from which they can give and take with Heavenly Parent. It is the love through which we can sever the lineage of Satan, our false owner who took us away from our parent, and become one with Heavenly Parent with our mind and body united. After that, we need to recover the original homeland.

The original homeland refers to the original garden of Eden before the Fall. It signifies the place where perfected families can enter and live together with Heavenly Parent free from any traces of the Fall. That family expands to become the fatherland of Heavenly Parent, which is also the homeland and fatherland that we human beings need to seek out one day. From the viewpoint of the heavenly tribal messiah, it refers to the hometown where he or she has completed (the Blessing of) the 430 couples of his or her tribe. It is the place where Heavenly Parent can come to dwell.

In the Bible there is the parable of the prodigal son. He asked his father for his share of the inheritance and set off to wander in distant countries. At first, he felt like he could achieve anything he wanted. However, he squandered away all his wealth, and he ended up having to eat the feed for pigs to fill his empty stomach. Then he began to miss his parents back home. In the end, he worked up the courage to return to his hometown, and his parents were joyful to see the son they had thought dead, and they held a feast and placed a gold ring on his finger and welcomed him home with open arms. The place we need to find is the original homeland, where our Father, Heavenly Parent, is waiting for us.

Next, we need to construct the kingdom of heaven on earth and in heaven, which is the original ideal of creation. Heavenly Parent's original ideal of creation was for two people to unite as one and construct the kingdom of heaven. That kingdom of heaven is realized not only on earth; it also must be realized in heaven. On that foundation, the corporeal and incorporeal worlds can become one completely united nation. Consequently, the incorporeal Heavenly Parent can come down to earth, enter the physical bodies of perfected blessed families and experience human character. On the other hand, the corporeal human beings can achieve oneness with Heavenly Parent and experience divine character, thus living in the corporeal and incorporeal worlds simultaneously.

Because the Fall originated in the family, restoration also must take place in the family. The time has now come for us to achieve it. Until now there has never been a historical age like this. We have entered the age when the family finally can settle down, centering on Heavenly Parent and True Parents. That family is expanded by restoring the tribe. Our task as blessed families is to restore the land, the region where our tribes live, and return it to Heavenly Parent as the original homeland, and to realize the original ideal of creation that is the kingdom of heaven on earth and in heaven.

❋ Points for contemplation

1) How am I training my body and mind to unite with my spouse in everyday life, in order to become the object partner with whom Heavenly Parent can share true love?
2) What are the things that my family can do to construct the corporeal and incorporeal worlds of the kingdom of heaven on earth and in heaven?

4
The Path of the Central Representative Families of the Cosmos
— The Path of Filial Child, Patriot, Saint and Holy Son and Daughter

True Parents' Words

Family Pledge #2:

Our family, the owner of Cheon Il Guk, pledges to represent and become central to heaven and earth by attending God and True Parents; we pledge to perfect the dutiful family way of filial sons and daughters in our family, patriots in our nation, saints in the world, and divine sons and daughters in heaven and on earth, by centering on true love.

True love refers to love that appears where there is unity between mind and body, between husband and wife, and between parents and children. If you fail to practice this standard of true love, you surely will be in trouble when you go to the spirit world. That is how fearsome the Family Pledge is. You should always live by it.

If in your family, the father were to violate even one part of the Family Pledge, the mother and children all would be jointly responsible. The entire family would have to take joint responsibility for it.

The significance of Eve's Fall was that it brought about the Fall of Adam's entire family. This part of the Family Pledge includes the phrase "by attending God and True Parents." We human beings were originally to attend and honor God and True Parents, but we were driven away due to the Fall. Because of the Fall, we lose the value of our existence unless we attend God and True Parents. God is the vertical true parent and the True Parents are the horizontal true parents. We are to be born from the union of these two sets of true parents. God is the vertical parent, and perfected Adam and Eve are the horizontal parents. On the foundation of these two sets of parents becoming one, we also can achieve unity and be connected to God. For this reason, nothing can be accomplished unless we attend God and True Parents. We are pledging to represent and become central to heaven and earth by attending God and True Parents. For this, our family must determine to fulfill the dutiful family way of filial sons and daughters in the family, patriots and virtuous women in the nation, saints in the world, and divine sons and daughters in heaven and earth, everything that Heaven desires. ["The Value and Significance of the Family Pledge," *Pyeong Hwa Shin Gyeong*, 257.259]

Sharing Thoughts

Long ago, in a place called Debar in Israel, there lived a man who owned a very expensive diamond. One day, a rabbi, who had been looking for a diamond to be used in decorating the synagogue, heard about the man and came to see him.

The rabbi asked him, "I heard you have a precious diamond. Will you sell it to me for 6,000 gold pieces?" The man agreed and went into the room. He soon returned empty-handed, saying, "I can't sell the diamond now. My father is sleeping." Then the rabbi asked, "Does the diamond belong to your father?" The man answered, "No, it is mine." He then added, "My father is sleeping with the key to the safe under his pillow, and I can't wake him up." The rabbi repeated his request, saying, "Six thousand gold pieces is a large sum of money. You will become a very wealthy man, so you should wake your father up." The man replied, "No, I don't care how rich I may become. I cannot wake my sleeping father." No matter how much the rabbi pleaded with him, the man did not wake his sleeping father.

The heart of this man who did not wake his sleeping father, even though he could have received a lot of money and become rich, is recorded in the Talmud as a demonstration of true filial piety toward one's parents.

It is said that the fulfillment of one's duty of service and kindness as a child toward one's parents is the eternal truth. If valuables and wealth are used, they come to nothing, but filial piety and patriotism are never used up, and they shine more brightly, the more they are used. That is why when loyal patriots for the nation were chosen in the past, they usually were selected from families known for filial piety. The people of the past believed that loyal patriots are born from the upright hearts of people who practice filial piety toward their parents at home. True Parents tell us that when we attend Heavenly Parent, we need to fulfill our duty of loyalty and filial piety.

Heavenly Parent is the vertical true parent, and perfected Adam and Eve are the horizontal true parents. Only when the two kinds of vertical and horizontal true parents lay the foundation of unity, can the environment be created on earth. The day this took place was Foundation Day of 2013. Blessed central families have been enabled to achieve individual unity of mind and body, depending on whether they have fulfilled their portion of responsibility in the environment, created thanks to the benefit of the age in which the vertical and horizontal true parents have united. Therefore, when the vertical Heavenly Parent and perfected human beings achieve oneness, the "representative family of the cosmos" is born. That representative family has children through true love and is confirmed as a blessed central family. From that position, the family of filial children, patriots, and holy sons and daughters centered on Heavenly Parent can be born.

✻ Points for contemplation

1) How am I attending Heavenly Parent and True Parents in my daily life?
2) Let us contemplate the difference between the vertical Heavenly Parent and the horizontal True Parents.
3) When a blessed central family completes the mission of heavenly tribal messiah, it can stand in the position of the original family of Adam and inherit the position of true parents. What kind of spiritual experiences has your family had while carrying out heavenly tribal messiah activities?

5
The Path of the Original Family

— Perfection of the Four Great Realms of Heart,
Three Great Kingships and Realm of the Royal Family

True Parents' Words

Family Pledge #3:

Our family, the owner of Cheon Il Guk, pledges to perfect the four great realms of heart, the three great kingships and the realm of the royal family, by centering on true love.

The four great realms of heart and the three great kingships would have been fulfilled had Adam and Eve not fallen. But for the Fall, they would have fulfilled these and become God's royal family. This part of the Family Pledge refers to restoring fallen people and making them into the royal family. The families who receive the Marriage Blessing need to fulfill this mission. Conjugal love should take place where the four great realms of heart and the three great kingships are achieved. For a man and a woman to receive love from each other, they need to stand in such a position. Otherwise, they are not to love each other. Yet these realms and kingships cannot be realized without love. That is why man absolutely needs woman, and vice versa. ["The Value and Significance of the Family Pledge," *Pyeong Hwa Shin Gyeong*, 259.260]

The place where human beings marry and consummate their first love centering on God is the fruition point and center of all perfections. Therefore, marriage is the union of heaven, earth and humankind, and it perfects everything: the vertical and the horizontal, the left and the right, and the front and the back. Through marriage is perfected the ideal of the true love of true children, siblings, husband and wife, and parents, in short, the four great realms of heart. The position of Adam and Eve is the position of the second ancestors and second creators, who are the most beloved substantial object partners of God. They are supposed to inherit everything that God desired to experience as the first creator, and experience the joy of being children, siblings, husband and wife and parents on His behalf. Hereupon, God is the first creator, Adam and Eve are the second creators, and their children assume the position of the third creators. The first, second and third creators—that is, God, Adam and Eve and their children—are then to stand in their official position centering on the four-position foundation and thus become the fundamental principle of existence that all humanity must follow. [*Sermons*, 259–43, 1994.03.27]

Sharing Thoughts

Psychologists say that the foundation of our nature is formed from age 1 to 6 and that our life view and values are mostly formed by age 12. The things that are most important for living our lives are the things we learn from our parents in our home. In fact, an expert educator named Taylor goes so far as to say that 92 percent of the influences on a child come from the parents, whereas other influences (church, school, society and nation) account for only 8 percent. He thus emphasized the importance of the parents and the home in children's education.

Nevertheless, many parents focus their money and energy on the education provided by the remaining 8 percent, and they neglect the education that takes place at home, even though it accounts for 92 percent of the total. [Source: Kim, Tae-won, *Yehwa Focus* (Focus on Sincere Culture) 2003]

Originally, Adam and Eve were supposed to grow up, receive the Marriage Blessing and form a beautiful family so that the model family they formed could expand to become all of humanity. Heavenly Parent is an invisible spiritual being, and as such it was His dream of creation that when Adam and Eve—whom He had created in His image—received the Marriage Blessing and became one, He would enter their physical bodies, thereby becoming a creator with substantial form. He created Adam and Eve to become the human ancestors and to give birth to descendants, thus becoming fruitful, multiplying and taking dominion over all things. Heavenly Parent as the first generation, Adam and Eve as the second generation, and His grandchildren as the third generation were supposed to come together as one to realize His kingship on earth and to pass down that tradition for all eternity. This was His purpose of creation.

Within a family in which the three great kingships (the kingship of Heavenly Parent, the kingship of the present parents, the kingship of the future children) have been realized, the four great realms of heart—parents' love, husband and wife's love, brothers and sisters' love, and children's love—can harmonize to form the model of the kingdom of heaven. Then what are the four great realms of heart?

The first is the love between husband and wife.

In the beginning, Heavenly Parent wished for Adam and Eve to grow up and achieve the ideal of oneness with Heavenly Parent. The love of husband and wife follows the order of creation, in which the absolute subject partner must create the absolute object partner and the absolute object partner also must create and perfect the absolute subject partner. In other words, the only woman among the innumerable women in the world who can call a man her husband and acknowledge his value as such is his wife. Only when she acknowledges him as her husband can his position be perfected. Similarly, the position of the wife is also perfected when her husband acknowledges her. Therefore, the love between husband and wife signifies leading a life in which you match yourself to your spouse to perfect your position because he or she is the one who can perfect you and who has the authority to do so.

Second, the heart of the parents is important.

As has been mentioned above, the position of parents is not determined by the parents themselves; the position and value of the parents are determined by their children when their children call them their parents. In short, the parents' value is determined by how much they have guided their children toward perfection. Therefore, they need to guide their children toward perfection, for only then can it be said that their lives as parents have been well-lived.

The third is the heart of the children.

Children stand in a position in which they can become parents in the future. Children who receive their parents' devoted love and are in the position of responding to that love with the heart of hyojeong (filial heart), doing their best to be filial are acknowledged as filial children by their parents. In this way, they inherit the position and right of parents of the future as well as the right of lineage, right of inheritance, right of equal status and right of participation.

The fourth is the heart of brothers and sisters.

The human Fall in the family of Adam and Eve caused Cain and Abel to become divided and to fight. Heavenly Parent, the original parent, wishes for the brothers to become one and return to the original parent. Therefore, we need to not only give birth to our own biological children but also find and establish their lost brothers and sisters in the Cain realm and unite them with our children as siblings. In short, we need to make them live for the sake of their other brothers and sisters. This is because our position as an individual is not something we can create by ourselves. Our individual position is acknowledged and perfected only when we walk the path where we can win our brothers and sisters' recognition.

If these four great realms of heart are broken, the realm of heart of husband and wife becomes imperfect, the realm of heart of parents becomes imperfect, the realm of heart of children becomes imperfect, and the realm of heart of siblings becomes imperfect. The foundation on which we can realize these four great realms of heart is our own family.

The perfection of our character also can be achieved in a family in which three generations live together. It is possible when we understand the heart of grandfather and grandmother, mother and father, and brothers and sisters, and share love with them. That is why True Parents recommend that three generations live together in one home.

✻ Points for contemplation

1) To help your spouse reach perfection, you need to live for his or her sake and satisfy his or her needs, rather than trying to receive something from him or her. In your family, what do you think are the needs of your spouse that you need to satisfy?

2) Let us contemplate the points on which we need to make efforts in our present situation to spiritually experience the four great realms of heart as blessed central families who live attending Heavenly Parent at our center.

6
Perfecting the World of Freedom, Peace, Unity and Happiness

– The Great Cosmic Family Is Heavenly Parent's Ideal

True Parents' Words

Family Pledge #4:

Our family, the owner of Cheon Il Guk, pledges to build the universal family encompassing heaven and earth, which is God's ideal of creation, and perfect the world of freedom, peace, unity and happiness, by centering on true love.

God's ideal is that the world becomes one family, or household, under God. If those who have actualized the four great realms of heart and three great kingships recite the Family Pledge, there should be only one family under God rather than two families, or many. By building the universal family encompassing heaven and earth—the ideal of God's creation—we should establish that one family under God. To give you an example using air, when there is a lack of air in a low-pressure system, air from a high-pressure system flows in and fills it up. Similarly, water in a higher place automatically will flow down to fill up a lower place. Equilibrium is the ideal. In the world today, there are advanced nations and underdeveloped nations. In the advanced nations people have a lot, and end up discarding leftover things, whereas people in underdeveloped nations lack many things, especially food. They may even starve to death. Twenty million people die of starvation each year. Do you think that is God's Will? What the advanced nations are doing is oppressing the universe's natural system of interaction. If this continues, the advanced nations will be unable to avoid divine punishment. Heaven will not let this go unnoticed.

Already signs of judgment are appearing in various places. One of the signs is the prevalence of sexually transmitted diseases, and another is drug and alcohol abuse. Both free sex and homosexuality are the madness of the lowest of the human race. God detests such behavior the most; Satan, on the other hand, praises such behavior the most.

I, Rev. Moon, am leading a movement to save the tens of thousands of people who are dying of starvation and malnutrition each day in the underdeveloped nations, even if it means making people go hungry in the consumer paradise of advanced nations such as the United States. Despite disorder in the human race, the natural world is constantly trying to maintain equilibrium.

When we pledge to "build the universal family encompassing

heaven and earth, which is God's ideal of creation, and perfect the world of freedom, peace, unity and happiness," the word "freedom" here does not mean only the freedom of an individual, but the freedom, peace, unity, and happiness of all the people of this world as one family under God. It refers to a world whose people are living in happiness. That is why we should develop movements in all villages, towns and cities throughout the world. In any place of wealth, we need to set up structures through which it can be shared. ["The Value and Significance of the Family Pledge," *Pyeong Hwa Shin Gyeong*, 260–262]

Sharing Thoughts

One of the most urgent problems in the world is poverty. Even though we live in an age when science is so advanced that we can even send spacecraft to Mars, there are so many people who are dying of starvation. It is such a serious problem that, even now, more than 20,000 people die of starvation every day. There are people who die of hunger even in the United States, the nation that is said to be the wealthiest in the world. The situation of the poorer countries in such areas as Africa is indeed so devastating that it is beyond explanation in words. When all is said and done, this problem of starvation is like a time bomb that could bring truly serious crises to humanity. That is why the food problem of humankind is a task that must be solved in order to construct the ideal world of peace.

True Parents have long worried about this food problem and therefore took an interest in the ocean. They cast fishing lines into the sea, offered jeongseong, and thought so much about how to solve the food problem of humankind. They even took action to solve it.

True Parents lost sleep at night thinking about the solution to the food problem of humankind. They devoted all their energy into developing low-cost, highly nutritional food. Then they came to know the fact that more than a fifth of the fish caught worldwide is either thrown away or made into fertilizer. Upon learning that the wasted, disfavored fish were actually full of good, high-quality protein that was even better than that of beef, they thought the situation was deplorable and drew up plans to make the fish into fishcakes or sausages to be handed out in Africa. They came up with an idea through which they could provide the fish in a delicious, fresh state, and thus resolve all the problems at once. In short, they collected the fish and ground them into fish powder. Both the storage and transportation of the fish powder are quite simple. Therefore, it was perfect for the warm climate of Africa. Moreover, it was full of high-quality protein and was made into food that can save starving people.

In this way, True Parents are working to realize the ideal of one global family by solving the food problem of humankind. Therefore, we need to know clearly the meaning of the unity, peace, happiness and freedom spoken of in the Family Pledge.

Unity refers first to the unity of mind and body in an individual, then the unity of individuals, and, further, the unity of groups, nations, the world and the cosmos, centered on the fundamental ideals of Heavenly Parent. Only on the basis of that unity can this world create a structure in which everyone can consider others' viewpoints and thus create peace. Peace in turn brings about happiness. It makes you love. And people sing of the true freedom of living for one another under Heavenly Parent. In this vein, the dream of Heavenly Parent and True Parents is to realize the "One Family under Heavenly Parent" which they have eagerly awaited.

❉ Points for contemplation

1) In Korea we call our members *shikgu*. The root meaning of *shikgu* refers to those who eat meals together. What can I do to bring about this community of *shikgu* in which people of all races live together in harmony?

2) Let us think about the unity we need to achieve in our families. And let us contemplate methods by which we can bring about peace, happiness and freedom for one another.

7
Progressive Development

– Leading a Life of Realizing the Heavenly Kingdom and Unity

True Parents' Words

Family Pledge #5:

Our family, the owner of Cheon Il Guk, pledges to strive every day to advance the unification of the spirit world and the physical world as subject and object partners, by centering on true love.

In our daily life we should have a consciousness that the spirit world is the subject partner. Unless we reach perfection on earth—the object partner—we shall not be able to establish the foundation for perfection when we pass into the spirit world. There is a direct relationship between the two worlds. Only when the spirit world is linked to us every day, every year, throughout our entire life, it becomes our second sphere of activity and place of residence when we go there. How many times a day do you think about the spirit world? If we think about the whole world, right now are there more people in the spirit world or more people alive on earth? When you thought right now, how did you think? Did you think about the spirit world? You cannot think only about this world. We need to remember every day that the subject partner is the spirit world. [*Sermons*, 260–305, 1994.05.19]

The spirit world is the subject partner, yang, and the physical is the object partner, yin. In the same way, the mind is in the subject partner position and yang to the body, which is in the position of object partner, yin. The body represents the physical world, and the mind represents the spirit world. If we act in such a way that we do not recognize the mind and the world of the mind as the subject partner, we are bound to go to hell. If we have lived in such a way that our body has led our mind, we now should live so that our mind leads our body and subjugates it. I am saying that such a time has come. ["The Value and Significance of the Family Pledge," *Pyeong Hwa Shin Gyeong*, p. 264]

Sharing Thoughts

True Parents received a letter of appreciation from the head office of McDonald's in the United States. Why do you think they received it? Had they perhaps bought the right of operation for the famous McDonald's with a lot of money? Actually, it was because they had eaten so many McDonald's hamburgers. In other words, they did not want to waste a single moment that they could spend on their work to accelerate the progressive development of the unity between the spirit world, which is the subject partner, and the physical world, which is the object partner. They made all haste to accelerate it. In short, True Parents spared almost no time for meals. Such is the busy life they have led. Seeing that they had less than 36,500 days to live, they continued to work hard, eating McDonald's hamburgers to save time.

On more than one occasion, the hoondokhae session begun by True Parents in the early morning was continued throughout the day, and they of course skipped breakfast, and also lunch and dinner, to speak to the members. True Father usually spoke five or six hours, and sometimes he spoke for ten or even more than 20 hours. Not only did True Parents not stop for meals, they did not even stop speaking to go to the bathroom; such was their life of continuous struggle to advance the providence by even one step. In this way, they lived their entire lives for the unity of the spiritual and physical worlds, seeing that they had less than 100 years on earth. Only when this kind of effort is made and such endeavors are carried out, can the unity of the spiritual and physical worlds be achieved. We too should live every day of our lives with the same thoughts and attitude toward life as True Parents. By so doing, we should make every effort to "live our lives to realize the heavenly kingdom and unity."

In October 2009, True Parents declared the Age of the Association Connecting the Spiritual and Physical Worlds. In other words, they announced the age of the association by which the spirit world and physical world are connected as one. In accordance with the progress of the providence, the wall that separated the spirit world and the physical world has been completely abolished. The age has been opened where spirits in the spirit world can freely travel to and from the earth. The spirit world and the physical world are no longer two separate worlds. They have become one connected world. When the age of substantial Cheon Il Guk unfolds, the Association Connecting the Spiritual and Physical Worlds will stand at the central axis on this earth and finally govern the entire created world. That means that when substantial unity is perfected by connecting the spiritual and physical worlds, the providence will be governed based on the heavenly ways and heavenly laws.

❈ Points for contemplation

1) If we were to live for 100 years, our lives would be 36,500 days long. If we subtract the time spent on eating, sleeping and playing, what is the number of days that we actually can work? Have we ever struggled to realize the heavenly kingdom and unity like True Parents who even begrudged the time they spent on eating?
2) True Parents tell us to inspect ourselves every day to keep step with the spirit world. How many times a month do I inspect myself?

8
Life of Conveying the Blessings of Heaven
― Becoming Families That Move Heavenly Fortune

True Parents' Words

Family Pledge #6:

Our family, the owner of Cheon Il Guk, pledges to become a family that moves heavenly fortune by embodying God and True Parents, and to perfect a family that conveys Heaven's blessing to our community, by centering on true love.

What have True Parents done? They became the family that can stand in God's place and move heavenly fortune. In the same way, you must become one with True Parents and become families that can move heavenly fortune and connect Heaven's blessing to the people around you. You cannot do this by yourself; you need to make the families around you like your family. You must pledge to become a subject partner family who can do that. [*Sermons*, 267-153, 1995.01.04]

Not only True Parents but also all of you must become true parents. True Parents have become a big tree, but in the same way that cells multiply, you must become the same kind of cells. You must resemble True Parents' big tree. You who are following True Parents must resemble that tree. You must resemble the origin. [*Sermons*, 259-319, 1994.04.24]

You are a family that embodies God and True Parents. The families that embody God and True Parents are the families that mobilize heavenly fortune. When we say that we pledge to "become a family that moves heavenly fortune … and … conveys Heaven's blessing to our community," we are not saying that we want to be blessed by God and enjoy a good life just for ourselves. We are saying that we are all ultimately to become part of the royal family and that everyone should be a citizen of God's kingdom of Cheon Il Guk. We are making a vow to become a channel of God's blessing, sharing His blessing equally with all the people of the world. The family of God and the True Parents is one family. There is only one set of True Parents. However, since there are many blessed families throughout the world, God wants all of them to become channels that share the blessings of God and True Parents with others. You should strive to become such a family. This means that you are trying to enable everyone to receive many blessings. ["The Value and Significance of the Family Pledge," *Pyeong Hwa Shin Gyeong*, 265–266]

Sharing Thoughts

There are many people living on this planet. At the beginning of each year, a great number of them, regardless of whether they are from the East or the West, show much interest in checking their fortune for the year based on the year of their birth, their horoscope, Tarot cards or their name. Though they are trying to find out what their fortune will be like for the new year, in the larger picture they are trying to find out about their fortune in relation to their fate. Just as individuals have their own fortune, families, nations and the world also have their own fortune. And in the same vein, all of heaven and earth are influenced by heavenly fortune.

Even if a person is born with good fortune as an individual, when his or her family suffers misfortune, he or she also has to endure it. Similarly, even if a person is born with good fortune as an individual and also as a family, when his or her nation's fortune starts going downhill, he or she also is affected by it. Furthermore, national fortune or the situation of the entire world is determined by the direction and progress of heavenly fortune, which encompasses all principles of the world. Establishing the heavenly way in the world signifies shaping the fortune of an individual or nation and the world, of course, to be in tune with heavenly fortune.

Then how does heavenly fortune find its way to someone? When one stands in a lowly position of humility in an environment desired and yearned for by Heaven, heavenly fortune naturally finds its way to him or her. To such a person, everything he or she desires and yearns for is supplied automatically. Just as air and water flow down and fill the lower places, heavenly fortune follows the same principle and flows down.

Knowing this principle, True Parents make the wind of heavenly fortune blow. If there is low pressure, the wind of high pressure is made to blow. When we pray with utmost devotion and sincerity and ask for help and always sacrifice ourselves to serve others, even if we are in a region of low pressure, heavenly fortune meets Heavenly Parent's love of high pressure and blows upon us like a storm.

For us to receive heavenly fortune, we first need to know the path by which heavenly fortune travels. It is not a place where people like to go, where people enjoy themselves and eat and drink to their hearts' content. In fact, it is a place that people abhor. It is a place where one needs to fulfill one's responsibility, no matter what it may be, and then return glory to Heavenly Parent and be grateful for being able to do so.

Then what kind of a person should you be to receive heavenly fortune? Just like Heavenly Parent, you must be the champion of love who can love heaven and earth. At the same time, you must be able to transcend not only individuals or families but also peoples and national boundaries. In addition, when you find yourself in a place that is greater than your living environment, instead of trying to make that place small enough to fit your own space, you should be able to place yourself out there in the bigger place. The Family Federation for World Peace and Unification is pursuing a world of the culture of heart that transcends language, race and nationality.

There is no one who works on a wider range than True Parents. That is why heavenly fortune comes to them. For this reason, we should go beyond receiving heavenly fortune by educating ourselves to lead a life of living for the sake of others, and we should become "families that can move heavenly fortune" so that we can connect even our neighbors to love.

❉ Points for contemplation
1) Do you know what realm of fortune you are in at the present?
2) Contemplate on what it means to receive heavenly fortune, to move heavenly fortune and to share heavenly fortune.

9
Living for the Sake of Others
— Constructing the World of the Culture of
Heart by Living for the Sake of Others

True Parents' Words

Family Pledge #7:

Our family, the owner of Cheon Il Guk, pledges, through living for the sake of others, to perfect the world based on the culture of heart, which is rooted in the original lineage, by centering on true love.

Becoming a person who lives for the sake of others is the basis for the formation and construction of the cosmos. Even God exists for the sake of others. There is not one thing among all things in the cosmos that goes against this principle. A person who stands in this core position of the subject partner and the origin of formation is welcomed by the cosmos and even God Himself.
[*Sermons*, 255-176, 1994.03.10]

Love cannot be attained alone. Where does love come from? It does not come from you but from the other person, your object partner. That is why you should bow down your head and live for the sake of your object partner. This is where the principle of Heaven to "live for the sake of others" comes from. Since something extremely precious is coming to you, you need to live for the sake of others and raise them up so you may be fully able to receive the love they are trying to give to you. Only when you practice the philosophy of living for the sake of others, can you be loved. [*True Family and the Family Pledge*, p. 264, 1986.03.14]

The concept of eternity is impossible if you live only for your own sake. Taking an object in action, for example, the greater the force that pushes it and pulls it from the opposite direction is, the faster it goes around. God, the King of wisdom, established the principle of living for the sake of others so that we can last for all eternity. [*Sermons*, 75-322, 1975.01.16]

That is why a person who lives for the sake of others cannot come to ruin. Moreover, a person who lives for the sake of others is constantly coached by the spirit world. It makes that person form relationships with new things again and again. And because that person forms connections with new things, he or she naturally becomes famous and widely known worldwide. [*Sermons*, 292-28, 1998.03.22]

Sharing Thoughts

A person who likes to run, for example in a marathon, experiences a "runner's high." That term is made up of two words: "runner" (a person who runs) and "high" (feeling the best). In other words, it means the greatest satisfaction and pleasure a person can feel while running.

Similar to this "runner's high," there is something called a "helper's high," which is the pleasure you feel when you help someone. This term is also a combination of two words: "helper," meaning someone who helps others, and "high," meaning feeling the best.

If we were to pick an example of someone who overcame adversities in the twentieth century, we would think first of Helen Keller. She won both the respect and sympathy of the entire world as a representative figure who overcame human limitations. Only a year after she was born into the world, Helen Keller suffered a fever that left her unable to see anything, unable to hear anything, and unable to say anything. Thus, she became a disabled person who had to suffer this triple handicap throughout her whole life.

However, she overcame her adverse circumstances and entered Harvard University, where she mastered not only German and French but also Greek and Latin, and she left behind many literary works that deeply moved the hearts of people all over the world.

Until Helen Keller could become such a person, however, she was helped not only by her parents but also by her governess, Annie Sullivan. For 35 years till her death, Annie devoted everything to helping Helen. If not for Annie, the Helen we know never could have existed. They were more than just a teacher and her student; they had strong faith in each other, based on trust and love, which made them live for the sake of each other.

After helping someone, we usually experience a feeling of pleasure for a few days or a few weeks. Annie Sullivan, however, experienced this helper's high all her life, for she dedicated every moment of it to help Helen overcome her adversities and live a happy life.

If True Parents' teachings were to be boiled down to one phrase, it would be "live for the sake of others." Not only the love between man and woman, but also the relationship between parents and children shines even more brightly when they live for each other. This is also true for international relations. The life principle of everything in this world is that everything lives for the sake of one another. The teachings of all the saints also ultimately emphasize living a life that is not self-centered but lived for the sake of others and the greater good, a life of giving and sharing with others.

Therefore, we should not make assertions for our own sake. If we do not live in a world where we all live for one another's sake, a peaceful world cannot be realized. That is why True Parents had to establish the principle of living for the sake of others. True love and true ideal both begin from living for the sake of others. In addition, true peace and true happiness also begin from living for the sake of others. That is the fundamental principle of the creation of heaven and earth, and the world of the culture of heart desired by Heavenly Parent. What is the world of the culture of heart? It means a culture of living for the sake of others, where compassionate impulses are substantialized centering on Heavenly Parent.

❇ Points for contemplation
1) Why should we live for the sake of others? Am I living for the sake of others?
2) The world of the culture of heart is the compassionate impulse generated when, in resemblance to Heavenly Parent, you live for the sake of others. Try to contemplate the world of the culture of heart.

10
The Ultimate Task of Blessed Families
– Oneness with Heavenly Parent through Love

True Parents' Words

Family Pledge #8:

Our family, the Owner of Cheon Il Guk, pledges, having entered the Completed Testament Age, to achieve the ideal of God and human beings united in love through absolute faith, absolute love and absolute obedience, and to perfect the realm of liberation and complete freedom in the kingdom of God on earth and in heaven, by centering on true love.

When you participate in love, you rise to the position of equal status right away. People think that God is high up above and that we human beings are low creatures, but what happens when God says that He cannot go on anymore because of His great desire to love? When He says that He cannot endure not loving someone,

we could even climb to the top of His head. If you were a woman with a husband and you sat on his shoulders, would there be anyone who would look at you and say, "That woman is crazy!"?
[*Sermons*, 87-325]

God is the root of love, the root of life, the root of lineage and the root of the kingdom of heaven on earth and the kingdom of heaven in heaven. Had Adam and Eve not fallen, God would have entered their hearts when they married and realized a loving oneness with them. God would have become the vertical True Parent, and Adam and Eve would have become the horizontal True Parents. We would have been born with the flesh and blood of these two sets of parents. Our mind would have become the vertical self and our body the horizontal self, and we would have led lives based on one heart, one body, one outlook and one harmony.

In such a way, we are to perfect the unity of our mind and body by achieving unity with God in love and thus becoming His sons and daughters. Once we are in this parent–child relationship, we become God's princes and princesses. We can enjoy a parent–child relationship with God and inherit everything from Him. When we, as His children, become husbands and wives and unite totally based on true love, we become a family that lives by attending God. That family becomes a base for peace and the ideal. When a man and a woman, each being one half, unite together, they become the base through which they fulfill God's ideal love as His partners. ["The Value and Significance of the Family Pledge," *Pyeong Hwa Shin Gyeong*, 269–270]

Sharing Thoughts

What do absolute faith, absolute love and absolute obedience mean? First, what does absolute faith mean? It means not standing in a self-centered position. In other words, it refers to the life in high-noon vertical alignment. Vertical alignment signifies the time at 12 o'clock sharp, when the sun that rose from the east shines down on the earth at an exact right angle to the planet's axis. At that moment, all things are affected 100 percent by the light of the sun. That moment, as seen in a clock, is the moment when the second hand, the minute hand and the hour hand are all aligned in the 12 o'clock direction, at an exact right angle with the horizon. At that moment in time, because everything falls 100 percent under the light of the sun, there are no shadows. In short, the state of being aligned one hundred percent with Heavenly Parent's influence, with not one whit of the self involved, is called vertical alignment, and the place where this takes place is called the position of absolute faith.

Absolute love comes next. Absolute love refers to placing the object partner at the center and investing everything into him or her and giving love for his or her sake. True love does not begin from you as its motive; rather, it begins as an expression of your heart's desire to live for the sake of your object partner.

The third is the position of absolute obedience. Absolute obedience is a term used in the world of perfection. In the world of perfection—the world of true love—your partner engages with you to help you in the process of reaching perfection. Interaction in the perfect world happens with this intent. In this context, "absolute obedience to your partner" means being fully receptive to your partner so that you may accomplish the process of your growth towards perfection. Accordingly, your position is perfected when you "obey" your partner. Absolute obedience also can be expressed as the position of absolute positivity. Heavenly Parent is a being who possesses only absolute positivity. That is why Heavenly Parent has been able to continue His work for human salvation for 6,000 years without giving up.

To sum up, absolute faith, absolute love and absolute obedience can be said to refer to the state of complete oneness in which you attend Heavenly Parent at your center, don't assert yourself, walk the path of living for the sake of your partner, and live a life of absolute positivity, which is an attribute of Heavenly Parent.

The Korean flag is quite special. At the center of the Korean flag is the *taegeuk* symbol, which symbolizes Heavenly Parent. This mark looks like a yin-yang symbol that is made up of two colors, red and blue. The red in the upper part symbolizes heaven, and the blue beneath it symbolizes the earth. The symbol, however, is not stationary, for yin and yang are constantly rotating around each other. Through this, we can see that yin and yang coexist harmoniously and beautifully in Heavenly Parent. He possesses both elements of yang and yin; yang refers to the masculine elements, and yin refers to the feminine elements.

The incorporeal Heavenly Parent exists with the dual characteristics of yin and yang. His yang part was substantialized in the form of Adam, and His yin part in the form of Eve. The human beings Adam and Eve were to be perfected and become husband and wife, at which time Heavenly Parent was to enter their bodies and become one with them. Such was His dream. Even in the Bible, it is written, "Do you not know that you are Heavenly Parent's temple and that Heavenly Parent's spirit dwells in you?" If human beings had become perfected, they would have become Heavenly Parent's temple. In the end, the appearance of perfect human beings is the parent–child oneness Heavenly Parent wanted, with Heavenly Parent as human beings and human beings as Heavenly Parent. By so doing, perfected human beings would have become the second substantial object partners of Heavenly Parent. What does that mean? It means inheriting the best things owned by Heavenly Parent, or rather, everything owned by Him. Then of all the things owned by Heavenly Parent, what is the best? It is true love. That is why becoming the substantial object partners of Heavenly Parent means to love all things and to gain the right to love the entire universe, just like Him.

Heavenly Parent and humankind were originally in a relationship of parent and child, and as such they should not have been separated from each other. However, human beings disobeyed Heavenly Parent's words and fell, thus falling to a position from which they could not return. Now, we need to find our parent and return to our hometown. That is the place where Heavenly Parent and humankind become one. It is the place where we can give and take the true love of Heavenly Parent and where we can feel the joy we originally were created to feel. It is a place where we cannot stay centered on the flesh, for our hometown can interact and expand only when we live the kind of life our original heart desires.

True Parents achieved oneness with Heavenly Parent and became His embodiments, and in order to carry out the providence of restoring His lost children, they walked the path of suffering their entire lives.

❈ Points for contemplation

1) Contemplate the path of absolute faith, absolute love and absolute obedience.
2) Think about the oneness of Heavenly Parent and humankind in love in comparison to your own life.

Chapter 8

Life of Faith

1
True Meaning of Life of Faith
– Becoming the Substantial Object Partner of Absolute Goodness

True Parents' Words

Faith means living in attendance to God, living together with God and attending Him. If we do not walk such a path, we feel uneasy. We feel physically uncomfortable, and we meet obstacles in our environment. A life of faith is a life of living together with God and attending Him. The sun rises in the morning, reaches its zenith at noon, and sets in the evening. This is unchanging. It will not change in tens of thousands of years. If an orbit goes awry, everything goes awry. We need to go out and find the mind of love, the path of true love. The person who inherits true life and true lineage becomes part of God's family and always lives with God. Living with God also means living happily with nature and coming and going happily in our daily lives. [CSG 8.1.1:16]

I have brought four great truths to the world of faith. First, I clarified the relationship between God and human beings. I also gave a clear explanation about the portion of human responsibility and indemnity—things that no one in history had known about before. We did not know why human beings are as they are today. I made this point clear. I then explained why life is difficult for conscientious people, while evil people live well. No one has known about the law of indemnity or the problem of Cain and Abel. Finally I explained why, even though people seek goodness, situations often get worse, little by little. This is an issue of lineage; it is due to our blood being tainted by Satan. This question has been unresolved due to the fundamental ignorance concerning the problem of lineage. All the problems of the world are related to the issue of lineage. [CSG 8.1.1:3]

Sharing Thoughts

Human beings were originally Heavenly Parent's children who were supposed to attend and live together with Him, their parent. When He created His children, Heavenly Parent wished to look upon them as the parent and feel joy. Therefore, we, His children, are meant to return joy to Him, our parent. Moreover, taking dominion over the entire world created by Heavenly Parent with love and making it overflow with true love was the mission that humankind was supposed to fulfill. However, humankind was unable to walk this path due to the fall. That does not mean that the mission and purpose to be fulfilled by humankind are now invalid. Heavenly Parent has continued unceasingly throughout history to seek out human beings who could achieve them.

Life of faith refers to a life of attending Heavenly Parent. To attend Him, we need to expel evil and pursue goodness. That is why when we lead a life of faith, we endeavor to erase the evil parts of our lives and fill them with goodness. The last wish of humanity is to become beings of complete goodness. As the Bible says, since Heavenly Parent is perfect, He hopes for humankind to be perfect as well. Since Heavenly Parent is absolutely good, He wishes for us human beings, His children, to also be absolutely good and kindhearted. Heavenly Parent does not want humankind to stand in the position of evil, moaning in anguish and being subjected to the accusations of Satan.

In the Bible, there was a man named Job who followed Heavenly Parent's Will to the letter. He was a rich man with great wealth and was respected by those around him. As the head of a family with a wife and several children, he was a happy man who lacked nothing. Satan, jealous and envious of him, accused Heavenly Parent, "Job believes and follows You because You bestow blessings upon him. If You were to take away all those blessings, he would betray You."

Thereupon, Job was tested in all kinds of ways. He suddenly lost his children and his wealth, and sores erupted on his skin. His wife said to him, "Curse Heavenly Parent and die." However, Job replied, "Shall we receive the good at the hand of Heavenly Parent, and not receive the bad?" He meant that if all his sufferings were Heavenly Parent's Will, he would submit. Job's friends, who had come to visit him on his sickbed and console him, made him hurt even more by saying that he had brought all the pain and suffering upon himself.

In the end, he also overcame such ordeals and miseries with faith, saying, "Though Heavenly Parent will kill me, I know that He governs over all of this." Then Heavenly Parent bestowed even greater grace and blessings upon him than before. Job regained his great wealth and had new children. In fact, he was blessed to the point that his three daughters all grew up to become so beautiful that "Job's daughters" became a byword. We can learn much from the absolute faith and belief of Job, who overcame such severe ordeals.

A life of faith is a life of believing and of seeking for hope. The right way to practice a life of faith is to firmly believe in the fact that we are Heavenly Parent's children and to offer our faith and hope to Him. Such a path leads us to meet Heavenly Parent; entering the center of His love and care for us by following that path is the definition of the life of faith.

Faith also involves belief, reverence and attendance. Whom should we believe in and attend? The answer is none other than Heavenly Parent, the parent of humankind, and True Parents, who have come to earth to save humanity. Then how should we believe in and attend Heavenly Parent and True Parents? We should do so by giving joy to Heavenly Parent and True Parents. However, it takes more than mere thoughts to make them joyful. We need to attend

Heavenly Parent and True Parents as the subject partner of faith in our everyday lives and create a united world of heart, first by offering jeongseong incessantly. After that, we need to practice what Heavenly Parent and True Parents want us to do. We should help our object partners to walk the right path they wish to follow and to grow, giving them love on behalf of Heavenly Parent. His Will is to save human beings as their parent, and with that hope He is walking the path of absolute faith, absolute love and absolute obedience toward humankind. We too, as His children, should establish the standard of absolute faith, absolute love and absolute obedience to Him, our parent, and also to True Parents.

If human beings can follow the Will of Heavenly Parent and True Parents by doing so, they will be able to harbor the heart of Heavenly Parent and True Parents in their own hearts at all times and love other people, and thus walk the path of perfection.

❈ Points for contemplation

1) Let us contemplate together the question of where we can find the identity of our lives.
2) The perfection of human beings refers to inheriting the parental heart of Heavenly Parent and True Parents. What is the path by which we can inherit that parental heart?

2
Stages in a Life of Faith
—Becoming Perfected as a True Person by Believing and Doing

True Parents' Words

Hope always supports faith. What does faith demand? If a person has perfect faith, faith demands that he match it in value with substantial effort. Faith means standing for and believing in the person who has matched the ideal of creation, who is in accord with principled law, and who has not fallen but has reached perfection and then is acting accordingly. The one who is victorious in this kind of faith will realize his hope. God's love comes naturally to the one who achieves victory in faith and hope. [CSG 8.1.4:2]

God has toiled up to the present day, seeking to find what was lost. It is not because He is unable to take dominion over human beings. Similarly, God has been fighting Satan and his accusations not because He has no authority. God fights in this way in order to establish the Principle. In this great struggle, God actually permits Satan to act; then He does the great spiritual work of rearranging what Satan has done. Satan cannot accuse God for rearranging what he himself has dominated first. Thus the wisest person is the one who knows how to get even Satan to run God's errands. Such a person will be the ultimate victor. [CSG 8.1.4:9]

What was the starting point for True Parents? It was true love. In the end, love becomes the critical issue. Any family, tribe, people, nation or world that advances, based on true love, is automatically united. History should have followed the one direction of true love. But instead history has followed a messy, zigzag course. True Parents are called to completely change this situation after going through the levels of the individual, family, tribe and nation. [CSG 8.1.4:20]

Sharing Thoughts

A life of faith signifies attending Heavenly Parent and True Parents and practicing the Word. It is the path of achieving perfection of character by making the Word flower within us. Faith means living our lives centered on Heavenly Parent at all times. Based on that center, we need to fulfill His ideal of creation. It means for us human beings not to fall but to lead our lives in accordance with the Principle and become perfected. Therefore, Heavenly Parent comes to those people who have this center intact within them. Practice and centered life are like the two sides of a coin and must be carried out simultaneously. Other religious organizations always speak of faith rather than practice. However, FFWPU advocates attendance and practice. Accordingly, we need to go beyond having a strong faith and attend Heavenly Parent at our center and follow and practice the path He wishes of us. Lot's wife, who appears in the Bible, is famous for not heeding the warning of the angel when she and her husband were fleeing from the destruction of Sodom and Gomorrah and looking back, whereupon she was turned into a pillar of salt.

Sodom and Gomorrah were fallen, immoral cities, and they ultimately incurred Heavenly Parent's wrath. Consequently, He said that He would punish those cities. Abraham persuaded Him not to destroy the cities if ten righteous people could be found within them, but in the end no righteous people could be found and the cities were destroyed.

Heavenly Parent sent angels to save Abraham's nephew Lot and his family. The angels told Lot and his family in advance to leave the city and never look back. However, Lot's wife did look back and was turned into a pillar of salt. Heavenly Parent burned the two cities of Sodom and Gomorrah with fire and brimstone, and the cities were completely destroyed.

In this story, Lot's wife did not obey the words of the angel. When they were told not to look back, they actually were being told not to regret giving up their lives in Sodom and Gomorrah or feel a lingering attachment to the wealth they had left behind. Those were things they could receive again when they became one with Heavenly Parent. In short, she died because she was unable to obey the direction not to look back.

The next stage in our life of faith, after attending Heavenly Parent at our center, is the stage of practice in which we rid ourselves of fallen nature. We all have fallen nature. That is why we are contradictory beings stained by the Fall, and egoism is rampant in our families and societies. Therefore, we need to have a desperate desire to rid ourselves of it. We need to think of the bitter tears of the human ancestors Adam and Eve, who were driven out of Eden in the beginning of time due to the Fall. And we must think of Heavenly Parent, who looked upon Adam and Eve in their plight with sorrow. Pondering the heart of Adam and Eve, who were unable to be with Heavenly Parent, and the heart of Heavenly Parent, who was unable to embrace them, we need to resolve to rid ourselves of the fallen nature lodged within us at all costs. The fallen nature that human beings came to have through the Fall includes five aspects: comparison, arrogance, jealousy, indiscretion and falsity. We need to drive this fallen nature out of ourselves. To do so, we need to believe in and practice True Parents' words.

When we discover that fallen nature gradually is being expelled from us, we also will discover that Heavenly Parent is governing us more and more. We will come to realize that Heavenly Parent has dominion over us. After going through the stage of practice where we rid ourselves of fallen nature, we go on to the stage of becoming perfected through true love. Ultimately we will stand in front of

Heavenly Parent as His true children. In order to be able to do so, we must be perfected through true love. To become perfected through true love, we first need to find and establish the standard of loving our object partners. We must walk the path on which we can achieve perfection by filling the needs of those we meet as our object partners with the love of Heavenly Parent and True Parents and by helping them to grow. When we establish that standard, our object partners bestow on us the status of the parent. We need to win their recognition so that they feel, "You are truly a person who resembles Heavenly Parent."

Heavenly Parent's purpose for creating human beings was for them to practice His words and achieve perfection through true love. Furthermore, it was for them to become true couples who are united as one through Heavenly Parent's true love. In this way, Heavenly Parent's hope can be fulfilled. Becoming perfected as a true couple signifies perfecting His absolute love.

❋ Points for contemplation

1) The human Fall refers to the severance of the relationship between Heavenly Parent and humankind. Therefore, faith is about reconnecting that severed relationship. Accordingly, the first point of faith is to adopt an attitude of life centered on Heavenly Parent in order to reconnect that relationship between Him and humankind. What should we do in our everyday lives to become substantial

embodiments centered on Heavenly Parent?

2) When we set our center, we need to practice what that center wishes for us to do. Let us deeply contemplate the life of practice centering on True Parents' words.

3
Life of Faith and Spiritual Experience
– A Life of Faith Is a Process of Spiritual Experience

True Parents' Words

Profound empathy with God is a requisite of a life of faith. Through our profound experiences we can fathom God's character and feel the internal bond of deep heart we have with Him. Only through spiritual experiences can we feel these things. Through our spiritual life we can experience a euphoric sense of well-being. Moreover, unless we have this kind of experience, we cannot be filled with new hope for the ideal. Despite receiving fierce persecution from the Romans, even being fed to lions, early Christians were able to persevere in their path of faith. This was not due to some abstract belief but because they had profound spiritual experiences that allowed them to transcend the hardships they faced. [CSG 8.1.5:15]

Do you have mystical experiences in your life of faith or spiritually experience God's presence? There are some among you who frequently see me spiritually during prayers or in dreams and receive directions from me. This should happen 100 percent of the time. This is the strength, the pride and the treasure we have. Up to this point, no religion has gone through such an intense kind of experiential process. This is why religions are confused and have become secularized. However, the Unification Church knows that God stands at the very end. Even if the storms and floods of life rage against us and we are about to die, the amazing fact is that we have become men and women who can leave behind a legacy of hope for tomorrow. [CSG 8.1.5:1]

Sharing Thoughts

The life of faith is the process of spiritual experience. It is the process of becoming one with Heavenly Parent by spiritually experiencing His heart and circumstances, and the process of becoming one with True Parents by spiritually experiencing their will and wishes. Only through the path of spiritual experience can we learn about their true selves. Through spiritual experience, we can know of the joy or sorrow of Heavenly Parent and True Parents when they are joyful or sorrowful. To be able to do so, we need to attend Heavenly Parent within us, and in turn we need to enter Him and live together with Him.

There is a movie titled *Quo Vadis*. The title is a Latin phrase that means "Where are you going?" This film was made in the United States in 1951 by the famous director Mervyn LeRoy. The movie is about the time after Jesus' death on the cross, when his disciples went to Rome and were severely persecuted while spreading the words of the Gospel.

With the spread of Christianity in Rome, people began to refuse to worship the emperor or to condone murder. Rome began to oppress such Christians. The Roman emperor, Nero, dealt harsh punishments to Christians, such as feeding them to starved lions.

In Rome, the Church of Domine Quo Vadis can be found. Jesus' first disciple, Peter, was running away from Rome because he feared the persecution of Emperor Nero. When he reached the place which is now the Campanian Plain, he saw a vision of Jesus, walking toward him in the midst of a bright light with a cross on his shoulders. Peter was startled and asked, "Lord, where are you going?" Then Jesus answered, "Since you have abandoned my sheep, I am going to Rome to be crucified again." Hearing these words, Peter repented with all his heart and returned to Rome to propagate the Gospel, where he was finally arrested and crucified upside down to die a martyr. In commemoration of it, the Church of Domine Quo Vadis was erected at that place.

As can be seen, the path of truth and enlightenment is not a comfortable one. It is a path of difficult and painful suffering. However, it is the path by which one returns to the place that one left behind, with faith, courage and love. It is choosing the thorny path over the path of victory and glory. Nevertheless, it is the path of the conscience and not one riddled with lingering attachment to the life lived on earth in the flesh. It is the path where love is perfected through the growth of the spiritual self.

To be able to follow that path, we need to spiritually experience Heavenly Parent in our daily lives, which is possible only through a strict life of faith. We need to be able to shed tears boundlessly without realizing it while carrying out our daily tasks, because we suddenly feel the heart of Heavenly Parent and the bitter sorrow of True Parents washing over us. We should not be shedding those tears because we feel wronged and sad for being persecuted by the world. We should shed tears in our concern for Heavenly Parent, who has been seeking us throughout human history with bitter sorrow and grief. In our life of faith, we need to grasp and spiritually experience the circumstances of Heavenly Parent and True Parents in such a manner. We need to experience them to such an extent that the circumstances and sorrows of Heaven overwhelm us and move us to tears without our realizing it. We need to be overwhelmed to the point where we are choking with tears and at a loss as to what to do.

The details we can experience spiritually in our life of faith while shedding tears of repentance are Heavenly Parent's circumstances by which He sought us human beings. They reflect His heart as He continued to make infinite sacrifices for us and His heart-filled love that desires to give infinitely to us. The people who experienced this before anyone else were True Parents, and we too must become the children who can follow in their footsteps and spiritually experience it.

When we are able to undergo spiritual experiences through our life of faith, we will experience them at every important moment of our lives. We can know whether what we are doing will succeed or fail, by praying about it while carrying it out. When such an event takes place, your heart will be joyful and your body will be refreshed. Such efforts should make us completely forget ourselves in our life of faith, to feel as if we are not doing enough, even when we are offering ourselves on the altar, and to feel sorry for not being able to do more. That is indeed the most important part of the spiritual experience we need to undergo in our life of faith.

❈ Points for contemplation

1) Let us think about what kind of life of faith we need to lead in order to spiritually experience the heart of Heavenly Parent and circumstances of True Parents.
2) Let us deeply contemplate what we need to do to raise the level of our spiritual experience, centering on True Parents' words.

4
Living for the Unity of Mind and Body
– A Life Pursuing the Harmony of Mind and Body

True Parents' Words

Love is essential for the unity of mind and body. When parents come to love their children, they willingly endure hunger, hard work, ragged garments and going places they don't want to go. While walking the path of such love, the mind and the body take the same unifying direction. It is the only way to unity, the only means to unity. If you take this as the standard for daily life and for your entire life, you will not perish. This I guarantee. [CSG 8.2.6:2]

We must fix our gaze on Heaven. Had human beings not fallen, had everything been right in the fundamentals, we could have lived with our gaze trained below 90 degrees. Nonetheless, due to the Fall, we must fix our eyes on Heaven. It is not suitable for people of faith to look below 90 degrees; we need to gaze at Heaven. Therefore, those who stare at the ground while walking are bound to decline. Similarly, those who move with a self-centered mind will decline. We need to correct everything, beginning with our way of life, our body, our mind and our heart. Then where should we set our heart? It is not to be set inside the course of history. Instead, we should place it in the heart of Adam and Eve before the Fall. Through that heart and along with Heaven, we have to digest all the feelings we experience in our current life and in the trends of our time and resolve everything together with Heaven. Sons and daughters who are able to do this must emerge on this earth. [CSG 8.2.6:1]

Sharing Thoughts

We human beings have a mind and a body. Heavenly Parent wishes for our mind and body to be united. The oneness of the body and mind signifies that our character has become refined and that we have no conflicts in our mind. After our character is perfected, we are given the right to live centering on the divine character when we go to the spirit world.

The mind is the subject partner, and the body is the object partner. Since the mind should be the center of the body, the mind should have resolve and be able to control the body. A person who can do so is a perfected human being whose body and mind are united as one.

In the history of Israel, Moses was one of the great leaders. The ancestors of today's Israelis were the Hebrews, who wandered around many places in the course of history and finally settled in Egypt. For more than 500 years, they lived mingling with the Egyptians. Then the people of Israel were forced to live in misery, either as the slaves of Egyptians or as manual laborers. Though they wished to escape from Egypt, they could not because the Egyptian soldiers were securely guarding the borders.

Moses was the leader who succeeded in leading these Israelites, living year after year in such agony, to escape from Egypt. At the time of their exodus from Egypt, they overcame many difficulties by such means as the miracle of the Red Sea and the victory in the war against the Amalekites, and they reached Mount Sinai through the guidance of Heavenly Parent.

While Moses was up on Mount Sinai praying and receiving the Ten Commandments from Heavenly Parent, the people of Israel came to distrust Moses and made a golden calf and worshipped it as their god. Upon seeing this, Moses threw down the tablets in his wrath and broke them. Those tablets symbolized the promise between Heavenly Parent and the Israelites, and at the same time the Messiah who would come in future. Moses breaking the tablets in anger meant that the promise with Heavenly Parent was broken, and it was simultaneously a warning that the Messiah who would come in the future might fail. In the end, Moses died in the wilderness without setting foot in the promised land of Canaan. Moses teaches us the lesson that one can act against Heavenly Parent's Will and providence when one's mind and body are not united in oneness.

Since the mind of human beings is the place where Heavenly Parent can visit, our own mind can represent Him. Therefore, our heart can express Heavenly Parent's heart on His behalf. Our mind and body desire to be united as one, not only so that to unite within ourselves but also so to unite with Heavenly Parent.

That is why our mind must be in oneness with Heavenly Parent. Our body also must be in oneness with Heavenly Parent, as must our will. Unless we are in oneness with Heavenly Parent, the value of being "I" cannot be determined. Within us are lodged Heavenly Parent's heart and hopes.

At that moment when we are connected to Heavenly Parent, our body represents Heavenly Parent. Moreover, at that very moment, our life can become one with the universe. Due to the Fall, however, humankind has never reached such a state. Satan, who made humankind fall, is blocking the way toward mind–body unity by utilizing our own bodies against us. He made our body take dominion over our mind and do whatever it wants, and he made us indulge ourselves in physical indolence and pleasure, just as our body desires. The body says to the mind, "Don't do anything that is difficult and bothersome." And it tells the mind to do things that are animalistic and exciting.

Satan, who is blocking the way between Heavenly Parent and humankind, was originally an archangel. Heavenly Parent is the subject partner and the archangel is His spiritual object partner. Because the mind symbolizes heaven and the body symbolizes heaven's object partner, Satan, who fell centering on the intentions of the flesh, is using the body of human beings as his foothold in carrying out his work.

Therefore, the mind must recover the original heart with which Heavenly Parent created humankind, and the body must come under the dominion of that original heart and be established upright. That is why it is important to train the mind to ignore all conditions demanded by the body. Whereas the mind likes things centered on the development of reason for the perfection of character, the body likes pleasures centered on the flesh. Hence, for our mind to have dominion over our body, we need to hold hoondokhae through which we can recover the original Word of Heavenly Parent. We also need to constantly nurture our loving heart by offering early morning jeongseong and visiting people, even though doing so would torment our body. When we can regain the original form of human beings that Heavenly Parent wished for us to have, true peace finally can be begun.

✸ Points for contemplation
1) Let us ponder ways by which the mind can take dominion over the body, based on our own experiences.
2) We have been told that when our human character is perfected, we

can spiritually experience the world of divine character. Let us then contemplate what needs to be changed and what we need to do in our daily lives to cultivate our character.

5
Inheriting the Traditions of Cheon Il Guk

— The Traditions of Cheon Il Guk Show the Eternal Value of Humanity

True Parents' Words

What do you have that you can be proud of? Can you be proud of your money or your education? What can you be proud of? Since True Father's Seonghwa, he has lain in the BonHyang Won, and I go there every day to offer jeongseong. In Korean cultural tradition, when a parent of a noble family passes away, the children mourn at their parents' graves for three years. You do not go back and forth from your home; rather, you live in the mountains by the tomb. You do not eat decent meals nor do you wear decent clothes. You cannot light a fire, even during the cold of winter. In Korea, a lot of snow falls in the winter. Yet for three years you live by the side of your parent who is buried there. After doing this, you can be called a filial child. What about you? You should be doing hoondokhae every day, reading Father's words with this heart of attending him every day. It is for you to inherit the tradition that True Parents want you to uphold. [CBG 13.2.2:10]

We must establish Heaven's tradition. You should become people who study True Parents' words every day at hoondokhae and live accordingly. You need to understand that the result of your life will depend on how absolutely you attend True Parents, whether in your workplace or in your daily life. If you live your life with absolute faith, absolute love and absolute obedience, Heaven will give you great blessings. [CBG 13.2.2:14]

True Father's words are the truth. They are the Principle. You must study them and live by them in order to be able to build the world of love based on the culture of heart and offer it to True Parents. I hope that you will do your utmost to accomplish this. I am sure that all of you know what it means to live according to the teachings of True Father, who is now in the spirit world. Please make a pledge before True Father that you will stand as mature sons and daughters. [CBG 13.2.3:4]

Sharing Thoughts

Heavenly Parent sent True Parents to be born on earth for human beings, who lost their parents and are wandering aimlessly. True Parents, born as the only begotten son and only begotten daughter, performed the Feast of the Lamb, after which they continued to follow a difficult and toilsome course of life to liberate Heavenly Parent, save humanity and construct a world of peace on earth. They also bestowed traditions that humanity must always uphold.

We blessed families in the age of Cheon Il Guk must treasure the traditions established by True Parents as we would our own lives, endeavor to pass them down to our descendants, and make sure that they are passed down eternally. We should make the tradition of hoondokhae, which True Parents revealed to us through jeongseong and prayers, the most central part of not only our families but also our churches and many other gatherings.

In addition, True Parents established the tradition of the culture of heart for us. True Mother, in particular, observed the three-year period of memorial jeongseong after True Father's Seonghwa in 2012, during which she stayed by his side every day. Observing this kind of memorial period is usually done by a child after losing his or her parent, by building a small hut by the side of the parent's grave and living in it for three years without carrying out any activity, in order to stay together with the deceased parent. In short, it is a traditional method of practicing filial piety. Believing that one was unable to fulfill one's duties as the child by losing one's parent, one walks the path of suffering in order to fulfill one's duties as the child after the parent's death.

In place of all humankind, True Mother every day stayed at BonHyang Won where True Father was laid to rest, and offered jeongseong by his side for three years. She paid reverence in the early morning of each day at BonHyang Won and welcomed the rising sun on Mount Cheonseong, stroking the grass as she held conversations with True Father in heaven. She personally set the table for his meals, three times a day, as she had done when he was alive, and ate together with him and discussed her day with him. Looking afar to Cheongpyeong Lake reflecting the moonlight of evening, she sometimes remembered his achievements. Even while governing all parts of the providence, large and small, she stayed by his side every day without exception during the memorial period. By so doing, she was able to newly establish for us the tradition of hyojeong culture, based on the culture of heart. She proposed this hyojeong culture as the new leading mindset through which our members can be reborn.

Through her three-year period of memorial jeongseong, True Mother even moved the heart of Heavenly Parent to resolve the difficult problems in the Unification Church and let us welcome the miraculous coming of the spring of the providence. Thus, in the latter half of 2017, the age of the heavenly FFWPU, in which we can attend and uphold Heavenly Parent, was opened not only in Korea but also in Japan and the United States.

In addition, we who have received the blessing of heavenly tribal messiah from True Parents need to fulfill the mission and responsibility given by Heaven. The heavenly tribal messiah is the blessing of blessings bestowed by True Parents. We have been commanded to go beyond resembling True Parents and to lead the life of true parents. Throughout their life course, True Parents always shed blood, sweat and tears to accomplish their mission as the Messiah. Blessed families also must fulfill their mission and responsibility as heavenly tribal messiahs to realize a peaceful world and the dream of humanity as one great family.

Lastly, we all must form the community of the culture of heart, harmony and unity. We could join the Unification Church through the joint influence of Heaven's choice, our ancestors' meritorious deeds and our own nature. Though numerous ordeals and severe suffering blocked our way, we could build the community of heart centered on Heavenly Parent and True Parents. Now, along with the declaration of Cheon Il Guk, the entire world has the responsibility to create one community of the culture of heart. If we can widely expand the culture of heart of living for the sake of others, with hyojeong personally demonstrated by True Parents as our basis, the substantial Cheon Il Guk surely will be realized.

The traditions of Cheon Il Guk never can be revealed without True Parents. The joy and happiness of blessed families can have no meaning without True Parents. Constructing the substantial Cheon Il Guk is the wish of Heavenly Parent and True Parents, as well as the wish of blessed families.

Points for contemplation

1) Let us contemplate what we need to do to internalize the traditions of Cheon Il Guk within ourselves, centering on True Parents' words.

2) Let us think together to find what we can do jointly for us all to fulfill the mission and responsibility of heavenly tribal messiah.

Chapter 9

True Parents' Remarkable Achievements

1
True Parents and Declaring the New Truth
– Declaration and Substantialization of the New Truth

True Parents' Words

The Unification Principle is neither a philosophy nor a theology. It is the Principle of God. It is the unchanging truth of God. Once you have encountered the Principle, you need to adjust your life to live in accordance with it. At the very least, you need to lay a foundation on which to actualize the Principle. Then Satan cannot invade. When someone has achieved complete oneness with the truth, Satan cannot tear that person away from God and claim him or her as his own. For instance, if God, Adam and Eve had united completely centering on the truth, there would have been no room for Satan to invade. The truth needs to be substantialized. Living human beings need to sustain and embody the truth. Otherwise Satan can steal it and misuse it. This is why I never reveal a new part of the truth until all conditions have been

met and the truth has been substantialized to a certain degree.
[*CBG* 5.1.4:9]

We must center on the Principle and unite with it. We should not leave the Principle on the shelf but should keep faith in it and substantiate it. By perfecting ourselves as the substance of the Principle, we become sons and daughters whom God can love.
[*CSG* 1.1.3:16]

Sharing Thoughts

An extreme miser went to a Jewish rabbi and asked for counsel. Though he had plenty of money, he was experiencing various difficulties in his relationships with people, even with his family members, and he was worried about his own happiness. The rabbi took the miser to the window and asked him if he could see outside well. The miser answered in the affirmative. The rabbi next took him to a mirror and asked him what he saw there. The miser answered that he saw only himself. Then the rabbi said to him:

"Though they are made from the same glass, one side of the glass in a mirror is coated with mercury and so you cannot see through it, whereas the window is not coated with mercury and so you can see through it to the outside. Unless you let go of your egoism and greed, you cannot find the truth, and not only will you be unable to see the true beauty of the world but you also will be unable to find the true happiness of life."

Though the miser had earned more than enough wealth and honor, he was worried because he had not attained happiness in his life, which was because he had lived centered on the pursuit of material value. To attain the true happiness of life, it is important to cast away greed and egoism and to pursue internal value.

Originally, religion and philosophy were the fields that helped one to pursue the internal value of life and find the way to greater happiness. Religion and philosophy taught that everyone should live for the sake of one another and show concern for one another, thereby pursuing not only prosperity and happiness but also enlightenment and happiness in the next world through spiritual maturity.

Religion and philosophy emphasized that one should realize the desires of the mind before pursuing the desires of the body, and they taught about leading a balanced way of life. They also taught that, in domestic life, one should stay loyal to one's spouse by upholding chastity and true love, and that one should lead a life of happiness together with one's children. Moreover, they taught that the love in the family should be expanded to the society, so that everyone can live for one another's sake and fulfill their own given roles in organic relationships of cooperation. Even in regard to nature, they taught that people should form a sustainable relationship with it with love and interest.

However, human beings of the modern society have denied the

path of internal happiness taught by religion and philosophy. Instead, they are pursuing lives of comfort and convenience and engaging in infinite competition to satisfy their sensual desires. They are making others unhappy through individual egoism, domestic egoism, regional egoism and national egoism, and pursuing their own desires without scruples. This is what is making us unhappy.

In light of this, True Parents emphasized that the fields that taught human beings about pursuing greater happiness, such as religion, philosophy and science, must be united with one another. They wrote the Original Text of the Divine Principle and published the Explanation of the Divine Principle and the Exposition of the Divine Principle to teach us about the principle of creation, the Fall and the principle of restoration. Through the words of the new truth, they revealed that religion is an instrument of the providence that teaches us the path to internal maturity and that science is an instrument of the providence that teaches us the path to external maturity. Only when human beings learn about Heavenly Parent's Word, that is, the new truth, can they overcome the conflicts between the divided fields of religion, philosophy and science, and find the way to the path of balanced happiness. Our learning must be headed toward the new truth, which seeks both internal enlightenment and external enlightenment.

True Parents presented us with the path to universal happiness in accordance with the principle of creation. They said that all beings were created in pairs and that they exist for each other and must live for the sake of each other. They also said that we need to resemble Heavenly Parent and pursue the invisible values, and that we need to realize the perfected life in which the mind has dominion over the desires of the body. Human beings must become the owners who can love and take care of all things as the second creators. May we all gain a precise understanding of the words of the new truth declared by True Parents and become Heavenly Parent's children who can pursue happiness in a balanced way through the new truth.

❋ Points for contemplation

1) What is the value of the new truth spoken of by True Parents?
2) How should I practice the new truth for the happiness of my family and myself?
3) How should human beings practice the new truth for their neighbors, community, society and the world?

2
Interdenominational and Interreligious Work
– Path of Religious Peace

True Parents' Words

Currently Satan is polluting the world with the communist ideological system. Communism covertly encourages religious division and promotes religious wars. In addition, because the world is dominated by white people, who are at the core of the mainstream Christian cultural realm, Satan exacerbates the racial divide between blacks and whites. Now the danger is global in scale. God understands the historical age and the forces driving humankind in this era, so He is raising a movement to unite all religions. He cannot help but strive for Christian unity and racial reconciliation as a way to defend against communism and racial and religious hate-mongers. God has no choice but to carry out a movement for unity that will bring this world into oneness. A movement beyond denomination, one that transcends all Christian sects and all other faiths and defends against global communism, must emerge in these Last Days. Otherwise, there will be no way for Heaven to prevail. [CBG 11.1.4:8]

Sharing Thoughts

"I first set foot in Jerusalem in 1965. This was before the Six-Day War, and Jerusalem was still under Jordan's territorial control. I went to the Mount of Olives, where Jesus shed tears of blood in prayer just prior to being taken to the court of Pontius Pilate. I put my hand on a 2,000-year-old olive tree that could have witnessed Jesus' prayer that night. I put three nails in that tree, one for Judaism, one for Christianity, and one for Islam. I prayed for the day when these three families of faith would become one. World peace cannot come unless Judaism, Christianity, and Islam become one. Those three nails are still there." [excerpt from *As a Peace-Loving Global Citizen* p. 242]

During the Cold War, True Parents emphasized that religious believers should cooperate to carry out a movement to practice true values to resolve the threat of war and social conflicts. Even after the Cold War, they lent support to resolve conflicts between religions, which were gaining ground as the cause of terrorism and limited warfare, and they advocated the interreligious peace movement. Harmony and unity among religions were the long-cherished ambition of True Parents' life and the course of the providence.

Furthermore, they pursued the movement to bring together and hold dialogues not only with the mainstream religious orders but with other religions as well. On April 15, 1970, the Holy Spirit Association for the Unification of World Christianity was registered as a member of the Korea Religions Association, a pan-religious organization. True Parents actively carried out their religious unification movement to promote reconciliation, friendship and mutual understanding between religions. They stressed that, to realize world peace, we need to overcome denominationalism and clearly understand about Heavenly Parent, who is working in the background of all religions.

On April 25, 1983, True Parents founded the International Religious Foundation to support dialogue between diverse religions, academic activities and publication projects. The International Religious Foundation launched the 1st Assembly of the World's Religions at the Americana Great Gorge Hotel in McAfee, New Jersey, from November 15 to 21, 1985, and published the *World Scripture* anthology in 1991. To publish this anthology, more than 160 topics commonly found in all religious scriptures were chosen and compiled in one book. It was an amazing providence through which the contents of 28 major and minor religions, including Christianity, Islam, Hinduism, Buddhism, Confucianism and Taoism, Judaism, Jainism, Sikhism, Shinto of Japan, Zoroastrianism, and native religions of Africa, North and South Americas, Asia and the South Pacific were all brought together and compiled into one united *World Scripture.*

In addition, on August 27, 1991, True Parents founded the Inter-Religious Federation for World Peace (IRFWP) in Seoul in the presence of more than 2,000 religious believers from 34 nations. On February 6, 1999, they established the Interreligious and International Federation for World Peace (IIFWP) to connect the interreligious foundation to the international foundation centered on the United Nations. This interreligious and international vision later led the way to the founding of the Universal Peace Federation in September 2005.

To bring about peace in the Middle East, the powder keg of the world, True Parents intensely carried out the interreligious peace movement centering on the Middle East region. They invited more than 20,000 religious leaders from around the world to participate in the historic Peace March held in Jerusalem on December 22, 2003. They walked down the streets of Jerusalem together, hand in hand, and called for religious harmony and peace for humanity. They offered a prayer for peace together at the Al-Aqsa Mosque plaza, where only Muslims are allowed to enter, and also held a prayer meeting of supplication for peace at the plaza of the Judaic holy ground, the Wailing Wall. Overcoming the differences between religious orders, they presented the crown of peace to Jesus Christ and demonstrated interreligious peace.

On November 13, 2017, a meeting was hosted under True Mother's leadership to bring together religious believers and establish the Interreligious Association of Religious Believers for Peace.

All these providential activities are the means of practicing true love, through which all religions can transcend sects and denominations to save the world and restore peace under the common goal of realizing Heavenly Parent's hopes and ideals. Through True Parents' interdenominational and interreligious movement, we should come to understand the path of religious peace and world peace and take part in it.

❋ Points for contemplation

1) Let us deeply contemplate ways to bring about dialogue and cooperation between religions, which can contribute toward the realization of world peace.
2) Let us think of ways by which the heavenly tribal messiah community realistically can inherit the spirit of True Parents' interdenominational and interreligious movement.

3
The Victory over Communism Movement and the End of Communism
—The Path of Victory over Communism

True Parents' Words

I proclaimed the end of the Soviet empire. While I was incarcerated in Danbury, this proclamation was made publicly at an international conference of the Professors World Peace Academy in Geneva (Switzerland). The president of PWPA International was Dr. Morton Kaplan, a famous professor from the University of Chicago. I called him to Danbury and asked him to proclaim the end of the Soviet empire at the PWPA conference. Dr. Kaplan stated that he was a respected scholar who had written 17 books, and this proclamation would invalidate all his books. Hence, he could not do it. However, I said, "No! Wait and see what happens to the Communist Party in the next five years." Dr. Kaplan then suggested modifying the wording to say, "The Soviet Empire may be coming to an end." He suggested using the word "may." My

response was, "Do not use that word! Wait and see what happens to the Communist Party in the next five years. Go ahead and proclaim what I say!" For the communist world to crumble, we have to proclaim its end. I said it would crumble in less than five years. The world's scholars said they could not understand me; however, after the proclamation, they saw that the world was being transformed. They were unprepared for what has followed.
[CBG 8.2.3:2]

Sharing Thoughts

"Mr. President, you have already achieved much success through perestroika, but that alone will not be sufficient for reform. You need to immediately allow freedom of religion in the Soviet Union. If you try to reform only the material world, without the involvement of Heavenly Parent, perestroika will be doomed to fail. Communism is about to end. The only way to save this nation is to allow freedom of religion. The time is now for you to act with the courage that you have shown in reforming the Soviet Union and become a president of the world who works to bring about world peace." …

Former Soviet President Mikhail Gorbachev and the first lady used chopsticks to eat the *bulgogi* and *jabchae* we had carefully prepared. When he was served *sujeonggwa* as dessert, President Gorbachev repeated several times, "Korea has excellent traditional foods." He and the first lady appeared quite different from the days when he was in office. Mrs. Raisa Gorbachev, who previously had been a dedicated Marxist–Leninist lecturer at Moscow State University, wore a necklace with a crucifix. "Mr. President, you did a great thing," I told him. "You gave up your post as general secretary of the Soviet Union, but now you have become the president of peace. Because of your wisdom and courage, we now have the possibility to bring world peace." [excerpt from As a Peace-Loving Global Citizen, pp. 253–255]

From before the founding of the Holy Spirit Association for the Unification of World Christianity, True Father had to walk the course of suffering imprisonment in Daedong Security Station and Heungnam Prison under the communist regime. The mission work he carried out in North Korea in to stop the division of the Korean peninsula, which was meant to become the fatherland of Heavenly Parent, resulted in his suffering in prison. After True Father was miraculously released from prison when the UN made a bombing raid on Heungnam Prison, he lived his life thinking night and day about liberating North Korea, agonizing under the communist regime, through the Victory over Communism ideology of Heavenly Parent's ideal.

On November 10, 1965, True Parents began to carry out their Victory over Communism movement in earnest by launching the Anti-Communism Enlightenment Group. And on January 13, 1968, they founded the International Federation for Victory over

Communism. Under the goal of the "end of communism," the International Federation for Victory over Communism advocated the Victory over Communism movement not only in the major countries of Asia, including South Korea, Japan and Taiwan, but also on a global level. In Japan, the International Federation for Victory over Communism-Japan was organized separately to fight fiercely against the Japanese Communist Party.

In addition, True Parents sent European members to carry out underground mission work in the communist realm at the risk of their lives to propagate the Victory over Communism ideology of Heavenly Parent's ideal. Some of the members were tortured and even martyred under the communist regime.

In the 1980s, the Victory over Communism movement was expanded centering on North and South America. The Confederation of the Associations for the Unification of the Societies of the Americas (CAUSA), centered on former heads of state, was founded with the aim of bringing about unity and cooperation of the North and South American continents, and the Association for the Unity of Latin America (AULA), centered on Latin American leaders, also was organized.

The 1980s were a time when communism was expanding limitlessly. It was a time when no one could even imagine that the communist regime could collapse. On the foundation of the passionate activities of the international Victory over Communism organizations, True Father during his imprisonment at Danbury Prison instructed the scholars of the world to declare the end of communism. At the Second International Assembly of the Professors World Peace Academy, held under the chairmanship of political scientist Morton Kaplan of Chicago University, the "collapse of the communist empire of the Soviet Union" was officially declared. As prophesied by this assembly, held for five days from August 13, 1985, at Geneva, Switzerland, more than 50 guard posts along the borders of East Berlin in East Germany were successively opened on November 9, 1989, and the Berlin Wall that symbolized the Cold War was brought down. And in December 1991, the dissolution of the Soviet Union was declared, thus making the end of the Soviet empire a reality.

True Parents proclaimed right after the Washington Monument Rally in 1976 that they would host a rally in Moscow. True Parents resolutely held the Moscow rally from April 9 to 13, 1990—less than five years after the declaration of the end of communism was made in Geneva, Switzerland. More than 600 journalists, politicians and scholars from 60 nations, including more than 40 former and current heads of state, attended the rally, which was held in the Sobin International Trade Center.

During this period, True Parents had their historic meeting with President Gorbachev of the Soviet Union, who was in the position of the head of the communist regime. In a private meeting with him at the Kremlin Palace on April 11, True Parents expressed their support for the Soviet Union's policies of reformation and openness (*perestroika* and *glasnost*). They also supported the Soviet Union in continuing the transformation of its spiritual identity into a democratic nation based on Heavenly Parent's ideal. In addition, they held a wide-ranging discussion with Soviet authorities on such issues as forming friendly relations with South Korea, the reunification of Korea, and expansion of religious freedom within the Soviet Union.

Exposition of the Divine Principle speaks of the final battle between Heaven's side and Satan's side as the battle between democracy and communism. Throughout their lives, True Parents endeavored to educate and transform the leaders and youths of the communist realm through the Victory over Communism ideology of Heavenly Parent's ideal. Beginning heavenly tribal messiahs must know that the ideal world cannot be brought about through the communist ideology with its denial of Heavenly Parent, and that it will only give rise to struggles and conflicts between social classes. Therefore, we need to inherit the vision of True Parents' Victory over Communism Movement.

❈ Points for contemplation

1) Let us deeply contemplate the problems of communism, which denies Heavenly Parent as the Creator.
2) True Parents educated and supported the leaders and youths of the communist realm with the true love of Heavenly Parent. Let us think about how we can transform people in the environment of our heavenly tribal messiah community who believe in the communist ideology.

4
The Korean Reunification Movement
– Path of Peace and Unity

True Parents' Words

"Father! I am going to the South. I came to the North, but I was not able to fulfill the Will as I originally hoped. I could not avoid imprisonment, and the most painful thing about that was the feeling of defeat when I could not accomplish the goal. Now I am being chased to the South with other refugees. I know that even in the South I will receive persecution. No matter what, I will keep going on this path, even if my way is blocked for ten years or 20 years. I know that one day I will have to return to the North. If I cannot return there in person, I will have my descendants go there, and if they cannot go I will have my disciples go there." This was the resolution I made as I crossed the 38th parallel. [CBG 3.2.1:7]

Soon after its liberation, Korea was divided into North and South.

This happened because Christianity failed to unite with me. The division of Korea occurred because Christianity opposed me and the nation did not unite with me. Since the representatives of the nation and the representatives of religion separated from me, I needed you to unite with me as I endeavored to establish the foundation to indemnify their failures. Now we have established that foundation. We have reached the level at which South Koreans throughout the nation can align with me. [CSG 10.3.4:10]

Sharing Thoughts

As I approached the official residence, I found President Kim Il-sung at the entrance, waiting to greet me. The two of us simultaneously embraced each other. I was an anti-communist and he was the leader of a communist party, but ideology and philosophies were not important in the context of our meeting. We were like brothers who were meeting for the first time after a long separation. This was the power of belonging to the same people and sharing the same blood. ... Soon after I ended my weeklong stay and left Pyongyang, Prime Minister Yeon Hyeongmuk led a North Korean delegation to Seoul. Prime Minister Yeon signed an agreement to denuclearize the Korean peninsula. On January 30 of the following year, North Korea signed a nuclear safeguards agreement with the International Atomic Energy Agency, thus fulfilling the commitments that President Kim had made to me.

These were the results I accomplished by going to Pyongyang at the risk of my life. [*As a Peace-Loving Global Citizen*, pp. 261–266]

Communists are not different from those of us living under Heavenly Parent's love. In fact, Heavenly Parent hoped for communists to abolish communism and return to Heaven's side as soon as possible and contribute to world peace. In particular, He greatly lamented the fact that the Korean peninsula He had prepared was divided into North and South, communism and democracy. Because True Parents were also a part of the ten million people who belonged to families divided by the division into North and South, they knew the pain and anguish of their people better than anyone. They therefore dedicated their lives to accomplishing the liberation of Heavenly Parent's fatherland and the reunification of Korea with their own hands.

On November 30, 1991, True Parents visited Pyongyang for the reunification of Korea at the official invitation of President Kim Il-sung of North Korea. At the time, North Korean leaders were accompanied by bodyguards armed with weapons, and it was a tense situation in which True Parents could lose their lives with the pull of a trigger. True Parents did not hide the truth, however, but instead proclaimed it.

On December 5, True Parents visited their hometowns, Jeongju and Anju, and on December 6, they had their historic meeting with President Kim Il-sung at the Majeon Presidential Residence in Heungnam, South Hamgyeong Province. True Parents embraced

President Kim with brotherly love and did not treat him like an enemy. True Father reached an agreement with him about such matters as the denuclearization of the Korean Peninsula, the Inter-Korean Summit, the reunion of separated families, and the development of Mount Geumgang (Diamond Mountain). Thus, True Parents paved the way for the peaceful reunification of Korea.

While he was fleeing to the South after his miraculous release from Heungnam Prison, True Father offered a prayer at the 38th parallel. He resolved to liberate, at all costs, North Korea, which was agonizing under the communist regime. He resolved to realize Korea's reunification through his own efforts or the efforts of his children, or if that was not possible, through the efforts of his disciples. True Parents said that the reunification of Korea cannot be realized with weapons, because brute force can take away life but can never realize the ideal of true happiness.

In accordance with True Parents' teachings, from the 1960s members of the Unification Church traveled to every corner of Korea to propagate Heavenly Parent's true love and to teach the true view on life and values. Every time North Korea sent armed spies to South Korea and made a threat to attack, Unification Church members worked devotedly to educate the Korean people ideologically. The members of the Unification Church took the lead in the Korean Reunification Movement to safeguard the free, democratic Republic of Korea.

On May 15, 1987, at the Little Angels Performing Arts Center in Seoul, True Parents founded the Citizens' Federation for the Unification of North and South Korea, thus launching a pan-national movement for the peaceful Reunification of North and South Korea. They educated the people of South Korea on the grassroots level of local societies and prepared them for a post-unification general election of North and South Korea. At the time of the Seoul Olympics (1988), a festival of peace participated in by 160 democratic and communist nations, True Parents personally gave encouragement to athletes from the communist realm, thus opening the path to a future, peaceful reunification of Korea. They financially supported major nations in a close relationship with North Korea, such as the Soviet Union and China, and carried out exchange activities through academia and media.

After the meeting with President Kim Il-sung, True Parents carried out exchange and cooperation projects for peaceful reunification. On January 7, 1998, they drew up a plan for the development project of Mount Geumgang and launched Peace Motors as a company jointly invested in by the North and the South. In addition, in November 1993 they acquired the Botong River Hotel, situated in central Pyongyang, and began to run it themselves. At the Interreligious and International Federation for World Peace Annual Assembly held on August 18, 2000, at the Second Conference Room of the UN Headquarters in New York, USA, they urged the UN to take the initiative in creating a Peace Park in the Demilitarized Zone of the inter-Korean armistice line. Thus, they personally took the lead in resolving conflicts and tension on the Korean peninsula and in realizing peaceful reunification.

True Parents broke ground for the reunification of Korea through true love. They sought the path of peaceful exchange and cooperation and continued to pave the way of unification through which we can attend Heavenly Parent.

❋ Points for contemplation

1) True Parents regarded the peaceful reunification of the divided Korean peninsula as the providence of bringing Heavenly Parent's fatherland to settlement. Let us think about the value and importance for the future of humanity of the peaceful reunification of Korea.
2) Let us contemplate the ways in which we ourselves can practice the "spirit of true love" of True Parents, who taught communists at the risk of their lives.

5
Working for World Peace
– UN Renewal Movement and the International Peace Highway

True Parents' Words

The Lord who comes under these circumstances needs to unite the world, making it a place where there are no national borders and no racial barriers. He needs to unite all broken families and establish a kingdom of peace in this world that is beset by conflict between good and evil. He has to teach individuals to sacrifice for the family and nations to sacrifice for the sake of a unified world. This is the only way to achieve a unified world. Otherwise, all hope of reaching such a world will be lost. [CSG 10.4.1:11]

The present United Nations cannot achieve world peace. Every nation is fighting for its own benefit. This is not correct; it is not conscientious. That is why a religious assembly, centered on the conscience, should be part of the United Nations. The Women's

Federation for World Peace is working behind the scenes. Providentially, women should play a central role in bringing about world peace; otherwise people will continue to fight. Women need to form an organization that can stand at the center, embrace Cain and Abel, and create an atmosphere of peace throughout the world. [CSG 10.4.3:4]

Sharing Thoughts

Since the Second World War, the United Nations has done much work for world peace. However, the UN has forgotten its original purpose and is becoming an international organization that works to benefit the powerful nations. To resolve conflicts taking place in the world, the UN must become an organization that prioritizes the interests of the entire world and not just a part of it. When strong nations put their interests first and suppress other nations, the conflicts that arise thereof will only bring about more conflicts. And yet, there is nothing that today's UN can do.

For the realization of world peace, True Parents pursued the renewal of the UN. They said the UN must be reorganized under a bicameral system, with an upper house centered on religion and a lower house centered on political and diplomatic representatives. The representatives of the religious upper house must be people who can study the various religions with an open mind, centering on universal and ultimate values. They then can go beyond the interests of localities and nations and contribute toward world peace with the spirit of embracing all humanity. When they join forces and hold discussions with political leaders who have been dispatched to all nations, a conflict-free, peaceful world can be realized. A UN must be created that can stand against the injustices and crimes prevalent in the world and practice true love.

To that end, True Parents at the Interreligious and International Federation for World Peace General Assembly held on August 18, 2000, at the UN Headquarters in New York, made an official proposal for the UN to adopt the bicameral system. And on October 3, 2003, at the Manhattan Center in New York, they inaugurated the Interreligious and International Peace Council as a new UN-type organization. On September 12, 2005, they founded the Universal Peace Federation (UPF) as a new peace organization that can replace the UN, and they began to carry out their world peace movement even more actively. The Universal Peace Federation brought together from around the world ambassadors for peace who were selected as the standard-bearers of the world peace movement. UPF took up the role of protecting, safeguarding and educating the communities of the world to move toward a world of peace.

This UN renewal movement was a piece of shining wisdom for the concrete realization of world peace. It was True Parents' endeavor to bring together the knowledge of political leaders with the ability to analyze the international political situation and the wisdom of interreligious leaders with spiritual insight, so that they could work together to bring about true peace. True Parents sought the path by which all peoples can cooperate, transcending the walls of religion, ideology and race.

In addition, True Parents also advocated the International Peace Highway to transcend religion, race and nationality. They proposed the great work of uniting the entire planet as one by connecting Korea and Japan through an undersea tunnel and building a bridge over the Bering Strait that separates Russia and North America. They visualized a plan to usher in an age when people can travel freely and reach every part of the global village quickly, from the Cape of Good Hope in Africa to Santiago in Chile, and from London to New York. When human beings communicate and exchange visits with one another, transcending national borders, all boundary lines can be abolished. True Parents dream of a new future in which the cultures of the world mingle and religions came together as one.

For the International Peace Highway to be made a reality, many nations in the world need to cooperate. They need to be able to cooperate fully by not only giving financial support but also rising above their own political interests. The truth is, the money the United States spent on the war with Iraq is sufficient to build the bridge across the Bering Strait. This is a time to melt down weapons to make plows and plowshares. We should not be wasting assets amounting to billions of dollars on wars.

The International Peace Highway requires the sacrifice of those who possess more and who know more than others. It requires true love, which involves sacrificing oneself and giving everything one owns. The International Peace Highway will allow the world to communicate physically, and on that foundation the world in the future will be able to unite as one, centering on the ideology of true peace and unity.

❋ Points for contemplation
1) The reality of political issues is that they prioritize economic and political interests. Let's think about ways we can reform these issues according to True Parents' teachings
2) Let us think of projects, such as the International Peace Highway project, which are appropriate to our own local societies for overcoming political, financial, social and cultural conflicts.

6
Financial Activities for the Construction of a World of Interdependence
— Equalization of Economy and Life

True Parents' Words

In order for God to conduct the work of re-creation, we need to first prepare a proper foundational environment. Originally, in that environment human beings would be the subject partners and all things of creation their object partners. Yet as a result of the Fall, we do not have the original materials, that are necessary resources to re-create that environment where human beings can be re-created. Satan's side took them all away. Hence, we must recover them. We must re-create them. Since Satan deprived us of all the needed materials, we must recover them from Satan's world, even if it means going door to door like beggars. [CBG 10.1.1:1]

The time will come when there no longer will be a need for this policy, when there no longer is any distinction between developed and developing nations. Knowledge belongs to the entire universe; it can never belong to just one nation. That is why since the 1980s I have been promoting the sharing of technology, knowledge, material and financial resources. Currently I am promoting equality in education and technology. These days many developing nations are building technological research facilities in Germany. They are competing against one another to manufacture even individual small parts. What they need to do is to standardize their quality and sizes and then, having secured supplies of raw materials, invest time into manufacturing them. Yet because they are competing, they all are suffering tremendous losses. We now need to reconsider the international economic system and its entrenched divisions. The economy will not work well unless the world is united. [CSG 10.4.4:28]

God is not pleased with a nation that monopolizes science and technology—which He has given as a means of peace for all people—and uses it to exploit the world for its own interests. Science and technology were given to humankind for the happiness of all people. They are not only for certain white people to benefit from and use for weapons, while disregarding peace. It is from this viewpoint that I am talking about the fair distribution of technology. [CSG 10.4.4:30]

Sharing Thoughts

While traveling through Argentina, Blake Mycoskie came across children who had never worn shoes in their lives. Because they always were running barefoot on polluted soil, the children not only hurt their feet occasionally but also were exposed to parasites and diseases. Moreover, because shoes were a part of the school uniform, children without shoes could not even go to school and so were deprived of the opportunity to learn.

Blake became interested in these problems and wished to give continuous help to the children who were subjected to such a situation, and therefore he founded TOMS Shoes in 2006. Under the slogan "Shoes for Tomorrow," he adopted the policy of "One for one": When a consumer bought a pair of shoes, a pair was donated to a child in the third world.

TOMS is an example of a business that conforms to the concept of social enterprise or corporate social responsibility, which recently has become an issue. It means not just pursuing financial gains but also sharing the social public responsibility and helping one another to build a better life together.

In the originally created ideal world, everyone would obtain what they need and—going beyond the basic needs for survival, such as food, clothes and shelter—spend and consume valuably. Honest and upright products would be produced, and producers and consumers would be able to form a relationship in the market in which they put each other first.

True Parents said that we need to re-create the environment of this world, which was created through Heavenly Parent's love. However, the more advanced nations possess patents to the latest technologies in such fields as medicine and science, and they cultivate high-value businesses, whereas the less developed nations are busy maintaining their livelihood through labor-intensive industries because they completely lack the capacity to research and develop technologies. True Parents deemed this economic living environment of humankind as unprincipled and inhuman, and made efforts to restore it based on the Principle by establishing and running the Tongil Group in all regions of the world, including Germany, Korea, Japan, the United States, and China. This world's environment desired by Heavenly Parent was a political and economic living environment of interdependence, mutual prosperity and universally shared values in which people live for one another's sake and generously give to and share with others. That is why True Parents pursue the equalization of technology by publicizing and teaching patented technologies to less developed nations. They believe that corporations in advanced nations should not focus on creating their own gains and instead should show an interest in the development of cooperative firms connected to them. They also said that those corporations should be able to help nations that are in a dire financial situation.

The essential right of ownership of all matter lies with Heavenly Parent. As His children, human beings should use all things belonging to Heavenly Parent with discretion. This is known as the conversion of the right of ownership, whereas trying to own things competitively based on the egoism of human beings is the act of exercising the right of ownership under Satan's dominion. What blessed families need to endeavor to do is create an environment in which they can share and give generously with the heart of true love.

True Parents have continued to carry out financial activities centering on this philosophy of creating the environment and achieving equalization. They are endeavoring to develop and supply products for the health of humankind in such fields as beverages, health foods and pharmaceuticals; they are contributing toward the creation of a global realm of the culture of heart centered on Heavenly Parent by running travel agencies; and their resort business is leading the way toward a healthy leisure culture, as originally created. On the other hand, in Africa where there is a shortage of food, they built sausage factories and provided equipment and also taught methods of farming and cattle breeding. And with the intention of advancing science and technology in China to the level of the more advanced nations in order to realize world peace, they also pursued the Panda Motors project, which involved constructing a large automobile factory. Newly starting heavenly tribal messiahs should inherit this financial philosophy and spirit of True Parents and find a way to carry out financial activities of sharing and giving.

❈ Points for contemplation

1) Let us think of a way to resolve the problem of economic polarization in our nation or in the world through the philosophy of equalization.
2) Let us think of economic projects through which we can build the originally created economic living environment.

7
The Ocean Providence
– Ocean Providence and Development of Resources

True Parents' Words

The future leaders of the world will be those who can protect and preserve the oceans. The time is coming when humankind will invest and devote all its power, culture, traditions and national resources into developing the riches and treasures that lie at the bottom of the sea. However, the key point is who will be in a position to command the oceans and pursue that development. When I am faced with this problem, I ask myself, as the founder of the Unification Church and True Parent responsible for human history, what base of operations am I going to leave for the future of the church? That base is located at the seaside. For the future, the fishing industry and aquatic industry in the oceans have unlimited potential. [CSG 6.4.3:26]

I foresee many changes coming to the ocean-related industries. In the future, the industry will have to farm fish. Even though we are engaged in the seafood industry, I already recognized that it will be difficult for anyone to sustain their marine business in the years to come unless they combine it with tourism and develop some sort of ocean recreation industry. Everything that we do requires money and raw materials. However, above all, we must cultivate human resources and develop our personal networks. For whatever work or business we do, we need people. Especially in the marine field, our main challenge is to find people who regard work on the ocean as God's calling. We need people who will love the ocean throughout their entire lives—during their youth, middle age, and senior years—and who, before they die, will teach their sons and daughters and even their grandchildren to also love the ocean. [CBG 10.2.4:11]

Sharing Thoughts

I like to use the phrase "Alaska spirit." This refers to getting up at five o'clock in the morning, going out to sea, and not returning until well after midnight. The person stays out on the ocean until he catches the daily allowance. One cannot become a true fisherman unless he learns how to endure this way.

Catching fish is not a pleasure cruise. No matter how many fish may be in the ocean, they are not going to just jump into the

boat. It takes specialized knowledge and much experience. A person must know how to mend a net and how to tie an anchor rope. Once a person receives intense training to become a fisherman, he can go anywhere in the world and become a leader of people. Learning to be a fisherman is good leadership training.
[As a Peace-Loving Global Citizen, pp. 305–306]

True Parents emphasized the ocean as the base of life to be pioneered by humanity in the future. They devoted a great part of their lives to the ocean providence, proposing visions for the ocean and making investments unsparingly. They deemed the ocean as the central region of humankind's future life and the place where the food problem can be resolved.

The ocean providence was begun at Yamok-ri Pond and the seaside of Hwaseong, Gyeonggi Province. True Parents personally taught and trained the members on how to catch fish while visualizing the plan for the ocean providence. On June 26, 1963, at Incheon they began the project by launching the boat Cheonseung, which they had had built.

True Parents' ocean providence in Korea was then expanded centering on Jeju Island, Yeosu and Geomun Island. From the early 1970s, they ran a shipbuilding yard, a fish nursery and a tangerine farm on Jeju Island. They bought Jigwi Island, situated off the coast of Seogwipo on Jeju Island, and utilized it as the foundation for the ocean providence.

After 2003, they purchased Cheonghae Garden, located in the

Hwayang complex of Yeosu, and put it into operation as a training center, and they developed their ocean realm providence in Soho-dong by establishing the Ocean Resort and Hotel. Geomun Island was declared a holy ground on November 15, 2006, and True Parents built the Ocean Cheon Jung Gung there. After that, they sought to develop a leisure business in the oceans of Korea by bringing together Jeju Island, Chuja Island, Geomun Island, Cho Island and Yeosu. On that foundation they pursued the vision of the Pacific Rim ocean providence.

In the United States, they carried out their ocean providence centering on Gloucester, Alaska and Hawaii. Gloucester, Massachusetts, located in the northeast of the country, is a place well known for tuna fishing. When True Parents visited there, they went out to the sea early in the morning in the boat New Hope and offered jeongseong by fishing for tuna. In Alaska, they established the International Seafoods of Alaska Inc. in December 1979 to carry out the ocean providence of resolving the food problem. Hawaii was proclaimed as the central region in the Pacific Rim providence, and True Parents built the Kona Coffee Farm, a training center and a school in Mauna Kea to train people to carry on the ocean providence in the future.

In 1999, they purchased a piece of land of 680,000 hectares (more than 1.68 million acres) in Leda of the Chaco region in South America's Pantanal natural region and personally cultivated it. They built a farm and an educational center and school to make a foundation for the independence of the native population.

True Parents offered jeongseong by fishing throughout their lives with the single idea of saving fallen humanity. While offering their most devout jeongseong, they came up with ideas for various ocean projects, including ocean hotels, underwater residences and fish nursery buildings, and planned ocean businesses to resolve humanity's food problem. They put their plans into action by developing and producing fish powder, a high-protein source of food, and by catching krill, transforming it into processed foods and supplying them to less developed nations.

True Parents cared for and protected the oceans with their heart of love for nature. They personally developed the oceans, which cover two-thirds of the planet, as the settlement and treasure trove of food for humanity, and offered jeongseong for it. The ocean is the future and hope of humankind. May the newly starting heavenly tribal messiahs also inherit True Parents' love and vision for the ocean.

❈ Points for contemplation

1) Let us think of ways in which we can apply the various ocean projects developed by True Parents to our own localities.
2) At the ocean, let us personally feel the value and beauty of the world created by Heavenly Parent and offer jeongseong while deeply contemplating the oceans.

Chapter 10

Spirit World

1
Human Life That Spans Three Stages
— The Womb, Earth, and Heaven

True Parents' Words

When the time comes, we all must end our life in our mother's womb and begin our life on earth. Regardless of whether we desire it or not, the law of the universe operates this way. Then a new, vast and boundless world unfolds before us, one which we never had dreamed of or imagined. Our life in water ends and our life on earth begins. A span of ten months (by Korean reckoning) in the womb transitions into a span of 100 years of life on earth. People lead diverse lives and go through changes as they prepare for the spirit world, the world we go to after we die. That is why I tell you not to worry about dying. You are simply moving to a better place. [CSG 7.1.1:11]

Human beings live for ten months (by Korean reckoning) in the womb, 100 years in this physical world and for eternity in the spirit world. Our face has three levels: the mouth, the nose and the eyes. These represent the three ages of human life. Our mouth symbolizes the age in the womb, the material world. Our nose represents the age on the earth, the earthly, human world, and our eyes represent the age of heaven, the spirit world. The water in the womb of the mother is a universe of freedom for the baby. Even though the baby has to stay hunched up at all times and cannot kick wherever it pleases, and its nose and mouth are blocked, that place is still a universe of freedom for the baby. The vessel that supplies the baby with all that it needs joins at the navel, and the baby can breathe only through that umbilical cord. Yet that world is still a universe of freedom for the baby. [CSG 7.1.1:2]

After the age of water come the age of land and the age of light. In this regard, a person lives through three successive ages. The solar system, with the sun at its center, is always in daylight. On the other hand, night follows day on planet Earth. The spirit world is always in light. There are the ages of water and of air leading to the age of love. Love must never be extinguished. Like the light of the sun, love must be there at all times, night and day. Whether morning, afternoon or evening; whether at the North Pole, the tropics, the South Pole or anywhere else, love doesn't change. We will go to the spirit world to enter the age of love. The spirit world is like a storehouse for fruit grown and harvested during the four seasons. It is bathed in a light like that from the sun. [CSG 7.1.1:13]

Sharing Thoughts

The Family Federation for World Peace and Unification believes that Heavenly Parent created three stages of life for His children. The first is the mother's womb, the stage of water; the second is the physical world, the stage of earth; and the third is the spirit world, the stage of air. Blessed couples are those who have been given the Marriage Blessing of Heavenly Parent during the earth stage of their lives. The blessed family they create is a family which establishes heaven on earth in which three generations are unified, and peace and freedom are realized. Every moment of a blessed couple's lives will be recorded in the spirit world. You may feel that all your sacrifices and jeongseong on earth might be all in vain and go unrewarded. Do not worry. A blessed couple's lives of lofty values and ideals will be remembered by Heavenly Parent and inscribed in the universe.

Spirit world is a place full of love energy. You can travel the spirit world freely and create your own ideal place, if you trained yourself on earth with the love of children, of siblings, of husband and wife, and of parents. The images of the couples who lived a life of complete mind–body unity on Earth will take after Heavenly Parent. With that image, they will be able to enjoy infinite freedom. They will live a joyful life in the spirit world together with Heavenly Parent.

Thus, the people who understand the three stage of human life—the water stage in the womb, the land stage on earth, and the air of love stage in the spirit world—will live every day of their life practicing true love with the awareness of eternal value. This means that their life in the womb is the life preparing for the stage of earth, and their life on earth is the life that prepares them for the life in the spirit world. They do not live their life on earth just for the moment. Then what kind of world is the spirit world, and what kind of preparations do we have to make while on earth?

The spirit world is a world in which the spirits of perfected human beings harmonize with love. The incorporeal Heavenly Parent exists eternally in the incorporeal world after experiencing substantial love by residing in the physical bodies of true parents on earth. In other words, those who reached perfection on earth will rejoice the joys of perfect love when they meet the divine Heavenly Parent. Therefore, our life on earth is a period to perfect our spiritual bodies. Our spiritual bodies need to experience all realms of love. In order to do so we need to practice and manifest Heavenly Parent's blueprint of creation. The incorporeal Heavenly Parent consists of dual characteristics of yin and yang. A man and a woman should become substantiations of Heavenly Parent and create the energy of love through giving and receiving. Furthermore, when we fulfill the three great kingships and the four great realms of heart centering on Heavenly Parent, the incorporeal Heavenly Parent can enter the earthly realm to reside within our bodies and experience our characteristics in the physical world. Likewise, in our physical form we can experience Heavenly Parent's incorporeal divine characteristics. Through this, a love that is united between the spiritual world and the physical world occurs. In other words, the corporeal world and the incorporeal world become one and with this experience, we live eternally when we go to the spirit world. Therefore, on earth we should love a variety of people and perfect our love in order to achieve perfection of our characteristics. This is why True Parents made the motto of our earthly lives to "live for the sake of others".

True Parents have shown us what it's like to be an ideal blessed family united with Heavenly Parent. They have taught us that such a family can live in the spirit world while eternally reciprocating love with Heavenly Parent. Those who have embarked on the path of heavenly tribal messiah are encouraged to train themselves so that they can take after True Parents and achieve the eternal unity with Heavenly Parent in love.

❈ Points for contemplation

1) Life on earth is preparation for life in the spirit world. Let us reflect on the preparations for our life in the spirit world that we need to make during our life on earth.
2) Conjugal love between husband and wife on earth is the manifestation of one part of Heavenly Parent's integrated dual characteristics. In other words, Heavenly Parent wanted God's incorporeal blueprint to unfold on earth, the world of substance, through the love of husband and wife. What does conjugal love that is in alignment with this blueprint look like?

2
Life and Death
— Death Is the Beginning of Eternal Life

True Parents' Words

At the end of our physical life, we go through a second birth. This is death. The place where we experience our second birth, the place where we go after death, is the spirit world. As we enter that world, God, who is our third Parent, bestows upon us true love that represents the entire universe. We are supplied with the true love of God's ideal. Because there is ideal true love, there is no conflict and everything and everyone is united. At the moment of death, we leave behind our second world, the world of air, and we need to connect with our third world, the new world where we are designed to breathe love. We leave behind the love of our parents and of our siblings, go to the spirit world and ultimately enter the world of true love in harmony with God, the Original Being. Since the Original Being planted the seed, the fruit needs to return to the Original Being. [CSG 7.1.3:5]

It doesn't matter how talented, intelligent, or great a person you are. The spirit world is a realm where all such knowledge can be obtained within a week. In the spirit world, you can see with the light that exists in your heart. Through this light, you automatically understand all the relationships you engage in. This is because, by looking with your heart, you can build relationships in which you are either the subject partner or the object partner. [Sermons, 210-312, 1990.12.27]

Sharing thoughts

There is a young man who was dying of cancer. His family members and the doctor were with him. His father was crying as he wiped the sweat off his son's forehead. Then the son grabbed his father's hands and said: "Father, thank you. Because of everything you did for me, I was able to attend Seoul National University. It is all thanks to your efforts."

After some time passed, the son continued to speak: "Father, thank you. You saved me from drowning in a river when I was young. You and Mother were so joyful when I received the university acceptance letter. I can remember it vividly. But Father, why have you never talked to me about death? Why have you never talked to me about the kingdom of Heavenly Parent? Now

I fear everything." With these words, the son closed his eyes, never to open them again.

The thing the young man regretted the most was not knowing Heavenly Parent and His kingdom. What do you think about this? People normally understand death as the end of physical life. However, we who live the life of faith and know Heavenly Parent understand that death is not the end.

We have learned that our physical body may die, but we continue living in the spirit world. That is why we have to rethink life and death and clearly set our attitude toward them. We do not need to fear death, for it signifies the beginning of the second life. Rather, we should embrace death with joy and anticipation, regarding it as a new beginning. This is why we have to work diligently to cultivate the person inside us who will exist in the spirit world after physical death.

Why do human beings pass through this process of death? First, it is because their physical body can only experience love in a limited way. We need more than our physical body with its limitations to become the partner of love to Heavenly Parent, who is absolute, unique, eternal, and unchanging. That is why we have to transform into an incorporeal being who resembles Heavenly Parent. Second, it is in order to synchronize our ideals of true love with the entire universe. That is why death should be embraced not with fear but with anticipation, knowing that it is the door of happiness through which we can take ownership of true love at the level of the universe.

It is to move out of the finite physical world and into the infinite realm of the spirit world. The entire universe becomes a place where you can travel with true love. Death is the doorway to such a world. Death is like being born again. As such, we should embrace it with joy, not with fear and mourning.

How will we live in the spirit world after our physical body dies? Once we enter the spirit world, we live receiving from our parent, the Heavenly Parent, true love that represents the entire universe. In the physical world we breathe air, but in the spirit world we breathe love. Death is the moment that marks the transition from the second stage of life, the stage of air, to the third stage of life, the stage of love. We move beyond the love of children, siblings, husband and wife, and parents, and we enter the true love of Heavenly Parent, who is the owner of the great universe. Our life, which began from Heavenly Parent, reaches a conclusion and once again returns to Heavenly Parent.

Originally, human beings were created to live in a realm of resonance with Heavenly Parent. We were created to live a life of mind and body resonance. If we live centering on love in the physical world, our love is in alignment with the standard of love in the spirit world. Thus, we can feel the spirit world, even while living in the physical world. Just as we perfect our life on earth after being brought into this world through our parents and living with them, we are brought to the spirit world through Heavenly Parent, who is the original body of love in the spirit world, and we live eternally within that world of love. That is why death is the beginning of eternal life and our transition from the finite world to the infinite world. We should live our life on earth as preparation for our life in the spirit world.

❋ Points for contemplation

1) Let us contemplate the teachings of True Parents about how we should embrace death.
2) Let us reflect on ways to help people properly understand the nature of death.

3
The True Identity of the Spirit World
— Spirit World Is Our Original Homeland

True Parents' Words

The spirit world is the original garden of God's eternal ideal. How wonderful is the original garden? It is beyond description. Even if you were to gaze at just one of the secrets in the palace of the heavenly kingdom, you would not tire of the sight even after ten thousand years. Your lifetime on earth is a mere instant. The spirit world, on the other hand, is eternal. Compared to your life in the spirit world, your life on earth is shorter than a breath. [CSG 7.2.1:2]

The spirit world is an eternal place that seeks eternal elements. A spirit person who has experienced love on earth will unfailingly and automatically be drawn into that world. That person gravitates to the part of the spirit world that has as much love as he felt here on earth. Then what kind of place is the spirit world? It is a world of harmony brimming with love, where everything is imbued with love. It is not wrong to assert that this entire universe is put in motion by a single press of the button of love. [CSG 7.2.1:5]

It is important for you to understand the spirit world. What happens when you learn about what your ancestors from thousands of years ago are doing in the spirit world? By understanding clearly that you inevitably will face the same fate, you can transcend difficult problems on this earth. Because I know all this, I do not despair, no matter what persecution I receive. Because I know much more than this, because I know where the highest value lies, I can ignore and overcome all difficulties. [CSG 7.2.1:1]

Sharing Thoughts

A Christian doctor visited a gravely ill patient. The patient asked him, "Doctor, will I be able to recover?" The doctor said, "Well, it seems unlikely." Then the patient said, "I'm afraid of death. Do you know what lies ahead, beyond the grave?" The doctor answered honestly, "No. I don't know anything about what will happen after death." At that moment, the door was flung open and, wagging his tail, the doctor's dog ran inside and jumped onto the doctor's lap.

The doctor turned to the patient and began to speak. "See. The dog is unfamiliar with this room, but he jumped right in without fear because he knew his master was inside. I don't know what will happen after death, but I can tell you one thing with certainty, that Heavenly Parent is there. That is sufficient. Let go of your fear and place your trust in Him. When the door opens, you will travel into the world of light without any fear in your heart."

What is your understanding of the spirit world? In the spirit world, everyone experiences infinite joy and happiness as the children of Heavenly Parent. If Heavenly Parent laughs, everyone laughs. If Heavenly Parent runs, everyone runs. Heavenly Parent has been creating people that represent the universe. These people include white people, black people, and Asian people. Everyone is the same. Human beings are like the cells in Heavenly Parent's body. We are all like cells to Heavenly Parent. The spirit world is composed of people who are Heavenly Parent's partners. This is why we have to become one of Heavenly Parent's people.

The spirit world is also an infinite world that transcends time and space. If you say, "I want to meet a person who lived with such and such a heart on earth!" then you can meet that person instantly. In the spirit world, your thoughts can materialize. You also can meet anyone, however far that person may be, with the power of true love. The power of true love allows you to visit your homeland in an instant. The spirit world is an infinite world; it is a place where you can travel freely through true love. True love is faster than anything. Once our mind and body attain the unified foundation of love, we can visit everywhere in the spirit world. The spirit world is a place filled with the element of love. It is filled with love like earth is filled with air. Human beings breathe air on earth, and they breathe love in the spirit world. The spirit world is not a place where you give and take shallow love. The love reciprocated in the spirit world is the true love.

In the end, everyone has to go to the spirit world. The spirit world is the original homeland and everyone's final destination. The physical world is the homeland of our physical body, and the spirit world is the original homeland of our spirit. That is why we have to spend our time in the physical world to prepare for our life in the spirit world.

The spirit world is the place where we become unified by the power of true love. Those who wish to live there have to attain mind–body unity through true love. However, people's minds and bodies, religion and politics, and the spirit and physical worlds are divided because true love has not yet emerged. In the end, everything has to be united centering on true love. Individuals, families, societies, nations, the world, and the universe—everything can be connected. We must realize this through our own efforts. Otherwise, the original heaven on earth and in heaven cannot begin. That is why we must have a clear picture of the spirit world. We have to work hard. Blessed family members should perfect and liberate themselves so that they can march forward straight into Heaven without imperfections holding them back.

❋ Points for contemplation

1) Let us reflect on the differences between our lives in the physical world and the spirit world. Let us contemplate this through the teachings of True Parents.
2) Let us reflect on True Parents' teachings which refer to the spirit world as "the world filled with light" and "the world overflowing with love."

4
Experiencing the Spirit World through Prayer and Jeongseong

– Experiencing the Spirit World in Our Lives through Jeongseong

True Parents' Words

Those who have practiced a life of prayer will know this. When you pray, a great and mighty power will come to you. Thus, through that power, the eyes of a person who prays can see in both the physical world and the spirit world. God has carried out His providence through the religious foundation to make a connection between the supernatural realm of substantial ideology and humankind. By stimulating people's core emotions, He causes them to desire to go to such a realm. By so doing, God is trying to connect us to the transcendental plane. [CSG 7.3.3:4]

In general, people who are spiritually adept may not have clear perception with regard to the truth. They start out strong on one side, but they are weak on the other side. Since they are not consistent throughout, they cannot make their way forward. At one time or another, they will roll over and fall down. Conversely, if the side of truth is big but the spiritual side is small, that person cannot keep going. Therefore you need to make an effort to balance these two aspects in your daily life. The Bible says to worship "in spirit and truth;" that is, with prayer and with truth. This means you need to reach a level where you can balance the two aspects and harmonize them. Human beings are meant to mediate between the spirit world and the physical world. You therefore need to become people who can mediate by standing at the center of the spirit world and at the center of the world of truth. Unless you become such people, you cannot attain the position of perfection. [CSG 7.3.3:3]

Sharing Thoughts

There is a saying in Korea, "Sincerity can move Heaven." It means that your sincerity may touch Heavenly Parent's heart and help you to reach your goal. How much sincerity would we need to touch Heavenly Parent's heart? Have you ever offered jeongseong so sincerely that you have touched Heavenly Parent's heart? Do you want to offer prayer and jeongseong and know what you have to do?

Our mind has a door. This door is called the "mind door." Our prayer and jeongseong should be done during the time when this door is open. If you have prayed a lot, you will understand that it feels different depending on which time of the day you pray. There is a clear difference between praying in the early morning, when everything is quiet, and praying in broad daylight. If you pray deeply, you will understand that your prayer will be different depending on the time of the day. Therefore, you should select your time carefully when you pray. With careful selection, your prayer can resonate better with Heavenly Parent. When praying at an effective time, your mind door will open more easily. True Parents revealed to us that human beings can experience the emotions of Heavenly Parent when Heavenly Parent's mind door and the person's mind door are both open and move together in perfect synchronization. We can only enter this state of being if we train ourselves with many prayers.

In the next step, we need to develop our mind field. We can develop our mind field and discover the direction that leads toward it only if we first discover Heavenly Parent, who stands in the subject-partner position. However, experiencing Heavenly Parent is not an easy task. The only way to connect myself to Heavenly Parent is to focus my mind and start from the heart. If we start from the heart, the heart naturally will know the way. It will follow the path as magnets know which way is north. No matter which direction you started praying at, your body will turn automatically if you enter this mysterious state. From this, we can know that the mind door exists. There are even places that are better for praying than other places. Likewise, there are places with many evil spirits. Such places are yin places. Places that are full of yin energy or yang energy are essentially that way because of the kind of spirits that dwell in there. You can have complete knowledge of this after a few experiences.

We should reflect on how we have followed True Parents so far, and what kind of efforts we have invested to live an ideal life. We have to think about where we are now and where we need to go. For that, we must be able to experience the spirit world while in the physical world. To experience the spirit world means to experience and live together with Heavenly. That is why we always have to offer prayer and jeongseong and remember that Heavenly Parent is always with us. If you continue such a life of prayer and jeongseong, you will speak, though you don't try to, and you will naturally move, though you don't try to move. In other words, when you start the day, you can think first about what lies ahead and through prayer ask Heaven for answers. You will feel great joy if your day turns out as you were directed by Heaven in the morning through prayer. Things like this can happen when your prayers and jeongseong increase your level of resonance with the spirit world and your thoughts and the spiritual inspirations become the same as reality.

We have to experience the spirit world often in order to enhance our spiritual senses. Just as water is like air to the fish, love is like air to the people who are in the spirit world. We have to practice breathing love in the physical world. Experiencing the spirit world can be helpful in this regard. By practicing this, we will be able to breathe love together with Heavenly Parent and establish a relationship of experience with Him. Hence, our faith will materialize in our everyday life. That is why we should always offer prayer and jeongseong and open our mind door to live centered on true love.

When the heart of Heavenly Parent and the heart of a human being are unified through experiences, we will be able to experience the spirit world even in the physical world.

❈ Points for contemplation

1) Plan your day in the morning through prayer. At the end of each day, through prayer think about what happened during the day and write down if there were any changes.
2) Let us reflect on how to clarify our mind centering on True Parents' teachings on the mind door and mind field.
3) Let us reflect on how to develop a habit of praying, and how to focus our life on Heavenly Parent.

5
Life in the Physical World to Prepare for Eternal Life

— Life in the Spirit World Is the Fruit of the Life in the Physical World

True Parents' Words

Blessed marriage and eternal life begin from True Parents. They cannot exist without True Parents. True Parents need to resolve these astonishing matters and bring about the unification of the spirit world and the physical world, as well as unity within the earthly world. The world is bound to first oppose me and then follow me. Without going before God and receiving the royal seal, the unity of the spirit world and the unity of the physical world cannot be achieved. No matter how much the earth opposes me, it cannot block the way I am meant to go. The time will come when the angelic world and the spirit world will be mobilized. Ancestors will be mobilized to bring paralyzing nightmares and to grasp the necks of those who do not follow me, similar to what Satan has been doing. [CSG 7.3.4:1]

When you go to the spirit world, no one tells you to go to hell. You go there on your own. You go to the place that matches your own level.

Even in the case of Unification Church members, though the goal is to go to the same realm, where you come to dwell will depend on your spiritual state. Then in what ways are blessed families different? The members of a blessed family cannot be separated from each other, no matter how hard they try. When you pass to the spirit world, if the wife failed to fulfill her responsibility, the husband must take joint responsibility and resolve this. Whether the wife has done wrong or the husband has done wrong, or whether it is the sons and daughters who have done wrong, they are all involved. Since the kingdom of heaven is a place where the family must enter together, the family must be united. If a member of that family has done wrong, the whole family must wait until the wrongdoing of that family member can be resolved and atoned for. That is why, one way or another, each family member needs to reach perfection on this earth before passing into the spirit world. [CSG 7.3.4:11]

Sharing Thoughts

Two men visited a rabbi to have a conversation. One man wanted to repent for stealing someone's property. However, the other man was certain that he had led a life of relative goodness because he hadn't committed any major crime. The rabbi said to the first man, "Go outside and bring me a large rock." Then he spoke to the other man. "Go pick up ten small rocks."

The two men did what the rabbi told them. Then the rabbi said, "Now, carry those rocks back to where you found them." The men stepped out of the rabbi's house. The man who had one large stone could easily remember where he had picked it up. However, the man with many small stones could not remember where he got them. The rabbi spoke to the men: "Sin is similar to this. You who brought the large stone must have repented for your sin many times in the past. However, you with many small stones may not have committed a serious crime, but you have forgotten about all the small wrongs you committed. Everyone in this world commits sins, large or small. You will not enter Heaven unless you repent for each and every one of them."

True Parents have taught us many times that it is important for us to use our time in the physical world to prepare ourselves for the life in the spirit world. However, life's challenges can overwhelm us and we find ourselves neglecting this preparation. True Parents have emphasized that a good life is necessary for a good death. A good death means that you are starting your life in the spirit world in the best spiritual state possible. Living a good life means that your preparation for the spirit world has been impeccable. Anyone who lived his life in the physical world for the sake of others has no reason to fear death. Happy are the people who helped others walk the path of happiness. Anyone who lived a true life of shedding tears for others' pains and limitations lived a life of eliminating his fallen nature. Anyone who gave a piece of his life to another person has experienced transforming his life to that of a divine life. Such a life is a shining example of what a life of living for the sake of others can be.

We need to live a life that can be recognized with high regard once we go to the spirit world. That is why we have to live each day of our physical life preparing for our life in the spirit world. If our family as a whole does not attain this level of life, we will find ourselves stuck in a less-than-perfect stage. Ripened fruit is stored in a warehouse, whereas rotten fruit is thrown into a trash can. Living just for the moment may feel sweet, but we must remember that what lies ahead is a bitter reality with unfulfilled responsibilities. However, those who invest their physical life for the sake of their eternal life may experience hardships and difficulties, but their efforts will be rewarded with great joy and happiness.

We have to use our time in the physical plane to prepare a victorious foundation for our life in the spirit world. We need to live a life that can be recognized favorably in the eyes of heavenly law. We need to be clearly aware that "a victorious foundation is laid not with our thoughts alone but also with our actions." We must remember that our entrance into Cheon Il Guk will not be determined by our thoughts and concepts, but rather by our everyday life in the physical realm. When we go to the spirit world, we bring with us the results of our love. That is why we have to stack up as many results of love as we can to use in the spirit world. The fastest way to achieve this is to create a standard by which you have loved 430 families by completing your heavenly tribal messiah activity.

✤ Points for contemplation
1) Let us reflect on what we can do to connect the world of thoughts and the world of action.
2) We determine what kind of life we will live in the spirit world. Loving many people and being accepted as their spiritual parent surely will make our life in the physical world a fruitful one. Let us silently reflect on this.

Chapter 11

The Path of the Heavenly Tribal Messiah

1
Heavenly Parent's Standard of Jeongseong

— Heavenly Parent Is Not a Magician

True Parents' Words

When God created this universe … people read the story in the Bible and think that God created this universe with the flip of a finger. However, if that's to be the case, then we can't say that this universe has much value of love. The universe wouldn't have any value that deserves our love. We can have a much deeper relationship and fellowship with the universe if God had invested a tremendous amount of effort into creating it. [*Sermons*, 87-318, 1976.06.27]

Christianity today still believes in God as found in the Bible. However, there is faith even within God. As long as Heavenly Parent, Himself, has endless concepts for creation, He has the conviction to bring it into realization. Even God has things that He has absolute convictions about. [*Sermons*, 3-18, 1957.09.08]

If Adam smiles, God smiles. If Adam frowns, God frowns. Where Adam goes, God follows. Where Adam is, there God is. That is why the perfection of God follows the perfection of humans. That is the kind of perfection about which everyone is happy. Everything is meant for that perfection. In other words, everything exists for the sake of that perfection. Those who belong to a religion say that they practice their religion for human perfection. However, what do they mean by perfection? It means the perfection of love. [Sermons, 96-210–212, 1978.01.22]

What is the supreme objective of God? It is to relate to human beings as His own sons and daughters. It is the world where what human beings feel is felt by the universe and ultimately by God. God wanted us to be one with Him and, through that unity, experience His amazing love. This is the ultimate purpose of God's creation. [Sermons, 3-26–27, 1957.09.15]

Sharing thoughts

The book of Genesis in the Bible says that Heavenly Parent created heaven and earth in six days. Genesis tells us of a Heavenly Parent who can do and make anything He wishes, like a magician. It seems that all it required for Him to create everything in the universe, including us, was a mere utterance of the words: "Let there be." We should not think that Heavenly Parent's creation was completed easily in a day.

A long time ago, there was a king. The king was getting many complaints, which placed a lot of pressure on him. There was a head of a local county who sexually assaulted many women. The story of his actions spread throughout the country. The king finally decided to have both of his eyes pulled out, and this was to be the punishment for those who commit a similar crime. The kingdom was quiet for a while until a criminal was caught and brought to the king. Furious, the king ordered the sentence to be carried out on the criminal. However, it turned out that the criminal was none other than the king's only son.

The subjects of the kingdom wondered if the king would carry out the same punishment for his beloved prince. On the day when the punishment was to be carried out, the king ordered the criminal to be taken out of the prison. Then he gave the order: "Pluck his eyes out." The people of the kingdom nervously watched the execution of the sentence. When one eye was pulled out and the other was about to be pulled, the king said, "Wait. His other eye is here." Then he pulled out one of his own eyes and gave it to the executioner. The people of the kingdom were so greatly moved by the king's resolve that no one dared to commit any crime.

Heavenly Parent is an omniscient and omnipotent being of love. It would seem that He can do anything He wishes. However, Heavenly Parent exists in accordance with His principles and laws.

Heavenly Parent must abide by the principles and laws that He created. That is why Heavenly Parent is unable to do anything that is in violation of His principles and laws. It is the same as the king in the story who could not forgive his son who committed a crime in violation of the law that the king had created.

Heavenly Parent created the universe in strict accordance with His plans, laws, and regulations. Heavenly Parent did not create the universe solely through His words. Heavenly Parent did not create the universe simply by waiting for days. He invested unfathomable time and effort in every stage of His creation. Heavenly Parent did this so that His creation is also in accordance with the principles and laws that He defined. That is why True Parents said, "The universe is the culmination of Heavenly Parent's sincere jeongseong." [Sermons, 18-52]

Heavenly Parent does not want to be an omnipotent and omniscient being who is far away from human beings. He wants to be our parent. He invested an unfathomable amount of time and effort into guiding human beings back to Him. For 6,000 biblical years, He has been raising central figures to guide His lost children back to His embrace. He has been investing so much sincere jeongseong to lead his providence of restoration through indemnity. At each stage, He guided the human beings through His central figures, praying that humanity would advance to the next stage of restoration. He spent untold amounts of time waiting for His creation to come to fruition. He felt the same heart of a parent who is waiting for the child who ran away from home. Then, after 4,000 years, when Jesus Christ, His only begotten son, was born on earth, Heavenly Parent was filled with immense hope that the day of reclaiming His children was near. However, His tears of hope became those of pain and remorse when Jesus was crucified. He had to wait another 2,000 years for True Father, His only begotten son, and True Mother, His only begotten daughter, who could wipe the tears from His cheeks and bring salvation to humanity. Heavenly Parent's tears fell like a waterfall in 1960, the year the Holy Marriage Blessing took place. Now, the realization of His dream is finally at hand again, thanks to True Parents. We are now at the stage where Heavenly Parent, who existed as an incorporeal being, can wear the body of True Parents to rule this world directly. When their children suffer, the parents' suffering is many times greater than that of the children. Then the parents offer sincere jeongseong to Heaven to alleviate their children's pain. Heavenly Parent is omnipotent and omniscient, but these characteristics alone cannot create love.

✲ Points for contemplation

1) Heavenly Parent followed the principles and laws that He created while walking the course of human salvation. What kind of principles and laws should parents have within their family? Let us reflect on this question.
2) Heavenly Parent spent a long time trying to restore His lost children. What kind of jeongseong should we offer to Heaven in order to shed ourselves of our fallen natures and go to our Heavenly Parent?

2
True Parents' Standard of Jeongseong
– A Standard of Devotion Never Before Seen in the History of Humankind

True Parents' Words

People who cannot love other people and nature cannot love God. Nature is the symbolic body of God, and humans are God's body in substance. Therefore, only the people who are capable of loving people and nature can love God. [Sermons, 70-182, 1974.02.09]

To be loved by God, we have to understand how precious are the things that are loved by God. To be a human being loved by God, we must experience the joy of loving all of His creation. We have to experience this to the level where we even forget about our own existence. Even our own life has to be spent for all of God's creation. Only then, can we deserve His love. [Sermons, 133-26–27, 1984.07.01]

I, too, worry about how I can invest my life to offer jeongseong to Heaven. I lament for the reality that I cannot offer more loyalty to Heaven when my body is beat and my hope fading. I offer jeongseong to Heaven with the determination that I will spend each day like 1,000 years. When offering jeongseong, you must set a standard for yourself that no one else can fulfill and that you are completely inseparable from. You have to offer jeongseong with a standard that surpasses that of your countless ancestors or those who walked a similar path. Then how do we set a standard that, when completed, would allow us to leave the physical world without any regret? We have to offer as much jeongseong as possible. If your jeongseong is a valley, it has to be the deepest there is. If your jeongseong has a peak, you have to reach the highest point. For this, we must be able to repent while sleeping, repent while eating, and repent throughout the day. We have to have that kind of heart. [Sermons, 26-122–128, 1969.10.19]

Sharing Thoughts

It was shortly after the beginning of the Korean War. U.S. soldiers were retreating into a deep valley when they heard the crying of an infant. One of the soldiers tried to save the baby covered in snow. The soldier was shocked when he uncovered the snow from the baby and discovered the baby's dead mother, completely naked, still clutching her arms around her newborn. The mother must have been trapped inside the valley while fleeing southward to safety. She took off all her clothes and covered her baby. Then, to protect the baby from freezing to death, she wrapped her arms around the baby, choosing to save the infant at the cost of her own life. Flooded with emotion, the U.S. soldier dug a grave for the mother and raised the baby boy as his own son.

Once the son became a young adult, the soldier told his son the truth about the rescue. They visited the grave where his mother had been put to rest. The son who had gained newfound knowledge about how he came to life knelt before the grave and began to cry. Endless tears fell from his eyes and wet the ground on which his mother was buried. After a long time of sobbing, the son finally stood up. He took off his clothes one by one until he was completely naked. He swept off all the snow that was covering his mother's grave. Then, still weeping, the son covered the grave with his clothes and said, "Mother, how cold you must have been!"

Our parents are the ones who gave us our life. Without our parents, we would not have been born into this world and could not have grown into the person we are today. Our parents sacrificed themselves and raised us with love and jeongseong. The grace we received from our parents is as wide and far as the ocean, but our parents will no longer be with us by the time we realize the true value of their sacrifice.

Heavenly Parent is our parent. Heavenly Parent has sacrificed much in order to save us, just like the mother in the story. He is investing an unfathomable amount of jeongseong to reclaim his children.

To Jewish people, Heavenly Parent is a formidable entity whose name has to be uttered with fear. To them, Heavenly Parent was the dispenser of punishment to those who violated His law. Two thousand years ago, Jesus revealed to us that Heavenly Parent is not a punisher but our Father. Then True Parents revealed to us that Heavenly Parent is not just our Father but our Heavenly Parent.

True Parents know about the jeongseong of Heavenly Parent more than anyone else. That is why they have lived a life of immense jeongseong, in order to express their gratitude for Heavenly Parent's jeongseong. True Father met Jesus at Mount Myodu near his hometown when he was 15 years old. Jesus passed on his unfinished mission to True Father, who accepted the mission. True Father became one with Jesus when he conveyed his sorrowful heart to Father. The old headquarters church in Cheongpa-dong in Seoul has wooden floors. When True Father prayed on the second floor, the wooden floor would be completely drenched with his tears, and the water often would drip down to the first floor. When he went to the ocean, he spent his time communicating with Heavenly Parent and planning the course of the Providence with prayer and jeongseong.

In the early days, he often would hear testimonies given by some of the elder members. Every time, Father would pay more attention to the story than the person giving the testimony. Father would feel for the member who went through a course of pain and suffering. This was his way of uniting with the members. The members whose stories Father listened to attentively testified that they determined to live up to True Parents' level of jeongseong. Providence sometimes is delayed through a sacrificial event. When this happened, Father always consoled the heart of Heavenly Parent who wants to restore His children as fast as possible.

Confucius taught that "Jeongseong is the course of heaven, and to realize jeongseong is the course of humankind."

True Parents spent their entire lives realizing Heavenly Parent's dream. They willingly walked the course of pain and suffering to become Heavenly Parent's body in substance and to restore His lost children.

❋ Points for contemplation

1) Let us reflect on True Parents' sincere jeongseong toward Heavenly Parent for the salvation of humankind.
2) We must follow True Parents' footsteps to achieve perfection. In this regard, to whom should we offer our jeongseong?

3
Sincerity Moves the Universe

— When We Offer Jeongseong, Even the Created World Is Moved

True Parents' Words

Everything a Unification Church member touches, whether it be of a secular material or something that's in the church, is a holy thing. You have to handle such things with respect, knowing that the thing you are interacting with is a holy thing. If you are handling an antique, think of that object as the holiest thing in the world. Know that the object you are using is an object that God created. At the same time, you should want that holy object to touch you the same way you touch it. You need to feel that the object will be grateful to you for touching it. Even when you are sitting on a chair, you must feel that you are sitting on the best chair in the world, that you are sitting on a holy object that is the best in human history. In short, you should treat everything as holy. Handle everything as a holy object. [Sermons, 102-112–118, 1978.11.27]

It is said that if you are sincere enough, you can enter a mysterious state in which you can feel the joyous emotion of the object. If you find a person who has offered more jeongseong to Heaven than you, then you have to hand over that object to that person. If something that belongs to you can be used for the nation, then you should give it to the nation instead of your children. If it can be used for the entire world, you should give it to the world. That is justice. That is the right way to use your object. [*Sermons*, 31-252–253, 1970.06.04]

The shortcut to protecting nature is to develop a heart that loves nature. We must be able to shed a tear at the sight of even a blade of grass that we see as we walk along the road. We must be able to grab hold of a tree and weep. We must understand that God's breath is hidden inside a single boulder or a single gust of wind. To care for and love the environment is to love God. We must be able to see each creature created by God as an object of our love. With our spiritual eyes open, we could see that a single dandelion by the roadside is more valuable than the gold crowns of kings. [*As a Peace-Loving Global Citizen*, p. 314]

Sharing Thoughts

Professor Ueno at Tokyo University received a cute puppy with snow-white fur and beautiful eyes as a present. The puppy was named Hachi, and the professor loved him greatly. Hachi grew to be a healthy dog. Wanting to spend more time with his master, Hachi would walk to the train station with the professor every day. He also came to the station for the professor on the way back home. One day, Professor Ueno's life abruptly ended in the middle of a class. Not knowing this, Hachi came to the train station every night, longing for his master to come back. Days became weeks and weeks became years. He came to the train station every night for ten years. People were moved by his sincere loyalty and decided to pass this beautiful story on to the future generations by erecting a statue of Hachi in 1934. Hachi waited for the return of his master all his life and finally passed away one year after the completion of the statue dedicated to him.

In *The Book of Changes*, which is said to be a book frequently read by Confucius, there is a saying, "Sincerity can move the universe." It means that sincere jeongseong can move even the hearts of objects. It teaches us to be as sincere as possible while relating to nature. Just as we can see from the story, Hachi was so moved by the love of his master that he spent his entire life yearning to see his master again. Nature is a symbol of Heavenly Parent's image, and also another image of ourselves.

People use the term "pet" often. Pet could mean an animal that we can enjoy like a toy and throw away when we are tired of it. However, some people now use the term "animal partner." This is used not only for dogs but also for cats. The term "animal partner" derives from calling our spouse a life partner. Calling our pets "animal partners" elevates their status to be equal to ours.

It may seem that we human beings are in control of the universe. However, the universe will not want to be controlled unless it is taken care of with a loving heart. We discover the image of Heavenly Parent in nature. We need to develop our original character through such discoveries. Destroying nature ultimately will lead to the destruction of humanity. On the other hand, nature can be as warm as Heavenly Parent's embrace if we take care of it well. That is why we need to conserve our resources and protect nature. People in today's materialistic age have been destroying the environment and frivolously consuming natural resources. A society filled with people whose primary concern is ownership of material things will lead to the loss of humanity. However, nature will protect us if we protect nature.

❋ Points for contemplation

1) Have you ever thought of nature as the symbolic image of Heavenly Parent? We have in our possession things that are acquired from nature. Which resources should we conserve, and what kind of attitude should we have toward them?
2) Nature and humankind can live in harmony and mutual protection. The universe created by Heavenly Parent is designed to reward the people who conserve and protect it. Let us reflect on this matter.

4
Sincerity Moves People
— Jeongseong Moves People:
Ways of Communication That Inspire Others

True Parents' Words

Think of other people as the holy sons of God. You need to truly feel that you are conveying heavenly fortune to whomever you relate. The question is whether you can have the same heart with which God wants to relate to them. Think of others as holy people. Think of them as the holy body of God. In other words, you have to truly feel that whomever you meet is the best person, even like a saint, on earth. [Sermons, 102-112–118, 1978.11.27]

When listening to them, listen carefully. When speaking to them, speak with your blood, sweat, and tears. I know it sounds rather scary. You have to close in on them like this. My back would be completely wet from sweating whenever I gave a sermon in Korea. My shirt and underclothes would be drenched in sweat, and beads of sweat would drip from my hair. So be very sincere when you are listening to what they say. If you listen to an elderly lady, be prepared to listen to her story for 12 hours, even 20 hours. Stay up all night if you have to. … Unless you do that, the Cain won't join your side. The Cain-type people will not join you unless you allow them to spill out everything they accumulated in the satanic realm. [*Sermons*, 96-323, 1978.02.13]

Sharing thoughts

When do we feel respected? We normally feel respected when someone listens carefully to what we say. That is why Heavenly Parent gave us one mouth and two ears. In other words, we need to spend more time listening to others than speaking to them. Pay more attention to what others say to you than what you say to them.

Before the American Civil War, a young man came to a farm in Ohio to work. The young man spent hours milking the cows and taking care of other farm duties. He slept on a haystack and spent every waking hour sincerely worrying about completing his jobs. The farm owner's daughter fell in love with the strong and responsible young man, but her father forbade her from marrying him, saying he didn't have any money or future. In the end, the young man left the farm, leaving behind only his name, "Jim."

After 35 years had passed, the farm owner discovered a name carved on a side of the dry hay storage. The name read "James A.

Garfield," and there was another name written: "Jim." The young man who left the farm 35 years earlier with his heart broken by a farm owner who ignored him for his lack of money was none other than the 20th president of the United States.

We can learn from this story that the farm owner "judged the book by its cover" and failed to see the true value of the young man who was destined for great things. We need to have an attitude of sincerely understanding others. We need to understand what troubles them, what their problems are. To empathize with someone means to feel the other person's feelings. We have to invest a lot of effort into understanding the other person wholly. We can now see the true value of True Father's teaching.

> "In the past, they couldn't understand me. The people at the Headquarters said, 'Oh, man, Father is going to stay up all night listening to that grandmother's story again. Father, just kick her out!' That's what they said. Would they like you if you ignored them like that? She would have simply gone to her husband or her sons. You have to be liked more than she likes her own kin. You have to listen to what she says sincerely and speak sincerely. That is the secret. Be sincere in listening to their stories and sincere in speaking to them. How about you? You should also listen to an elderly lady; be prepared to listen to her story for 12 hours, even 20 hours. Practice listening to a person's story all night long." [Sermons, 96-323, 1978.02.13]

True Father's sincere way of treating others reminds us of the saying "Sincerity moves people." Anyone whose story was heard by Father for ten or even 20 hours, and then listened to his sincere words would have felt deeply appreciated by Father and happy to be with him. The members were happy to be around Father because he always listened to their stories sincerely.

❋ Points for contemplation

1) What do we like more: to speak or to listen? If we practice listening, people will want to tell us their stories. They can draw their own conclusion after they finish telling their story. Let us reflect on how we should treat others.

2) What do you think is the way to move people's hearts? Let us reflect on this question.

5
Sincerity Moves People
— I See in You the Face of Heavenly Parent

True Parents' Words

What were human beings originally created as? Human beings were created as the princes and princesses of God. Originally we were supposed to born as a baby, and, after completely maturing through the growth stages, we were to become God's body in substance. Then why did God create human beings? He did so to have relationships. Love requires a partner. To form love, the partner and I must stand in a position of relationship. Establishing the goodness of love absolutely requires a partner. This is why God created Adam and Eve as His body. What would have happened if Adam and Eve had attained perfection? Had they perfected themselves and entered the stage where they could receive the Blessing, what would have happened? They would have established the most universal and fundamental unity centered around one love. This would have led to their unity in body with God, and God and human beings would have had the first integrated beginning within this realm of the created universe. What is that beginning?

It is love. Love. Our beginning point should have been love. Then what kind of love is that love? It is the love of God. [*Sermons*, 18-149, 1967.06.04]

We all know the story of how Jesus washed his disciples' feet. You can't unite with your people unless you establish that kind of tradition. I have been doing just that. Once I heard that the children of my enemy were starving. I gave everything I had to them, save for my underwear and a bag. I lived the entire following week with nothing but underwear and a bag. Then I sold even the bag to raise money for them. Why did I do it? It was not because I was ignorant. It was because I had to walk the course of restoration, and for this I had to set an absolute condition that I loved my enemies. There are not many people who can do this. I did this because I had to live the words of the Bible: "Love thy enemy." [*Sermons*, 23-320, 1969.06.08]

Sharing Thoughts

"If I [Jacob] have found favor in your [Esau's] eyes, accept this gift from me. For to see your face is like seeing the face of Heavenly

Parent, now that you have received me favorably."

Esau was Jacob's older brother. When their father became very old, Esau was to receive his father's blessing and the right of inheritance. However, Jacob tricked his blind father and stole the blessing of the first son, which was to be bestowed on Esau. Then he fled to the land of Haran and lived in hiding for 21 years. After losing his birthright to his younger brother, Esau pledged—every single day for 21 years—to take revenge on his brother. After many years passed, Jacob felt bad for Esau who still was waiting to kill him. Jacob amassed a fortune, and after 21 years, he decided to return to his homeland. Jacob gave all his assets and property to his older brother, and at the first moment of their reunion, Jacob said, "For to see your face is like seeing the face of Heavenly Parent." At this very moment, Esau's cold heart, filled with thoughts of revenge, melted completely. Jacob did not utter these words just to avoid the impending doom. He thought of his older brother whenever possible. He prayed and offered jeongseong for his brother, and he tried hard to grow to the stage where he would be reminded of Heavenly Parent's face when seeing his older brother's face. Jacob was able to cleanse the hatred from his enemy's heart because he put himself in the position of Heavenly Parent's love. Even that enemy is someone who needs to be restored in Heavenly Parent's eyes. Esau, moved by his brother's love, threw away his knife and put his arms around Jacob, shedding tears of forgiveness.

True Father, too, invested a lot of effort to see the face of Heavenly

Parent in the face of his enemies. How else was he supposed to embrace Mikhail Gorbachev and Kim Il-sung, mortal enemies who had tried to have him assassinated? He was able to do so because he offered an immense amount of jeongseong to Heaven to see the face of Heavenly Parent in the faces of his enemies. He overcame his hatred for his enemies and saw them with the loving eyes of Heavenly Parent. Even they needed to be restored in Heavenly Parent's eyes. Gorbachev was moved when he saw True Father treating him as Heavenly Parent Himself.

True Father's meeting with Kim Il-sung was more surreal than Hollywood movies. Risking his life, True Father stood before the top leaders of North Korea and criticized Kim Il-sung's Juche ideology, telling them to believe in Heavenly Parent. True Father's action was as dangerous as criticizing Kim Il-sung openly in North Korea. However, Kim Il-sung embraced True Father because he knew the depth of True Parents' love and jeongseong. He was moved because True Parents offered jeongseong to Heaven so that they could see the face of Heavenly Parent in Kim Il-sung's face. The true love of brotherhood materialized because their hearts were both melted with the love of Heavenly Parent.

Now we can understand the meaning of "Love thy enemy." In the eyes of Heavenly Parent, even our enemies deserve to be saved. This is because Heavenly Parent's work of restoration must be completed with every human being. In that sense, it may be a little paradoxical to "see the face of Heavenly Parent" in your enemy's face. However, we can do this by not seeing others as mere human beings—instead, seeing them through the eyes of Heavenly Parent. Everyone is created in the image of Heavenly Parent. If you return to the original heart, the heart of Heavenly Parent, you can see His face in anyone's face.

True Father said that he gave everything he had when he heard that his enemy's children were starving. He told us that he was able to "walk the course of restoration" when he gave everything he possessed to the children of his enemy, whom he found extremely difficult to forgive. This is difficult to do unless you forgive everything from the bottom of your heart and see the face of Heavenly Parent in the face of your enemy.

We live in an extremely complicated web of relationships. We sometimes suffer because of enemies whose faces we cannot even bear to look at. What would happen if we worked hard to see Heavenly Parent's face in our enemies' faces? Wouldn't our relationship with people naturally improve? We should go beyond physical appearances and try to look at other people with the eyes of Heavenly Parent.

✼ Points for contemplation

1) We meet many people in our lifetime, including our family members. We should treat everyone with the heart of Heavenly Parent who wants to restore them. Let us reflect on this statement.
2) Are there any people whom you hate? How can we discover the face of Heavenly Parent in their faces? Let us reflect.

6
Sincerity Moves People
– Let Us Die Loving Our Enemies as Our Friends

True Parents' Words

We have to use the opportunity to love our enemy, to live out the words in the Bible, "Love thy enemy." Until now because of that, when I see someone come to our Unification Church who has no clothes to wear or whose clothes are mended over and over again, I give them money to buy clothes. I never had the chance to buy new clothes for my own parents. How could I think of my own parents? When I saw people who were thin from not being able to eat, even if I had food to eat I couldn't eat, because my throat became so choked up. The image of such starving people would remain in my head, not allowing me to eat anything. Whenever I had something delicious in my possession, I would keep it and give it to the starving person that I had seen earlier. It didn't matter if they were poor or ugly. I was grateful to every single one of those who came to visit me. I once even bowed to a three-year-old baby. I felt, "The entire world hates me, but you greet me with joy!" I offered him a full bow and felt the heart of God. [*Sermons*, 22-172, 1969.02.02]

Our path of the Principle does not begin with the desire to live but with the desire to die. We could die because an enemy frames us as an enemy of the state or because we are betrayed by our comrades, friends, or even by our loved ones. There are many things that could lead to our death. However, when we die, we have to die with a heart of living for the sake of the world. Do not die with enmity in your heart. Let us die while loving our enemies as our friends. In that sense, the prayer that Jesus offered to Heaven before the crucifixion is truly a great prayer. [*Sermons*, 34-48–49, 1970.08.29]

The people in Japan would have perished had I not known about God. During the Japanese colonial age, I was tortured by a Japanese police officer. He was my enemy. When Korea was finally liberated, he would have lost his life if I had revealed his past to the public. However, I kept quiet because I knew God. You will become God's enemy if you attack your former enemy who is waving a white flag in surrender. This is the universal principle of cause and effect. Because of this law, the Japanese people are now paying back their debt to me. [*Sermons*, 203-214, 1990.06.26]

Sharing Thoughts

Before he was released from the Gyeonggi-do police detention center in February 1945, True Father offered jeongseong to Heaven to lay a foundation for his future public work. During this time, he almost died from torture, but he never prayed to Heavenly Parent to help him. He was beaten severely, but he always asked Heaven to forgive them. Jesus, too, asked Heaven to forgive the people who crucified him.

After the liberation, True Father could have taken his revenge against the police officers who had tortured him. However, he told the Japanese torturer, his unforgivable enemy, to flee from his house because it was dangerous for him to stay there. True Father sometimes told us that there was one Japanese police officer who used to torture him whom he could not forget. His name was Kumada Hara. However, Father still helped Mr. Hara to flee when things became very dangerous for him. This was truly unthinkable. When the Japanese colonial period ended, the Japanese people who had mass-murdered Korean people quickly escaped from Korea. Some of them were captured and bound for certain death. In the darkness of night, True Father rescued the Japanese police officer who had tortured him and got him on board a smuggler's ship bound for Japan. Then True Father said, "Today I am rescuing my enemy who represents all of my enemies. In the future this will serve as a condition for the Japanese people to help me." It is not easy to forgive and rescue an enemy who almost tortured you to death. This kind of forgiveness is not completed in just one day. It is done through many days and nights of continuous sincere offering of jeongseong.

The Bible tells us, "Love thy enemy." Our thoughts alone are not enough to put these words into practice. The heart alone is also not enough. We need to invest a great deal of energy and forgiveness into actually loving our enemies.

The picture above was taken in 2004 during an interview with Mr. Kumada Hara. The story of Mr. Hara is a story of how True Father actually loved his enemy. Many Japanese people joined the church because True Father set this historic condition of saving a Japanese person.

The satanic world imprisoned True Father six times. Once he was imprisoned in the Gyeonggi-do police station for participating in the Korean liberation movement. At that time, the Korean peninsula had been divided into North and South. North Korea was quickly becoming a communist country, and the communist regime imprisoned Father three times. True Father was also imprisoned by the South Korean Christian government because he was accused of witnessing to the students of Yonsei and Ewha University. In the United States, True Father was convicted of income tax evasion, and received an unjustly harsh prison sentence for the size of the offense.

However, even these tribulations were not enough to change True Father's ideas and beliefs. True Father silently encouraged the prison system to hit him harder. He wanted to see in himself the true extent of his forgiveness for his enemies. Father's determination was solemn. "Hit me if you want. I will not hate you. Even while vomiting blood, I will know that I am being punished for all of humankind, past and present. I will forget. I will not remember any of this." Then Father cried to Heaven, "Heavenly Parent! Forgive them!" With such determination, Father passed the test that the satanic world had put him through. To pass the test, True Father put himself in the position of nearly dying.

One time during the Japanese occupation of Korea, True Father was tortured 12 hours straight, vomiting blood at the end. He was tortured until he was senseless, but he survived miraculously. Although he was beaten and tortured, he did not think of the perpetrators of his pain as his enemies. Thinking that it was his responsibility to wish them good fortune, he offered great jeongseong to Heaven on their behalf. That is why even the worst of the torturers who beat Father all night long was moved by Father's love and later apologized sincerely. This is the power of sincerity that moves people.

✤ Points for contemplation

1) Have you ever sincerely wished good fortune to those who hated you? Have you ever sincerely wished good fortune to those whom you hated? Let us reflect on these questions.
2) Have you ever had an experience with someone who misunderstood you and gave you a hard time until, after realizing your sincere heart, he apologized to you and became your friend? Let us reflect on this question.

7
Sincerity Moves the Self
― Our Jeongseong Changes Even Ourselves

True Parents' Words

When you look at the world, you need to see the holiness in everything. You need to see the holiness in everyone, every person you interact with. Not only that, you need to see the holiness that exists within you as well. If you treat your body with true sincerity, your body will feel that it is being respected. If you treat it with the heart of God, your body will feel happy. This will open the door in your mind for the love of God to visit. Continuing to train yourself in this way will enable you to hear the voice of your heart. Moreover, treating your body with a truthful heart, the heart of loving God, will enable the love of God to come to you. In addition, you should meditate before you go to sleep to repent for the sins you had committed during the day and feel that you have awakened from the deepest part of your mind when you wake up. [*Sermons*, 102-112–118, 1978.11.27]

Attain mastery over yourself before seeking to master the universe. [*Sermons*, 2-140, 1957.03.17]

There are 84,000 seconds in a day. [*Sermons*, 9-29, 1960.04.03]

You need to be truthful every second of the day. This is the way to live a truthful life. In this regard, there is only one person like me in the entire history of humankind. There has never been, and there will never be, anyone like me in all of history. [*Sermons*, 26-127, 1969.10.19]

You need to regard your life as precious, because you live only once. You have to spend each and every day in order to restore yourself and win every struggle that may come to you at any time. [*Sermons*, 26-132, 1969.10.19]

Sharing Thoughts

The 16th president of the United States, Abraham Lincoln, may be one of the most respected people in the world. Lincoln was born to a poor farmer's family in Hardin County, Kentucky, in 1809. His family was so poor, Lincoln could not continue his education past the second grade. The total number of years of education Lincoln went through was less than two.

When Lincoln was 20 years old, he worked as a general store clerk. His job consisted of selling merchandise, receiving money and counting it. It was relatively easy. One day, he was ready to close the store when he discovered that his cash register had three cents more that it was supposed to. He counted several times, but it was unmistakable. There were three cents more than there should have been. He carefully thought about what had happened during the day and soon realized that one lady had paid three cents too much for her purchase.

Lincoln closed the store and hurried to the lady's house. He told the lady about how he had received three cents too much, apologized to her, and gave the money back. The lady was shocked. "You would do all this for just three cents?" she said. The lady was tremendously moved by Lincoln's honesty. She grabbed his hands. "Many blessings will certainly come to you for being so truthful." She did not want to take the money back, but Lincoln insisted. In the end, Lincoln went back to his house after returning the money.

Honest in everything he did, Lincoln was well-known in the town as an exemplary, kind young man. One of the reasons why Lincoln was elected president with widespread support was his honesty.

We often are infinitely generous to our own mistakes while very harsh toward others' mistakes. However, the Bible teaches us, "Why do you look at the speck of sawdust in your brother's eye and pay no attention to the plank in your own eye?" We tend to analyze and criticize others' mistakes while ignoring our own mistakes. We tell ourselves, "This is how it's always been done" or "This is the tradition."

That is why True Parents taught us, "Before seeking to master the universe, attain mastery over yourself." Perhaps attaining mastery over ourselves is one of the hardest things we can do. Genghis Khan, the founder of the Mongol Empire, the largest empire in human history, said: "My enemy was not out there but inside me. The moment I overcame the enemy within, I became Genghis Khan."

That is why True Parents taught us that even our body becomes happy if we treat it with the utmost sincerity. They emphasized that a truthful heart invites Heavenly Parent's heart, and then it invites the love of Heavenly Parent. You need to be truthful every second of the day. This is the way to live a truthful life. When we close our eyes to meditate and reflect on every minute of the day before we go to sleep, we will be able to know how truthful our life has been.

❋ Points for contemplation

1) Have you ever treated yourself as Heavenly Parent would? If this is difficult, what do you think is the reason? Realizing your self-worth requires a lot of experience of sharing your breath with Heavenly Parent. You gain this experience by loving others with all your heart,

sympathizing with other people's emotions. Let us reflect on this.
2) Use 5 to 10 minutes to breathe in and out while feeling gratitude. What changes in your mind and body have you experienced?

8
Sincerity Moves Heaven
– Jeongseong Offered on Earth will Reach the Heart of Heaven

True Parents' Words

Your jeongseong can move even Heavenly Parent. You have to offer jeongseong with life-or-death determination. [*Sermons*, 35-331, 1970.11.01]

If you connect God with a rope of jeongseong, God is completely bound to you. There is no way to break the bonds created by jeongseong. That is why we have connected God's essence and substance to the Family Federation with cords of jeongseong. [*Sermons*, 17-251, 1967.01.29]

In the early days in Korea, the ground of every place where I offered jeongseong to Heaven was always wet with my tears. The wooden floor would be completely drenched. I shed an endless number of tears. That was how my prayers were. This is recorded in history. Nowadays I don't cry as much as I used to, but in the past, I couldn't take a single step without shedding tears. We need the help of the spirit world. Many of the people in Korea who joined the church have been guided to the movement through prayer. They came to the church all on their own. They were drawn to it. [*Sermons*, 97-197, 1978.03.15]

"God, please help me!" This was never my prayer before an important event. I knew it was the course I must follow, so I made the decision to do so on my own. You have to make that decision on your own. You should not expect help from anybody. You have to be the one making effort day and night. Even if you are in a position in which you could use some help, you have to think about others more than yourself. You have to give it everything you have, and when you feel like you have completely exhausted your energy and options, you have to pray to Heaven for guidance. This is the course of restoration. [*Sermons*, 24-115, 1969.07.13]

Do you know why God loves me? It is because I do not ask Him for help. Many times, God put me in a position of death, where my life was threatened. To complete the course of restoration through indemnity, He put me in such positions and turned away. [*Sermons*, 32-68, 1970.06.21]

Sharing Thoughts

A long time ago, there were two crippled orphans. One was called Jiseong and the other Gamcheon. Jiseong could not walk and Gamcheon was blind. The two decided to help each other out. Gamcheon acted as Jiseong's legs and Jiseong as Gamcheon's eyes. Gamcheon would carry Jiseong on his back, and Jiseong told Gamcheon where to go. The brothers went around the town like this and begged for food. Greatly moved by their efforts, Heaven gave them a present. The present was in the form of a gold nugget which Jiseong and Gamcheon discovered next to a pond. Each brother wanted the other to have the gold. They could not come to a conclusion as to who should keep it, so they decided to leave it where they found it. Then they told a person whom they met on the road where he could find the gold nugget. The person went to the place, only to find a serpent. Angered, he cut the serpent into two. When Jiseong and Gamcheon returned to the pond where they had found the gold nugget, they saw that the nugget was cut in half. They each took one half. However, they were afraid of running into a robber, so they gave them away to the orphanage where they were raised. Grateful for the two brothers' generous donation, everyone at the orphanage offered sincere prayers on behalf of the brothers. Thanks to their prayers, Jiseong was able to walk again and Gamcheon could see again.

What kind of jeongseong did True Parents do to move Heavenly

Parent's heart? Many blessed members regard True Father as some kind of superman. However, True Father was a son of Heavenly Parent with a physical body like the rest of us. He went beyond the limits of his physical body to reclaim the position of original parent for Heavenly Parent and for the liberation and salvation of humankind.

Even when his voice became hoarse, True Father never gave up speaking in the middle of his sermon. There were many times when True Father skipped meals so that he could continue speaking. He often skipped breakfast, skipped lunch, and even dinner, ending his talk around midnight. He lived his entire life like this. If this was the life of True Father, can we imagine what True Mother's life was like?

Hoondokhae was not only a time of reading True Father's teachings, but it was also a when Father offered jeongseong with his mind and body. The longest Hoondokhae went on for 23 hours. True Father risked his life many times in storms when he went ocean fishing. He experienced Heavenly Parent's sorrowful heart in trying to restore humanity. True Father spent years finding answers to some of the questions hidden in the Divine Principle. He would stop offering jeongseong only when he was completely satisfied with the answer he discovered. That is the type of person True Father was.

True Parents spent more than 18 hours day working for the advancement of the providence. They never had a day off in their entire life. They practiced this life of jeongseong because they knew that Heaven would know it. That is why they never wasted a second and always led lives of sharing their breath together with Heavenly Parent. They believed that each moment could determine their victory or defeat in the providence of restoration.

Their efforts have made every day of life a bright, shining day. By connecting to Heavenly Parent in every moment, they lived a public life which connected to the world with eternal value.

❈ Points for contemplation

1) What is sincere jeongseong? For whom do we offer it, and for what do we do it? Let us reflect on this.
2) What are the differences between the jeongseong that we offer and that which True Parents offer? Let us reflect on how we can overcome our physical limitations and offer jeongseong in which we do not put ourselves at the center.

9
Sincerity Raises Your Status
—Jeongsong Puts You on the Same Level as Heavenly Parent

True Parents' Words

You should meditate before you go to sleep to repent for the sins you committed during the day and feel that you have awakened from the deepest part of your mind when you wake up. Only then will you have a keener sense of spirituality. Your mind will be able to take control of your body if you continue practicing. In this state, you will be a person dedicated for the public's benefit wherever you go. With the heart of an owner, you can touch an object and feel the good and bad things about that object. This information comes to you like an electric current. Someone who continuously trains himself will meet someone and know instantly if that person is a good person or not. Such information enters your mind. You can see your own spiritual self walking around, if you see with your spiritual eyes. You have to train yourself to see and follow your spiritual self. You also will see that your spiritual self materializes itself. At this level, you can interact with good spirits in the spirit world, and the place you stand on becomes a place where God can stand as well. [*Sermons*, 102-112–118, 1978.11.27]

Raise your hand if you ever saw me in your dream. There are many. It's 100 percent. You will be likely to see me if you shed tears in yearning. Even if you are out on the street selling flowers, I will come to you and be your friend. Something like this has never happened in human history. I eventually will disappear in the future. When that happens, people with spiritual awareness will be able to see me, even from a long distance. Something like this has never happened in human history. What you feel with your spiritual senses will be felt by your physical senses as well. In all of human history nobody has been able to have that kind of experience. [*Sermons*, 94-241–246, 1977.10.01]

What does it mean that God never had a chance to act as a parent? It means that God and human beings have not been able to achieve an equal level. We have to advocate for the rights of God. What good are talks of equality and freedom when we are unable to interact with our Creator? Human beings have to experience divine spirituality in order to be able to stand on an equal footing with God. God's work of restoration finally will come to an end when God and every human being can unite and sing songs of joy in the universe of freedom. This is the hope of humankind as well. [*Sermons*, 11-24, 1960.12.11]

Sharing Thoughts

The spread of True Parents' teachings and the Unification movement to Eastern Europe was only possible through many sacrifices. Many Eastern European nations held onto communism and did not want any religion to take root in their territory. Missionaries who were sent to such countries were in danger of being sent to jail or even executed if they were caught. That is why we planned a special missionary operation called "Mission Butterfly." Missionaries who were sent to these countries did not expose each other's true identities. Many of the missionaries who took part in this operation had joined the church only a short time before. Soon after joining the movement, people were sent to Eastern European countries as missionaries. They volunteered to take this mission with a sense of calling that they must spread the message of the Divine Principle to communist countries. They did not have anyone there to help them. They had only their heart of sincere yearning for Heavenly Parent and True Parents.

Because of their determination, they were under the direct dominion of Heavenly Parent and True Parents. Whenever they were in a dangerous situation, True Parents would appear to them in a dream and warn them. They would hear Heaven saying to them, "Flee now!" There was even a case when a missionary had an ominous feeling, so he decided to bury his Divine Principle books in the ground. Just a few moments later, communist intelligence officers swarmed the house and searched it for any illegal materials. A few missionaries even experienced True Parents telling them in a dream where to go and whom to meet. In this way, Heavenly Parent and True Parents directly guided the missionaries' activities. Even though the missionaries did not have a long history with the movement, their sincere heart of yearning allowed Heavenly Parent and True Parents to help them personally.

There were tragedies as well. Some of the missionaries were discovered and captured by the Soviet Union's KGB or other Eastern European communist intelligence agencies. One of them left a note saying, "Father, Mother. This will be my last moment on earth. I will see you in the spirit world," before offering a bow in True Parents' direction. She was then carried out of the cell and executed.

That is why True Father wanted anyone who had seen him in a dream to raise his or her hand. Then he said, "You will be likely to see me if you shed tears in yearning. Even if you are out on the street selling flowers, I will come to you and be your friend."

He was teaching us that True Parents can visit us anytime, if we have a good heartistic foundation. Not only that, he told us he would visit us even after he went to the spirit world. He was referring to the very time in which we live today.

The Bible teaches us that Heavenly Parent is love, He is logos, and He is spirit. This is how True Parents, who have attained unity with

Heavenly Parent, can visit any member on earth and provide direct guidance. Members of the Unification Church around the world must realize how happy we should be for being able to receive True Parents' guidance.

It is also an extremely great blessing to have True Mother, who works tirelessly day and night in order to fulfill Heavenly Parent's Will.

❋ Points for contemplation

1) Have you had any experience in which True Parents came to you personally and gave you guidance? Or, have you had any spiritual experience after joining the Family Federation for World Peace and Unification? Let us reflect on this.
2) What do you think are the results of your sincere jeongseong? What kind of prayers do you offer to Heavenly Parent for your family and for your community? Let's reflect on this.

10
Heavenly Tribal Messiah

– Path to Become the Second True Parents,
the Blessing of Blessings

True Parents' Words

Humankind's wish is to meet True Parents. They wish to meet True Parents, even if it means that they have to walk the course of death. They may lose their entire history, the current era, and all their descendants, but it would all be worth it if it means they can find True Parents. In True Parents, they will find a new history, a new era and a new future. We have to understand that this is the value of True Parents. I said that people may lose their entire history, the current era and all their descendants, but that it would be worth it if they could find True Parents, and with them a new history, a new era and a new future. Why is that? Why is this so? It is because only after discovering True Parents can humankind hope to have a chance of resembling the original ideal for human beings. What does it mean to resemble True Parents? It means that we can love humankind and the universe with the heart of a parent, just like God, because they resemble True Parents. This is why, even after meeting True Parents, one cannot say he truly met them unless he has come to possess a true love that is similar to the love of God. [Sermons, 35-237, 1970.10.19]

You have to listen to the stories of my suffering and be able to feel as if the pain is your own. If you hear my sad story, you have to be able to feel sad and angry as if it is you who have been wronged. My history of pain and suffering is the ingredient with which I move your heart. You can raise your children to be filial sons and daughters if you have a history of suffering. However, your children will grow up as selfish people who only look after their own family if your suffering was only for the sake of your own family. On the other hand, your children will grow as the precious sons and daughters of God, who will say they will love humankind in God's place, if your history of suffering took place in your course of fulfilling God's wishes and bringing salvation to humankind. That is why parents should do more than just giving love to their children. They have to live for the sake of God's wishes and convey the love of God to their children in the process. [Sermons, 34-101, 1970.08.29]

Sharing Thoughts

You should feel most honored that you are living in the same age as True Parents. This is the blessing of the current age that never will be repeated in human history. The same unprecedented blessing was given to the Jewish people in Israel 2,000 years ago, when Jesus was born. The Jewish people have been walking the course of immense pain and suffering since then, because they failed to recognize the true value of Jesus Christ. That lost opportunity never returned to them.

It is the blessing of all blessings to be able to live, breathe, talk, and laugh in joy together with True Parents in the same day and age. Not only that, True Parents want to do anything for their children. We already know that True Mother has a very kind nature, and she wants to give her things to others. She does this because not giving makes her heart sad and uncomfortable. Many people come to visit her all the time. To each of them, True Mother tries to give as much as possible. This is the perfected love of a parent. She never feels happy or satisfied if she lets her guest leave emptyhanded.

No matter how many people come to visit her, she personally visits a department store to buy her visitors nice clothes, shoes, shirts, or even ties. She picks the colors and the design herself. True Mother sometimes even gives them her own clothes. She often finds herself in a predicament because she has given away so many of her clothes, she doesn't have good clothes to wear outside.

The following story is a good description of True Parents' life of living for the sake of others. After their Holy Wedding, True Father felt very sorry for True Mother, whom he couldn't take on a honeymoon or give any wedding gifts. They married in very difficult circumstances. Sometime after their marriage, True Parents went on a world tour. In the Netherlands True Father decided to buy a present for True Mother to make up for not being able to buy a gift at the time of their marriage. He bought a ring with a large diamond and gave it to her. One day, however, he discovered that the ring was missing from her finger. Father asked Mother, "It's been a while I saw you wearing that ring I bought for you." True Mother answered, "If you gave it to me, then it means that it's mine. So why do you ask what happened to it?" She smiled and brushed off his question. He later found out that True Mother had given the ring to a missionary from abroad and forgotten about it. True Mother truly was practicing true love. The heart of True Mother is wanting to practice and pursue true love, not materialistic values.

Our blessing of blessings is the fact that we were able to meet True Parents. Receiving the love and grace from True Parents, who offer jeongseong to Heaven on our behalf, is the greatest blessing in our life. That is why True Parents taught us that the greatest wish of humankind is to meet True Parents. True Father emphasized this point strongly by saying, "They may lose their entire history, the current era and all their descendants, but … it would be worth it if they could find True Parents, and with them a new history, a new era and a new future."

History here means the past. The current era is the present, and the descendants mean the future. The course of death refers to the worst-case scenario. It is of great significance to meet True Parents, even if it means that we have to walk the worst course that encompasses all of the past, present, and future. True Parents are responsible for not only our life in the physical world but also our life in the spirit world.

This is because meeting True Parents is an absolute prerequisite to resembling True Parents and becoming the people of Heavenly Parent's original ideal. Only after meeting True Parents, can we be raised as true children and become the second true parents. Therefore, we have to become heavenly tribal messiahs who spread the fortune of Heavenly Parent around the world as the representatives of Heavenly Parent and True Parents. We should then become true parents ourselves.

❋ Points for contemplation

1) Do you feel the need to meet your spouse and become true parents? Think about what you and your spouse are doing to realize this and share your thoughts with others.
2) What is the path of a heavenly tribal messiah? What should our goals be, and what should we perfect while on this path?

Bibliography

Editorial committee for the Collected *Sermons* of Sun Myung Moon, Ed. *Collected Sermons of the Rev. Sun Myung Moon*, vol. 2. Seoul: Sung Hwa Publishing, 1957.
Editorial committee. *Sermons*, vol. 3. Seoul: Sung Hwa, 1957.
Editorial committee. *Sermons*, vol. 9. Seoul: Sung Hwa, 1960.
Editorial committee. *Sermons*, vol. 11. Seoul: Sung Hwa, 1960.
Editorial committee. *Sermons*, vol. 17. Seoul: Sung Hwa, 1967.
Editorial committee. *Sermons*, vol. 18. Seoul: Sung Hwa, 1967.
Editorial committee. *Sermons*, vol. 22. Seoul: Sung Hwa, 1969.
Editorial committee. *Sermons*, vol. 23. Seoul: Sung Hwa, 1969.
Editorial committee. *Sermons*, vol. 24. Seoul: Sung Hwa, 1969.
Editorial committee. *Sermons*, vol. 26. Seoul: Sung Hwa, 1969.
Editorial committee. *Sermons*, vol. 31. Seoul: Sung Hwa, 1970.
Editorial committee. *Sermons*, vol. 32. Seoul: Sung Hwa, 1970.
Editorial committee. *Sermons*, vol. 34. Seoul: Sung Hwa, 1970.
Editorial committee. *Sermons*, vol. 35. Seoul: Sung Hwa, 1970.

Editorial committee. *Sermons*, vol. 70. Seoul: Sung Hwa, 1974.
Editorial committee. *Sermons*, vol. 75. Seoul: Sung Hwa, 1975.
Editorial committee. *Sermons*, vol. 87. Seoul: Sung Hwa, 1976.
Editorial committee. *Sermons*, vol. 90. Seoul: Sung Hwa, 1976.
Editorial committee. *Sermons*, vol. 94. Seoul: Sung Hwa, 1977.
Editorial committee. *Sermons*, vol. 96. Seoul: Sung Hwa, 1978.
Editorial committee. *Sermons*, vol. 97. Seoul: Sung Hwa, 1978.
Editorial committee. *Sermons*, vol. 102. Seoul: Sung Hwa, 1979.
Editorial committee. *Sermons*, vol. 133. Seoul: Sung Hwa, 1984.
Editorial committee. *Sermons*, vol. 203. Seoul: Sung Hwa, 1990.
Editorial committee. *Sermons*, vol. 210. Seoul: Sung Hwa, 1999.
Editorial committee. *Sermons*, vol. 255. Seoul: Sung Hwa, 1994.
Editorial committee. *Sermons*, vol. 259. Seoul: Sung Hwa, 1994.
Editorial committee. *Sermons*, vol. 260. Seoul: Sung Hwa, 1994.
Editorial committee. *Sermons*, vol. 267. Seoul: Sung Hwa, 1994.
Editorial committee. *Sermons*, vol. 292. Seoul: Sung Hwa, 1998.
Editorial committee. *Sermons*, vol. 294. Seoul: Sung Hwa, 1998.
Editorial committee. *Sermons*, vol. 301. Seoul: Sung Hwa, 1999.
Editorial committee. *Sermons*, vol. 302. Seoul: Sung Hwa, 1999.
Family Federation for World Peace and Unification, ed. *Blessed Family and the Ideal Kingdom II*. Seoul: Sung Hwa Publishing, 1998.
Family Federation for World Peace and Unification, ed. *The Holy Scriptures of Cheon Il Guk: Cheon Seong Gyeong*. Seoul: Sung Hwa Publishing, 2014.
Family Federation for World Peace and Unification, ed. *The Holy Scriptures of Cheon Il Guk: Pyeong Hwa Gyeong*. Seoul: Sung Hwa

Publishing, 2014.

Family Federation for World Peace and Unification, ed. *The Holy Scriptures of Cheon Il Guk: Chambumo Gyeong.* Seoul: Sung Hwa Publishing, 2015.

Family Federation for World Peace and Unification, ed. *Pyeong Hwa Shin Gyeong.* Seoul: Sung Hwa Publishing, 2009.

Family Federation for World Peace and Unification, ed. *True Family and the Family Pledge.* Seoul: Sung Hwa Publishing, 2001.

Moon Sun Myung. *As a Peace-Loving Global Citizen.* Washington, D.C: The Washington Times Foundation, Inc., 2009.

A GLOSSARY OF KEY TERMS

home church :
A style of community ministry that was emphasized in the Unification movement in the 1980s. Each blessed family had the mission to create a model home and family and seek to love and care for 360 families living nearby. Providentially the home church movement had the goal of restoring from Satan the authority of the eldest son.

tribal messiah mission :
The tribal messiah mission was the family ministry that followed home church. Starting in 1991, blessed families were called to return to their home towns and minister to their extended families and others in their home towns. Tribal messiahs worked to bless 160 couples to the Blessing. The tribal messiah age led to the restoration of the authority of parents.

family church / hoondok family church :
The age of hoondok family church was declared in 2005. From this time forward each blessed family was called to establish a hoondok family church, establish

a strong tradition of hoondokhae in their families, and put into practice what they learned through hoondokhae in ministering to their extended families and neighbors. Through hoondok family church the authority of the king was restored.

heavenly tribal messiah mission :
The role of heavenly tribal messiahs was first introduced in March 2012, and True Father emphasized it again in his final prayer. Working in their hometowns or another mission area, heavenly tribal messiahs can shorten the time required for the complete restoration of their lineage from a vertical period of seven generations to as little as one generation, by liberating and blessing 430 vertical generations of their ancestors, and gathering and blessing a horizontal tribe of 430 families, with three generations of their families working together.

home group :
A small group of people, often organized around a few families, who gather regularly as a community of faith, to pray, study, fellowship and minister together. In heavenly tribal messiah activities, a home group sometimes serves as a local pioneer church center.

small group :
see "home group"

midsize group :
A community of faith formed by combining a number of small groups which are in the same vicinity, to work together and support each other, by organizing education programs or community events, for example.

large group :
A larger local church or center which provides opportunities for weekly worship, workshops, and other support services. Parts of the congregation might separate off into small groups and create new pioneer centers.

jeongseong :

An act of devotion, service or care offered to mobilize spiritual support and protection as part of a life of faith. Jeongseong can include prayer, bowing conditions, fasting, taking special care of people, cleaning the church, cooking a special meal, writing letters, and many other types of offering of heart.

"To offer jeongseong means to do your utmost internally and externally. You must offer everything, combining your words, your attitude, your mind and thoughts, all your actions, everything in the internal and external realities of your life." [CSG 11.1.2.1]

hyojeong :

A heart of filial devotion, love given by children in response to the love they have received from their parents, and the exchange of heart between humankind and Heavenly Parent, who also stand in a parent–child relationship. A heart of hyojeong is the starting point of a world that expresses the ideal of creation.

hoondokhae :

Hoondokhae is a meeting where people gather to read, discuss and understand the teachings of True Parents. It is also a time for offering jeongseong of the mind and the body. By engaging in hoondok reading with the whole mind and body, we participate in "hoondok mind-body purification jeongseong."

Cheon Il Guk :

Cheon Il Guk is the shortened name for "Cheonju Pyeonghwa Tongil Guk," which is the "Cosmic Nation of Peace and Unity." Cheon Il Guk is the kingdom of heaven on earth, which we build by practicing what we have learned about love and living for the sake of others.

Seonghwa :

In the Unification movement, the transition from life in the world of air to life in the world of love is call *Seonghwa* (成和: completion and harmony) The end of life in the world of air is nothing to be feared, but is a time of ascending nobly to heaven. When we gather for a Seonghwa Service after somebody has ascended, we celebrate their life up until now, and rejoice for their coming life.

BonHyang Won :

True Father's final resting place above Cheon Jeong Gung is called *BonHyang Won*, which means "garden of the original homeland."

weonjeon / Paju Weonjeon :

Weonjeon is the word used to describe a memorial garden where Unificationists have been laid to rest. The Paju Weonjeon is a special weonjeon in Paju, Korea, for members of the True Family and early church members.

supporters :

Already married couples who received the Blessing through Heavenly Tribal Messiah activities, or other active supporters of FFWPU and/or related providential organizations.

registered members :

Members who attend worship services or donate at least once every six months.

associate members :

Members who donate (tithe if possible) and attend at least two worship services every three months.

regular members :

Members who tithe twice and attend at least six worship services every three months.

Editors

Wonju McDevitt (head editor, chief of staff, Dr. Hak Ja Han Moon's Secretariat)
Yun Young-ho (secretary general, FFWPUI HQ)
Yong Jin-hun (director, FFWPUI HQ Heavenly Tribal Messiah Academy)

Writers

Im Hyun-jin (Publishing Committee Chair, SunHak Universal Peace Graduate University)
Hwang Jin-su (SunHak Universal Peace Graduate University)
Do Hyeon-seob (SunHak Universal Peace Graduate University)
Kim Min-ji (Sun Moon University)
Moon In-seong (CheongShim International Academy)
Yong Jin-hun (director, FFWPUI HQ Heavenly Tribal Messiah Academy)
Lee Bok-jin (FFWPUI HQ Heavenly Tribal Messiah Academy)
Lee Gil-yeon (Korea University)
Park Ye-ran (advisory consultant)

Heavenly Tribal Messiah Special Textbook I
Hoondok Study Texts
Heavenly Tribe Hoondok

Published June 21, 2018

First edition © 2018
Layout by Sung Hwa Publishing Co., Korea
Published by Heavenly Tribal Messiah Academy
Printed by HSA-Books, New York, NY
June 2019